COMPARATIVE POLITICS

Elections, Parties, Democracy

COMPARATIVE POLITICS

Comparative Politics is a series for students and teachers of political science that deals with contemporary issues in comparative government and politics. As Comparative European Politics it has produced a series of high quality books since its foundation in 1990, but now takes on a new form and new title for the new millennium—Comparative Politics. As the process of globalization proceeds, and as Europe becomes ever more enmeshed in world trends and events, so it is necessary to broaden the scope of the series. The General Editors are Max Kaase, Vice President and Dean of Humanities and Social Sciences, International University, Bremen; and Kenneth Newton, Professor of Comparative Politics, University of Southampton. The series is published in association with the European Consortium for Political Research.

OTHER TITLES IN THIS SERIES

Democratic Challenges, Democratic Choices
Russell J. Dalton

Democracy Transformed?
Edited by Bruce E. Cain, Russell J. Dalton, and Susan E. Scarrow

Environmental Protest in Western Europe
Edited by Christopher Rootes

Social Movements and Networks
Edited by Mario Diani and Doug McAdam

Delegation and Accountability in Parliamentary Democracies
Edited by Kaare Strøm, Wolfgang C. Müller, and Torbjörn Bergman

The Presidentialization of Politics
Edited by Thomas Poguntke and Paul Webb

Losers' Consent
*Christopher J. Anderson, André Blais, Shaun Bowler,
Todd Donovan, and Ola Listhaug*

The Performance of Democracies
Edeltraud Roller

Elections, Parties, Democracy

Conferring the Median Mandate

MICHAEL D. McDONALD and IAN BUDGE

OXFORD
UNIVERSITY PRESS

Great Clarendon Street, Oxford OX2 6DP
Oxford University Press is a department of the University of Oxford.
It furthers the University's objective of excellence in research, scholarship,
and education by publishing worldwide in

Oxford New York

Auckland Cape Town Dar es Salaam Hong Kong Karachi
Kuala Lumpur Madrid Melbourne Mexico City Nairobi
New Delhi Shanghai Taipei Toronto

With offices in

Argentina Austria Brazil Chile Czech Republic France Greece
Guatemala Hungary Italy Japan Poland Portugal Singapore
South Korea Switzerland Thailand Turkey Ukraine Vietnam

Oxford is a registered trade mark of Oxford University Press
in the UK and in certain other countries

Published in the United States
by Oxford University Press Inc., New York

© Michael D. McDonald and Ian Budge

The moral rights of the authors have been asserted
Database right Oxford University Press (maker)

First published 2005

All rights reserved. No part of this publication may be reproduced,
stored in a retrieval system, or transmitted, in any form or by any means,
without the prior permission in writing of Oxford University Press,
or as expressly permitted by law, or under terms agreed with the appropriate
reprographics rights organization. Enquiries concerning reproduction
outside the scope of the above should be sent to the Rights Department,
Oxford University Press, at the address above

You must not circulate this book in any other binding or cover
and you must impose the same condition on any acquirer

British Library Cataloguing in Publication Data
Data available

Library of Congress Cataloging in Publication Data
Data available

Typeset by SPI Publisher Services, Pondicherry, India
Printed in Great Britain on acid-free paper by
Biddles Ltd
Kings Lynn. Norfolk

ISBN 0–19–9286728 978–0–19–9286720

1 3 5 7 9 10 8 6 4 2

To Alenna and Judith:
for patience, support and good humour
that spring from something
much dearer than marriage

Preface

How can representative democracy be made truly representative? Two mechanisms have been postulated for bringing public policy into line with popular opinion: convergence by vote-seeking parties on majority opinion, represented by the average (median) preference; and parties offering *different* policies that electors choose between, thereby giving the majority party a mandate for its policy. The book synthesizes and extends these ideas in the theory of a median mandate and applies them to the operation of twenty-one democracies from the early 1950s to 1995. In the process it demonstrates the compatibility of 'consensus democracy' with 'majoritarian democracy' and provides a unified account of the role of parties and elections in the modern world. Direct democracy—deciding specific policies through direct popular votes—is also discussed in relation to the median mandate conferred by general elections.

A few years ago it would have been impossible to investigate such questions in a range of democracies over an extended period. Available evidence was drawn from case studies of individual legislative sessions and specific governments and issues. Focusing on the short term and on specific examples of policymaking can be misleading. It may give a picture of confusion and chaos such as we uncover in Chapters 8 and 9. Bismarck is said to have observed that policy, like sausages, should not be observed in the making. It is the total democratic process, in the long term and in general, that ends up relating settled popular preferences to standing public policy, as we demonstrate in Chapters 10 to 12.

Our ability to focus on the comparative and long term owes much to the indices of policy outputs developed by Gøsta Esping-Andersen and Arendt Lijphart, the latter of whom kindly and speedily made them available to us. Much of our analysis in the later part of the book rests on these. The government expenditure data we use in Chapter 10 were collected at the Netherlands Institute for Advanced Study (NIAS) in 1995 with our colleagues Richard I. Hofferbert, Hans Keman, and Paul Pennings. We are delighted to acknowledge our deep intellectual and practical debt to them, which we hope will bear more fruit in the years to come. It is also a pleasure to acknowledge the essential support of NIAS in bringing us all together. This book represents a belated, but we hope worthy, product of our research efforts there. McDonald is grateful to Binghamton University for granting him a leave of absence and to the University of Essex, especially its collegial and energising Department of Government, for a research fellowship during which a first draft of the manuscript was produced.

Harvey Palmer and Guy Whitten generously provided us with their cross-national time series of economic expectations, which we use in Chapter 6. We hope our joint use of their evidence will stimulate a debate on retrospective economic voting based firmly on common ground.

Relating popular preferences to public policy would of course be impossible without information about the preferences of a variety of actors at diverse times and places. This essential information for parties, electors, and governments has been provided through the work of the Manifesto Research Group/Comparative Manifestos Project (MRG/CMP), latterly based at the Wissenschaftzentrum Berlin, and published in another book from Oxford University Press. Hee Min Kim and Richard C. Fording pioneered an approach to estimating government and electoral preferences from party stands that has been essential in estimating median positions. Jim Adams provided alternative mean/median measures of preference and compared them interestingly with ours.

Silvia Mendes helped collect and organize our data on elections, parliaments, and governments and was instrumental in the initial formulation of ideas about the median mandate. Aida Paskeviciute extended and corrected our initial data on party seats and votes. Chris Anderson listened, queried, encouraged, criticized, and re-encouraged as we moved the median mandate thesis forward from voters to parliaments, parliaments to governments, and governments to policies. His questions and criticisms improved our arguments and analyses in untold ways; his encouragement made pursuing them more enjoyable than it otherwise would have been. Robin Best and Zachary McDonald read and commented on the entire manuscript, with the effects of helping connect arguments and evidence across the stages of the representational process and of saving us errors and inconsistencies.

Preparing a manuscript loaded with data and figures is arduous for formatters and publishers! We thank Julie Snell for her impeccable work on the manuscript, and our editors at OUP—Dominic Byatt and Claire Croft—for their invaluable advice, help, and support.

We hope no one in this day and age will cavil at the idea that systematic evidence can be brought to bear on (partly normative) theories. Political theory in general, and mandate theories in particular, have always functioned as descriptions of democratic processes as well as justifications of them. To be able to justify democracy we have to know how it works. To be able to generalize about it, even at a normative level ('democracy is good'), we have to assume that it is not just embedded in particular countries but has a core of essential processes that occur in all democracies. We find this in the 'necessary connection' between popular preferences and public policy first suggested by J. D. May and drawn to our attention by Michael Saward.

Working democracy is not just a concept but also a series of processes directed to realizing it. These can be set down as a set of conditions for the emergence of a mandate whose presence in countries widely accepted as democracies can be checked. The absence of all or some of these conditions must then either cast doubt on the viability of the theory or of democracy (though we would surely prefer the former alternative).

It is in this sense that our comparative investigation casts light on the normative debate, pointing the way either to a reformulation of ideas about democracy or to best democratic practice. The essential step is to recognize in representative democracy not just a concept but a theory containing both normative and descriptive elements. The theory must be considered as a whole so that the invalidation of any element in it points to a rejection of the whole set of interconnected hypotheses. We are grateful to our theorist colleague Albert Weale for clarifying these and many other points in our argument and analysis.

These are all dealt with at different stages in our book. Part I sets out our theory and data. Part II examines the extent to which parties both shape and respond to electoral preferences over twenty-one post-war democracies. Between party preferences (even in government) and actual public policy, however, there is a large gap, which we illustrate in Part III for day-to-day policymaking. In Part IV we demonstrate how short-term processes lead to long-term equilibria both in political preferences and public policy, which are not only stable but closely related to each other. Democracy does work but in the long term and through power-sharing processes over time that restore democratic competition.

How our evidence builds to this conclusion is described, almost dialectically, in the following pages. Chapter 1 sets the process going by expanding on the theoretical concerns sketched above.

Michael D. McDonald
Binghamton

Ian Budge
Colchester

Contents

List of Figures xii

List of Tables xiv

I The Mandate Process 1
1. Choosing Governments or Identifying Preferences? The Role of Elections in Democracy 3
2. Mandate Theories: Government and Median 19
3. Communicating Preferences: The Public Policy Space 30
4. Research Questions for Comparative Investigation 49

II The Electoral Process 59
5. Choices Parties Offer 61
6. Mandates Without Obvious Majorities? 91
7. Representing the Median Voter 116

III The Governing Process 139
8. Who Controls Short-Term Policymaking? 141
9. From Declared to Actual Policy: Short-Term Influences on Government Policies 154

IV The Democratic Process 169
10. Long-Term Policy Regimes: Incrementalism Put in Context 171
11. Fluctuating Political Forces 181
12. Politics and Policy Regimes: Setting a Long-Term Equilibrium 203
13. Unifying Theories of Democracy Through the Median Mandate 227

Bibliography 243

Index 253

List of Figures

1.1.	The policy dominance of the median actor C in election, committee, or legislative voting	6
3.1.	Relating public policy space to private preferences	34
3.2.	The dynamics of dimensionality	41
3.3.	Hypothetical multi-dimensional policy spaces mapping party positions at an election	44
5.1.	U. S. party movements on a Left-Right scale, 1952–1992	63
5.2.	German party movements on a Left-Right scale, 1953–94	64
5.3.	Dutch party movements on a Left-Right scale, 1952–94	65
5.4.	Distinctiveness of choices offered by parties along the Left-Right dimension, by country, 1950–95	74
5.5.	Distinctiveness of policy options offered by parties on military alliances minus peaceful internationalism, by country, 1950–95	79
5.6.	Distinctiveness of policy options offered by parties on opposition to welfare minus support for it, by country over post-war period	82
5.7.	Distinctiveness of policy options offered by parties on support for free market minus economic planning, by country over post-war period	84
7.1.	Hypothetical conditions at four stages in the representational process, used here to illustrate how distortions and biases are evaluated	123
9.1.	Central government spending as a per cent of GDP, by nation in 1982 and 1992	156
9.2.	Central government support for welfare statism, by nation in the early 1980s and early 1990s	160
9.3.	Foreign aid support (1980s) and foreign aid relative to defence spending (1990s), by nation	163
10.1.	Long-run cross-national differences in six countries' public economies	174
11.1.	Responsiveness of median parliamentary Left-Right policy position to median voter Left-Right position over 266 elections in twenty-one democracies, 1950–95	188

12.1. Correspondence between mean Left-Right positions of median voters and median parliamentary party over twenty-one countries — 206
12.2. Correspondence between mean Left-Right positions of median parliamentary parties and of governments over twenty countries — 207
12.3. A validated overview of the long-term policy process under representative democracy — 216

List of Tables

1.1.	Equivalence between the median electoral party and the government in Britain, 1945–2000	7
1.2.	A possible voting situation in which party *B* wins on its overall programme even though a majority opposes its position on each specific issue	14
2.1.	Conditions for a government mandate to emerge	21
2.2.	Percentage of time in government and number of governments by majority status of governments and electorates in five SMD systems, early 1950s to 1995	22
2.3.	Percentage of time in government and number of governments by majority status of governments and electorates in fifteen PR systems, early 1950s to 1995	24
2.4.	Conditions for a median mandate to emerge	26
2.5.	Number and percentages of parliaments where the median legislative party was supported by the median elector, under SMD and PR systems, early 1950s to 1995	28
3.1.	Creation of an additive Left-Right scale from coding of manifesto sentences	37
5.1.	Policy moves initiated by parties over twenty-one democracies 1950–1995 which involve 'leapfrogging' other parties or moving out of a characteristic Left, Centre, or Right position	66
5.2.	Correspondence of party policy positions on specific issues with their general Left-Right positions	87
5.3.	The policy choices offered by parties in twenty-one post-war democracies	88
6.1.	Vote dynamics measured against baselines for long-term average vote as well as previous election vote, by differing types of electoral systems and governments	96
6.2.	Incumbent vote related to economic expectations under different electoral systems and government types: sixteen nations, late 1960s to mid-1990s	98
6.3.	Why retrospective voting is never unproblematic: the case of the economy	99

List of Tables

6.4.	Estimated Left-Right equilibrium positions of median voters by nation: early 1950s to mid-1990s	105
7.1.	Means and standard deviations of median voter, parliament, and government Left-Right positions, by country from the early 1950s to 1995	121
7.2.	Distortions in representing a median voter's Left-Right position, by country and electoral system type, overall and across steps in the process, from the early 1950s to 1995	126
7.3.	Biases in representing a median voter's Left-Right position, by country and electoral system type, overall and across steps in the process, from the early 1950s to 1995	128
7.4.	Proportionate reduction in distortions, by country and electoral system type, overall and at the negotiation and electoral stages, from the early 1950s to 1995	133
8.1.	Relationships between Left-Right positions of government policy declarations and Left-Right positions of electorates, parliaments, and governments	147
8.2.	Relationships, in three policy areas, between policy positions in government policy declarations and policy positions in that area of parliamentary Left-Right median, parliamentary policy median, and government, and relevant ministry	150
9.1.	Relationships between 1982 and 1992 central government spending as a percentage of GDP and Left-Right and economic policy positions of political and governmental actors, controlling for centralization and openness of economy	158
9.2.	Relationships between 1980s and 1990s welfare and international policies and policy positions of governmental actors, controlling for consensus democracy on both policies and for aged population in the case of welfare	162
10.1.	Policy regime estimated by mean spending on public economy, welfare, and international relations in twenty-one democracies, 1973–1995	175
10.2.	Policy regimes estimated by spending equilibria on public economy, welfare, and international relations in twenty-one democracies, 1973–1995	179
11.1.	Responsiveness of the median parliamentary party's Left-Right position to the median voter Left-Right position, by country	190
11.2.	Responsiveness of the government's Left-Right positions to the median parliamentary party's Left-Right position, by country	196

11.A.1.	Alternative estimation of responsiveness of the median parliamentary party's Left-Right position to the median voter Left-Right position, by country: median voter position measured with a three-election moving average of party positions	198
11.A.2.	Voters' median Left-Right positions as coded by Kim and Fording using the CMP data, versus voters' mean Left-Right positions as computed from Eurobarometer data	200
12.1.	Analyses of policy transitions from parliaments to governments to ministries in three areas	211
12.2.	Average central government spending estimated as a function of Left-Right positions of institutional actors, controlling for centralization and international economic openness	217
12.3.	Central government spending estimated as a function of economic policy positions of institutional actors, controlling for centralization and international economic openness	220
12.4.	Welfare policies estimated as a function of policy positions of institutional actors, controlling for aged population and consensus democracy	222
12.5.	Internationalism policies estimated as a function of policy positions of institutional actors, controlling for consensus democracy	224

PART 1
The Mandate Process

1

Choosing Governments or Identifying Preferences? The Role of Elections in Democracy

1.1 ELECTIONS AND GOVERNANCE

Elections are the distinguishing institution of democracy, translating individual voter preferences into collective choices that can in some sense be said to reflect them. The key questions about democracy therefore focus on elections, starting with the aggregation process itself. How are preferences reflected in votes? How are these combined to produce the overall election result? Once the election result is declared, what is its relationship, if any, with public policy? Does it determine it, in any way, or does it simply produce a parliament and government that then make policy themselves?

Classic theories of representation are in no doubt about this. They see democratic choice as a two-stage process. Voters choose legislatures and governments, which then, autonomously, make decisions for them. This is not dissimilar to 'consociationalist' or 'consensus' conceptions of democracy (Lijphart 1984, 1999), where party leaders negotiate policy compromises that deeply divided populations cannot agree on. In both cases the role of elections is to choose legislatures, which then independently shape both governments and policy.

Still building on the idea of a two-stage process, but shifting the focus from legislatures to government, current mandate theory sees parties as offering alternative policy programmes to electors. The most popular programme attracts majority endorsement and propels its sponsor into government with majority backing. The ensuing 'elective dictatorship' then carries through the promised programme, for which it is held accountable at the next election.

Mandate theory offers a way of coming to terms with the dominance of political parties within representative structures. As a result, it has guided most contemporary theorizing about, and most empirical investigations of, the way democracy works. From Downsian spatial modelling (Downs 1957) to theories of coalition formation (Laver and Budge 1992) the emphasis has been on how parties form governments.

The problem for government mandate theory once it moves into the real world is that only one democracy in the world—the USA—regularly produces a spontaneous majority choice of governing party. Elsewhere majorities are manufactured, if they are produced at all, either through the mechanics of the electoral system or by negotiations between potential coalition partners. This has led much research on democracy to concentrate on government formation as the key process in its functioning. Parties are carriers of specific policies (Castles 1982; Budge and Keman 1990). So once government composition is settled the policy mix to be adopted as public policy will follow automatically.

How exactly this relates to majority preferences, however, is obscure. This obscurity has been seized upon by 'consensus democrats', who refuse to be thrown by the dubiously majoritarian status of most governments. Going back to earlier 'trustee' conceptions of representation, they argue that the authority conferred by election enables party leaders, whether in government or in opposition, to negotiate necessary compromises, which they can then persuade voters to accept. This conception is not unrelated to the brokerage role assigned by Madison (1788/1911) and later American writers to policy bargaining within and between political institutions that goes on autonomously from electors.

The problem in both cases is the absence of any institutional mechanism ensuring 'a necessary correspondence between acts of governance and the equally weighted felt interests of citizens with respect to these acts' (May 1978; Saward 1998: 51; cf. Weale 1999: 14). Representatives and parties may be benevolent and consensual and consider the general good. But there is no mechanism to *make* them do so. They could thus be partisan, narrowly self-interested, and successfully manipulative and still get re-elected, especially given difficulties with accountability in coalition situations (Powell and Whitten 1993). As normative theorists recognize, what distinguishes democracy from benevolent despotism are precisely its institutional mechanisms for ensuring a *necessary* correspondence between government policy and individual preferences, not one dependent on vagaries of culture, elite temperament, or the goodwill of rulers.

More difficulties of a government-focused view of democracy are considered in detail in later chapters, both theoretically and with comparative data. These analyses point strongly to a radical solution for the conceptual and practical ambiguities associated with the traditional approach to elections— that is, abandoning the idea that elections really determine which parties govern. We can see them instead as specifying the policy preference of the popular majority. Operationally this is done by locating the position of the median or middle elector. With near 50 per cent of other electors to one side and near 50 per cent to the other, the median elector has the decisive role in forming a popular majority that must adopt his or her position—otherwise he or she will either abstain or vote with the other side. The power to force the median preference on the majority is desirable, not only because it provides an anchor point for majority opinion in the first place but also because it is the endorsed policy position that minimizes differences with all the others, given equal weighting of votes.[1] It thus provides everyone with the best they can get in public policy terms under the existing distribution of individual preferences.

Elections provide a mechanism for identifying the median preferences from the distribution of votes over the various policy alternatives offered by parties. They also indicate which party is its carrier (or comes nearest to being so). The electoral system should, and often does, ensure that this party also contains the median member of the legislature—determining of public policy therefore just as the median elector is of the popular majority and for the same reason. No legislative majority can be formed without that party.

It is important to recognize that identification and empowerment of the median position constitute a logical extension of traditional party mandate ideas rather than a replacement or a rival to them. As we shall see in Chapter 2, both 'median mandate' and 'government mandate' base themselves on much the same set of assumptions about party and electoral behaviour. The sole difference lies in the idea that the mandate is given to a single-party government by a cohesive popular majority. Median mandate theory recognizes that such a majority will exist only rarely and looks for an acceptable substitute in the other cases. For the reasons given above, it finds the substitute in the median voter position that then mandates its party carrier to effect it in office. At the extreme, where there *is* a popular majority, the two versions of the mandate merge, for this is the special case where the median voter is found in the majority anyway. All that median mandate ideas reject from the traditional mandate approach is its tendency to compromise with practice by endowing mere pluralities with the attributes of a genuine majority. That is unacceptable, as a plurality-based government is actually opposed by the majority of voters unless it is at the median.

These consequences depend of course on there actually being a median policy position. As we shall see this is facilitated by, but by no means dependent on, opinion being ranged along a single dimension of policy, usually a Left-Right one. We discuss the dimensionality of policy spaces in Chapter 3 both theoretically and with evidence from post-war democracies. Elections do seem to have the property of compressing political differences into a single set of Left-Right differences for the duration of the campaign and a brief time thereafter, however fragmented they become for most of the

---

[1] Note, however, that the same arguments would apply to a situation where votes were weighted by the intensity of feeling behind them. It is just that the location of the median would differ in this case.

interelection period. Even a fragmented interelection policy agenda however usually groups left-wing parties against right-wing parties on most central issues.

Its strategic position does of course make the median party a natural member of governments. In the extreme case of a party that gains a majority of votes, it will form the government itself with a direct mandate to carry through its policies. Coalitions tend to include median parties—in about 80 per cent of post-war governments (according to Laver and Budge 1992: 416). For the reasons given above such parties form a natural anchor point for the parties around them. Being in government naturally reinforces the ability of the median party to get its policy accepted. This is also, under appropriate election arrangements, the policy preferred by the majority of electors once they have constituted themselves as a majority.

We have not arrived back at theories of elections as determining government composition, and through that public policy, for two reasons:

1. Policy payoffs from being in government are not clear in many cases (Laver and Budge 1992: 423–5).
2. Twenty per cent of coalition governments do not include the median party. Unless we are to write the latter off as a negation of democracy, we have to recognize that a median party, representing the majority preference of the electorate, can influence policy in these cases too and for the same reasons. A legislative majority, whether narrow or wide, has to include the median party or at least secure its abstention, in order to get policy through. Since its support is essential it can bargain to have its own, electorally endorsed policy accepted by the government and, if not, defeat the alternative proposed.

Why this is so is shown in Figure 1.1, where actors prefer any policy closer to their own preference on a Left-Right continuum. This puts C, at the median, in the most powerful position. Policy-motivated actors both to left and right need C to form a majority. C can thus bargain for a public policy close to its own position, by threatening to join the alternative majority if C does not get its way. Compared to the policy positions of its rivals on one wing, C's position will be preferred by parties on the other wing in whatever coalition it joins. Thus C's position will constitute the point to which majority-backed

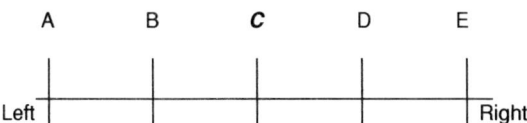

FIGURE 1.1. The policy dominance of the median actor C in election, committee, or legislative voting

policy always tends, where voting is determined solely by the desire to advance one's own policy-preferences.

Of course the matching of median party with median elector will occur only under a voting system that faithfully reflects popular votes in party proportions of legislative seats. Where the relationship is distorted the real median party may be excluded from median status in the legislature so the carrier of the popular preference is not given a policy-veto. What happens under these circumstances can be illustrated by the case of Britain in the post-war period.

Elections are a defective democratic mechanism in Britain because the popular majority are only occasionally allowed a pivotal position in the legislature. The single-member district (SMD) system operating in Britain generally awards a plurality party, which will have won 37–48 per cent of the national vote, the majority of parliamentary seats. It then forms a government that can do whatever it wants under the unwritten constitution, subject only to encountering extra-parliamentary resistance (Budge et al. 1998: 177–98, 681–700).

The situation may not be as anti-democratic or anti-majoritarian as it seems where the legislative majority and the governing party that it supports is also the median party judged in Left-Right terms. Table 1.1 shows the extent to which this has been so, during the post-war period.

Over the course of sixteen elections from 1945 to 2001 inclusive, the median party, even very broadly conceived, became the legislative majority

TABLE 1.1. *Equivalence between the median electoral party and the government in Britain, 1945–2000*

Election year	Post-election government party	Middle party Left-Right issues	Did middle party win?
1945	Labour	Liberals	No
1950	Labour	Conservative	No
1951	Conservative	Conservative (almost)	Yes
1955	Conservative	Conservative	Yes
1959	Conservative	Conservative	Yes
1964	Labour	Labour (almost)	Yes
1966	Labour	Labour	Yes
1970	Conservative	Conservative	Yes
1974(i)	Labour	Liberals	No
1974(ii)	Labour	Liberals	No
1979	Conservative	Liberals	No
1983	Conservative	Liberals-SD Alliance	No
1987	Conservative	Liberals-SD Alliance	No
1992	Conservative	Liberal Democrat	No
1997	Labour	Labour	Yes
2001	Labour	Labour	Yes

eight times, or after only half the elections. What is interesting and significant is that six out of the eight occasions when the middle party, broadly defined, got into office occurred between 1951 and 1970! In 1974 a relatively extreme left-wing Labour Party won a parliamentary majority, then an increasingly right-wing Conservative party got into government from 1979 to 1997. In other words, there has been a tendency for parties taking an extreme ideological position rather than one based on the 'middle ground' to win majorities from 1971 onwards. In that sense British governments have moved further away from reflecting majority opinion in the recent post-war period. Only 'New Labour', by shifting substantially rightwards, managed to reoccupy the centre in 1997 and 2001 and make itself a more consensual government.

The consequence of the mismatch between moderate majority preferences and extremist government policies from 1974 and 1997 is agreed by most commentators to have been a widespread loss of support for political institutions in general, popular cynicism about the real extent of democratic choice and unprecedented political apathy by 2001 when less than 60 per cent of electors actually voted in the general election of that year. Rule by the plurality party is justified in terms of 'working' mandate theories when they have to cope with the absence of a real majority party (cf. Powell 2000), that is, in all elections except for a few presidential ones in the USA. In this situation the party nearest a popular majority is justified by such theories in taking over government and putting its programme into effect unimpeded. Such a party may, however, like the Thatcherite Conservatives, be strongly opposed by the actual majority. Certainly the British electorate seems by its reactions to endorse the alternative view that compromises produced by empowering the median position are more acceptable. Regardless of who forms the government, the party 'carrying' the median preference of the electorate should have a pivotal voting position in the legislative. Even if it just follows its own policy preferences rather than taking on a more general representative role, the coincidence ensures that public policy corresponds as closely as possible to the expressed preferences of all citizens, and certainly to the majority of them. Few would characterize the workings of the 'elective dictatorship' in Britain over the last thirty years as being very democratic.

1.2 HOW ELECTIONS WORK FOR A DEMOCRACY

Democracy should entail popular specification of public policies. This is clear from a normative point of view (Saward's 'necessary correspondence' of policy and felt interests, Saward 1998: 51) and as a research conclusion from our own investigation later. In taking this position we draw on the oldest conceptions of democracy. Voting in Greek city states was held directly on policy proposals and governments were not elected at all but drawn by lot (Bonner 1967). This view is also of course the driving force in modern support for direct democracy, that is, popular voting on policies (Budge 1996). The specification of governments was only conflated with specification of policy in the eighteenth and nineteenth centuries, as a way of extending elective practices to large populations and territories. Electors in a large state could not decide directly on policy, as they could not meet together to discuss it (so it was argued). But they could elect representatives to discuss policies for them (Mill 1861/1910: 179–80).

With the emergence of political parties, electors could choose between or among policy stances as indicated by the parties' election programmes. The usual take on elections, however, places much more attention on which parties would form governments rather than policy adoption and implementation. For one thing, depending on the party system, forming governments often called for post-election party negotiations. For another, even single-party governments face many obstacles to implementation. The last two complications can obscure party responsibility and accountability for what had actually been done by the government. Policy is a parliamentary and governmental matter to be studied after the dust of the election has settled and the winners determined.

Viewed purely as mechanisms for selecting governments, elections appear as remarkably clumsy and approximate instruments, to the extent that most analysts and commentators are resigned to popular control over public actions not really being exercised (Powell 2000). SMD systems provide a strong incentive for two dominant political parties to contest elections within a district (Duverger 1954; Katz 1980; Riker 1982). The evidence on parliaments elected through SMD systems indicates that the mechanics of an electoral system can translate votes into seats in an odd way. This is a consequence of SMD's tendency to translate the vote percentage of the leading party into a seat percentage that is much larger. In this way, the SMD system frequently manufactures parliamentary majorities out of electoral pluralities. That alone is troublesome inasmuch as less than a majority of the people have given their consent—or a majority may actually be opposed (cf. the British case cited above). Even more troublesome for notions of popular control is the fact that certain geographical distributions of votes allow a second-ranking party in SMD systems to have its votes translated into a majority of the seats.

The manufactured majorities and other oddities of the vote-to-seat translation under SMD systems give force to arguments for using proportional representation (PR) to elect parliaments. Arguments in favour of a close party seat to party vote linkage in the legislature are very forceful. However, it is far from settled as to whether PR systems do provide a reliable connection between electorates and governments. The reality for parliaments elected through PR rules is that usually no party wins an outright majority of seats, and multiparty governments form on the basis of post-election bargaining, which may or may not square with the election results. Downs

(1957: 142–63) reasoned that voters in multiparty systems are not able to predict the party coalitions that form governments after an election. It is thus difficult for voters in PR systems to use their votes rationally, where the purpose is to put the reins of power in the hands of a party or parties that will do what the rational voter wants.

Theorizing and analyses of government formation in multiparty systems lend a good deal of credence to Downs' argument. Government formation in these circumstances is viewed in scholarly work principally as a matter of legislative consultation and negotiation, not much tied to election results. To the extent that election results do enter the theory and analysis of government formation in multiparty systems, it is mostly as backdrop. Parties use seats as a resource when trying to figure out what is in their best interest during the negotiations. Riker (1982) and DeSwaan (1973), for instance, suggest that one party might coalesce with another in a policy-blind calculation based on the spoils they can gain by forming a minimal winning coalition. A minimal winning coalition could be conditional on policy preferences, in the sense of Axelrod's conjecture (1970) that government coalitions are policy connected, that is, bring together ideologically adjacent parties. Even with policy connectedness, however, a centre party in a predominantly three-party system, such as the Dutch, could by itself and regardless of the election results choose whether it wants to push the policy position of government to the right or to the left.

All the evidence indicates that most governments form relatively autonomously of elections. So what role *do* elections play in democracy? Our suggestion is that they specify the median (majority) preference of the population, plus the overall policy structure or space within which it is embedded. Politicians and parties then operate within this revealed structure, which a properly functioning electoral system will reproduce in terms of party vote shares in the legislature. These will give a decisive voice on policy to the median party. Election results both empower the median position and inform politicians what it is, thus eliminating the possibility of strategic miscalculations messing up median-(majority-)based outcomes.

The electoral process therefore, if it functions properly in democratic terms, creates the 'necessary correspondence' required by normative democratic theory 'between acts of governance and the equally weighted felt interests of citizens with respect to these acts' (Saward 1998: 51). It does this in both a cognitive and empowerment sense. But in many ways the informative and communicative element comes first. This is because politicians would not even be able to react in strategic or power terms if they did not know the shape of the relevant policy configuration. They have to share a sense of what the underlying policy dimension is and how parties and electors are arranged on it, in order to decide on appropriate action and to form alliances. If they do not know what party is at the median for example, or if they all had differing perceptions of it, their resulting behaviour would be wildly erratic and certainly stand little chance of systematically translating electors' preferences into policy.

All this of course implies that there *is* a median position to be taken and an ordered structure of preferences underpinning it. Mathematical analyses have cast doubt on a median necessarily existing in Euclidean spaces of three or more policy dimensions (McKelvey 1979) and even with two policy dimensions (Schofield 1985). In terms of pure issue spaces a median position can only be absolutely guaranteed in one dimension and by extension, in policy-spaces with separable dimensions (Ordeshook 1986: 250) or with correlated dimensions (Adams and Adams 2000). This is already much, since actual issue spaces are usually of these types. Chapter 2 shows that the real-life world of representative democracy, where a limited number of political parties bind together policies into packages and simplify choices for electors, largely evades all these theoretical difficulties and to all intents and purposes guarantees the emergence of a median policy position.

The argument for elections having a policy specifying rather than a government specifying function does not depend therefore on the existence of a one dimensional election space. However it is facilitated by it. We argue in Chapter 3 that spaces of this type emerge from the Left-Right, bipolar, terms in which electoral debate is usually conducted. The election campaign itself is an active force simplifying and compressing other issues into such a space. The dynamics of political rhetoric and media simplification for a mass audience require straightforward summary comparisons to be made between national parties. In turn these squeeze out regional variants and group concerns, along with peripheral issues, by focusing on their central confrontation, which is interpreted in terms of a single Left-Centre-Right continuum.

Thus the median voter and his or her preferred party *are* identified by the election. Research reported below shows that this party tends also to be at the median on the majority of the separate issues into which the policy specialization of ministries and complementary division of legislative labour divide debate in the interelection period. This gives the party a general influence over public policies made by legislative processes, which in turn enables it to bring them closer to its own and hence to its median supporters' preferences and thus to those of the popular majority.

1.3 RE-EVALUATING ELECTORAL PROCESSES

Not only is a switch from a government-centred to a median-centred mandate theory practicable, it also confers other theoretical and normative advantages. These in themselves make a compelling case for adopting an alternative, policy-based view to the 'choice of government' one.

Suspend the thought that elections are about which party governs and the world of mass democratic governance looks very different. Instead of asking who governs, ask from what policy position does governance emanate? The answer is simple in a uni-dimensional policy space with political parties motivated by policy. The position in control is that of the median party in parliament, which Peter van Roozendahl identifies as the 'central' party (Van Roozendahl 1990; 1992). If there is a central party, which in a single dimensional space there almost always is but for the special case of the policy point falling between two parties, policy proposals favoured by the central party will be controlling.

What could this mean for the role of elections? It implies that their purpose is to communicate where the median voter stands. It means that voting is an expressive act with a guaranteed value: every vote counts not in deciding the winner but in identifying the median. It means that whatever value there is to majority rule, a majority will be in control. To the extent that their choice is not limited by sparse offerings from parties and otherwise remains undistorted by the electoral rules translating votes to seats, it means the median party will be at a position reasonably close to the median voter. It also means that as long as the dimensionality of election space and the positions of the parties along the dimensions are understood, the allocation of political responsibility is clear. It belongs to the policy position of the median party. Finally, it means that authorization to act for the popular majority takes place through empowerment of the median party, which after the elections is motivated by its own policy driven incentives to control public policy.

Many of these insights have a normative as well as empirical bearing on democracy, covering points traditionally made by mandate theory about the legitimation of some party policies compared to others and who has accountability for their implementation. The generalized formulation avoids the difficulties traditional mandate theory faces with regard to the legitimation and accountability of non-majoritarian or multiparty governments. In order to change policy or to punish non-fulfilment of promises, change the median position—a more practicable task than changing a coalition government *in toto* or even ejecting an entrenched plurality government.

This policy-based mandate theory of elections also makes a decisive contribution to a longstanding debate in political science: which election system is best, PR or SMD? It is clear that the latter, with its manufactured majorities based on the plurality (or even second) party, offers no guarantee in the short-term[2] of empowering the median and often in fact discriminates heavily against it. PR is more reliable in this respect.

---

[2] Taking a long-term view, the alternation of plurality-based governments under SMD, even where they are generally to the Left or Right of the electoral median, does produce an average policy effect that can approximate the average median elector position. In this sense SMD systems are more representative than they seem when one takes them government by government (cf. Chapter 12).

The traditional argument for SMD is that it aids the emergence of strong—often single-party—governments. Governments that ignore or flout the median preference are not normatively desirable however. They contribute to adversarial stances which can in the end lead to suboptimal policy mixes (Lijphart 1999). The alleged defect of PR systems, that they produce weak coalition governments, seems less serious when it is realized that policymaking emanates from the median rather than from the government position.

What does the policy-orientated view tell us is *not* important about elections? For a party to seek more votes by moving around the policy space is essentially futile with respect to disrupting the communication purpose of the election. If a party moves to the position of the median voter, and if voters believe the party movement is sincere, and if the party follows through, then no harm is done. The subsequent policy adoptions will fall in the vicinity of the median voter. On the other hand, if the party movement is just a strategic electoral manoeuvre without any follow through once in office and if voters fail to foresee that insincerity, the safety valve is that the other parties in parliament will line up along the dimension and oppose the policy proposals of the strategic party. That is, the true median party will re-present itself in parliament and take control from a party that achieved power on a purely insincere basis.

A policy-based view implies that incumbents should not necessarily be the targets of credit or blame for good and bad policy. What matters is the location of the median party particularly if it is a reasonable size. Taking a policy-based view also implies that Downs' worry (1957: 120–45) about identifying future governments under PR rules is not terribly relevant. A voter's interest will be served only by casting a sincere vote for an expressive purpose.

A final advantage of median-mandate theory is in toning down the sharp contrasts often drawn between direct and representative democracy. Direct democracy, though beset by many possible problems, clearly involves citizens in deciding public policy through devices such as referendums or most notably the initiative.[3] Hence it meets Saward's criterion of a 'necessary' connection between popular preferences and public policy better than the classic conception of representative democracy, where policy depends in the end on the will of legislators rather than on that of the people. Indeed, the attraction of direct democracy for many is simply that it seems more democratic in terms of popular control—giving a powerful impetus to the growing use of referendums in the modern world (Mendelson and Parkin 2001; Auer and Bützer 2001).

---

[3] Both referendums and initiatives involve electors voting for and against policy proposals. The former however are often called by governments at their own convenience while the latter can be called independently by the proposers of some policy change, thus putting the calling of a vote as well as participation in it into the popular domain.

The contrast seems overdrawn however when we bring in political parties and their role in presenting policy programmes to the public in elections, which are then taken as deciding between the competing packages. Given the central role of the parties in contemporary democracies they have really become 'party democracies' where the parties stand in elections on the basis of their programme—a programme to which governments formed by them and legislators attached to them are bound by convention and long-term considerations (Downs 1957: 95–104) to support during the interelection period.

All forms of mandate theory take this view of the way democracies function. The policy-oriented view underlying the median mandate stresses it even more than the others, however, since effecting the preferred policy does not depend on a majority actually emerging to support a single party government. Electoral endorsement of policy comes through clearly under all circumstances if it takes the form of a median mandate.

Even with this, a party democracy offering electors a choice between bundles of policies endorsed by each party, might still produce different results from voting on each policy individually. Table 1.2 provides a simple illustration. A party might gain majority approval on its programmes even though a majority of electors would vote against its position on each single issue. There is no simple way of saying which would be a 'correct' result over the range of policies in the table. It may be that certain types of issues, notably Left-Right ones, are naturally tied together in people's perceptions and hence best voted on *en bloc*, as a general orientation for policy. Issues outside this bundle, which have not as a result been really voted on in an election campaign, might be best decided by direct vote in a referendum.

TABLE 1.2. *A possible voting situation in which party B wins on its overall programme even though a majority opposes its position on each specific issue*

Voters	Issues		
	X	Y	X
1	a	b	b
2	b	a	b
3	b	b	a
4	a	a	a
5	a	a	a

Notes: The separate issues are X, Y, and Z.

The *a* and *b* entries are different alternatives on each issue, which may be positions endorsed by political parties A and B, respectively. If each issue X, Y, and Z is voted on individually and separately, alternative *a* (supported by political party A) wins. If they are voted on together (e.g. as a political programme), with voters giving each issue equal weight, alternative *b* (supported by political party B) wins, as voters 1, 2, and 3 will vote for party B on balance.

Resolving this question however is not really our concern here. What we want to emphasize is the way in which a policy-orientated view of modern democracies shifts the argument away from a simplistic confrontation of the merits of representative deliberation versus direct popular voting. What it shows is that both involve policy choices between the positions endorsed by parties (Budge 1996). But one may be a wider, more general choice than the other. Closing the gap with direct democracy is just one advantage of adopting a median mandate approach to representative democracy, to add to the others listed above.

1.4 EVALUATING THE MEDIAN MANDATE

The ability of median mandate ideas to meet many of the conceptual and practical problems that confront mandate theory in general make it hard to argue that a change in perspective is not worthwhile. In this life, however, the advantages of such a move are often balanced, if not outweighed, by the disadvantages. What are they in this case?

A first springs immediately to mind. The theory has something of a naïve, idealistic cast even if it also possesses some historical and normative force. It would indeed be nice if majority feeling were automatically reflected in policy processes whether or not a majority actually formed. But is this not too good to be true? *Can* parties be trusted to run with the preferred policy position? Will governments, with all their powers, really substitute the median position for their own (leaving aside the rare cases where they coincide as a single-party (electoral) majority government)?

The belief that elections are about winning office is so common that a first response to questions about democracy is that it makes governments dependent on winning elections. There is, however, even among those who appear to accept this truism, a large body of commentary on how undesirable it is. Madison himself provides one example. Perhaps his most clever and powerful argument was to claim that overlaying a democratic apparatus on a large territory and population was a good idea because from time to time, issue to issue, there would be cross-cutting cleavages and shifting coalitions so that there would be no permanent majority, that is, no permanent winner. In a contemporary commentary on Madison's idea, Guinier (1994) refers to the spirit of what Madison had in mind as 'governing by taking turns'. Before Guinier, Dahl (1956) referred to Madison's idea as democratic pluralism.

Buchanan and Tullock (1962) offered *The Calculus of Consent* as a theory of democracy. In it, they take as their premise that the unanimity principle is the ethically endowed democratic decision rule, majority rule a mere mechanism for efficient decision-making. As we have pointed out the median position is the best outcome everyone can hope for and hence can agree on. In a thoughtful and sobering commentary on the drift in thinking about modern democracy in the USA, Cain (1992: 273–5) warns of a new populism that puts so much stock into the idea of winning, clearly and decisively, that it threatens the idea of representative government. To the criticism of naiveté we would say that all of these commentaries are telling us that, in one way or another, putting exclusive power in the hands of winners is not the desired outcome. Therefore, it is not naïve to want elections to operate in policy terms. Can they?

Clearly even the most desirable normative outcomes have to face the test of reality. If the conditions for their application do not exist in working democracies, normative hopes cannot justify them. On issues of practicality, one could quibble with several of the conditions that would have to hold in order for the world to work according to our ideas. The diversity of policy positions offered by parties may certainly be too sparse. Just as surely, the electoral rules can distort the vote to seat translation thus separating the median position in parliament from the median among voters. And—a possibility already considered—policy disputes may not naturally line-up in the required policy space. Even if they did, all but the median party would have a strong policy incentive to rearrange to their own advantage that common way of viewing the world (Riker 1982). Finally, striving to achieve a preferred policy outcome is a dubious goal to specify for politicians. Even if the median party acts in its own self-interest by pursuing its own preferred policies, will it not be forced into compromises or outright abandonment of them, possibly in exchange for office?

Granting that all these criticisms have some validity in the abstract, we should nevertheless consider the empirical evidence before engaging in extensive arguments over their plausibility. That is what we are going to do in the following chapters of this book, with specially collected information from functioning post-war democracies.

1.5 PLAN OF DISCUSSION

Before doing so, however, we need to systematize and detail the general arguments rehearsed in this chapter. Here we have given the broad view. Now we need the detail, starting with the assumptions of mandate theories themselves, in Chapter 2. Not only do we summarize them in propositional form, we also make a preliminary check on whether some of their conditions are actually met in contemporary democracies.

Finding a median depends on the kind of issue space political debate and party competition is located in. A common tendency is to talk about it in Left-Right terms. Is this justified? And what are the other possibilities? Median positions have to be recognized in order to exert any effect. How far do parties and electors communicate preferences to each other within a shared issue space, rather than one fragmented by steep boundaries of knowledge and information? These questions are all considered in Chapter 3. Chapter 4 then focuses all these discussions into specific questions we can put to the evidence we have collected on established post-war democracies in the second half of the twentieth century.

It is not of course as if mandate theories are totally descriptive, to be rejected if actual democracies do not operate according to their rules. On the contrary, both the government and the median mandate share the usual normative-descriptive mix of political theory. Even if we find that contemporary democracies do not implement a government mandate for example this is not conclusive evidence that they *should* not do so. The mandate could still exist as a state to which they should aspire, because in some sense it might seem more democratic than what they have actually got.

On the other hand, since mandate statements also have a descriptive aspect empirical evidence does have some impact on the standing of the theory. This is especially true if an alternative, like the median, with equally good democratic credentials, does appear to match better with what these well-accredited democracies are doing. One can at least say that the median provides a better description of the way they work and hence seems easier to apply in practice. To this extent, an empirically supported mandate theory can be said to constitute a relevant functioning norm for democracy.

These considerations underlie the checks undertaken with comparative and overtime evidence in Parts II, III, and IV of the book. Parties are the crucial catalyst of electoral policy choices in modern representative democracies. In Chapter 5 we consider how good parties are in this role, particularly how far they offer 'a choice not an echo'. Because the government mandate fails all too often with respect to some of its own required conditions, an alternative or supplementary version has gained theoretical force. That is the idea that, if electors cannot reliably pick party governments on the basis of their future programmes, they can at least evaluate them on their record and reward or punish them accordingly. Chapter 6 reviews the electorate's ability to systematically hold governments to account in the context of 'economic voting', but concludes there is little evidence for it. On the other hand, Chapter 6 shows strong evidence that median voter positions could be empowered by translating them accurately into similar policy positions of governments. Chapter 7 investigates how, despite representational distortions deriving from limitations on party policy offerings, electoral system mistranslations, and post-election party negotiations, median voter and government policy positions are generally aligned. The key finding is that while distortions are readily apparent everywhere, across the steps of the representational process and more especially through time, the distortions tend to cancel one another out so that in the intermediate and long run distortions do not amount to much in terms of representational bias.

Part III examines the correspondence between median voter preferences and actual public policy. It begins in Chapter 8 with an analysis of the connections between parliamentary medians, governments, and ministries on the one hand, and on the other the policies that governments declare their intention to pursue while in office. Chapter 9 takes the next step and looks beyond government policy intentions to investigate how preferences of the various actors connect to actual policies. There is only weak evidence that declared policy intentions and actual policies follow in any sort of predictable way from the Left-Right or other policy preferences of median parties or median voters.

Those weak results force us to step back from the complexity of everyday politics and policy and reconsider the policymaking process in a larger democratic context. Having found in Chapter 7 that representation is distorted in numerous ways in the short run but is accurate in the long run, we look at the short and long run dynamics of policy and politics in Chapters 10 and 11. Our investigations show policy has a slow-moving dynamic while electoral politics and their impact on parliaments and governments are highly dynamic. We also find in virtually every one of our twenty-one democracies that highly dynamic politics are anchored in long-term equilibrium (Left-Right) positions. In Chapter 12, we investigate whether these long-term equilibria are responsible for setting the mark for slow moving policy, what we label the policy regimes, in our twenty-one countries. In three different policy areas—the size of a nation's political economy, the resources it expends on its welfare state, and its peaceful versus militarist orientation to international affairs—we find this to be the case. Further, the political preferences with the strongest and most consistent policy effects are those of the Left-Right parliamentary median.

We conclude with Chapter 13, showing how a median mandate theory pulls together strands of democratic theorizing that until now have stood as qualifications on democratic possibilities. Our account provides a rounded view of representative democracy centred on the median mandate. With that discussion we come full circle, back to the central propositions of mandate theory, which we now present and discuss in Chapter 2.

2

Mandate Theories: Government and Median

Mandate theory has a reassuringly familiar ring since it sets out the processes that most people see as making democracies democratic. Elections are competitive. Programmatic political parties present policy choices to electors in their attempts to attract votes and pledge themselves to carry out their programmes if they get into government. Governments have a limited term of office and can be held to account for what they have done (or failed to do). Not only does this account provide a broad description of the way contemporary democracies work, it also justifies them by asserting that governments are ultimately responsible to the people and under popular control.

Like most common-sense accounts however this one glosses over difficulties and ignores contradictions. Many citizens see their own democracy as falling far short of this ideal (Hofferbert and Klingemann 2002) with devious and corrupt political parties, unresponsive governments, and aloof bureaucracies. They may even view all democracies as sharing these defects to some extent. The most common complaint is that parties make election promises only in order to win votes and forget about them immediately after they arrive in power.

In contrast, comparative investigations have uncovered high fulfillment of specific election pledges (Rose 1980; Rallings 1987; Royed 1996) and a strong reflection of programmatic priorities in government expenditure (Klingemann et al. 1994). How far democratic processes as a whole fall short of popular ideals for them remains a moot point however—one which can only be resolved by the kind of systematic comparative investigation undertaken below.

Much of this is naturally taken up with reviewing the evidence we have collected from post-war democracies in all parts of the world. A first prerequisite however is to go beyond loose and possibly contradictory characterizations of the processes involved to systematic integrated statements of the conditions necessary for a mandate to work. Only by clarifying the theory can we be sure it applies under existing circumstances. Theoretical clarification also involves looking for and eliminating possible inconsistencies, thus making mandate descriptions and justifications more intelligible in themselves.

2.1 MANDATE THEORIES

As Chapter 1 pointed out, there is actually more than one kind of mandate theory available for discussion and analysis. In this chapter we specify two: a government mandate and a median mandate.

As we have emphasized, mandate theory, like many other approaches in political science, is both normative and descriptive. Its normative and descriptive aspects complement each other. As a normative theory, the mandate provides a justification for representative democracy as being uniquely sensitive to citizen interests. As a descriptive theory, it gives an account of how democracy works. In fact the two are connected. We could hardly justify democracy as institutionalizing the mandate if we found that democracies in practice do not work that way. As Riker (1964: vi–vii) has put it, political science research 'starts with a goal and searches for a way to attain it.... The scientific question is "What institutions encourage the chosen morality?" ' Empirical analyses enter because 'Description and analysis of causes (or more accurately, the analysis of occasions) are necessary for answering this question.' Our empirical checks leave the standing of the theory as a possible ideal largely untouched. But they do show which of its versions functions best as an account of contemporary democracy. Given the equal moral standing of both, empirical evidence favouring one rather than the other should swing the balance of acceptability between the two.

That at any rate is our stance in this book and the justification for the comparative investigation undertaken in Parts II, III, and IV. We make a modest start here with Tables 2.2, 2.3 and 2.5 below. But the main thrust of this chapter is theoretical: what exactly does mandate theory say? Under what conditions do its various versions differ from each other? As we shall see, they are essentially the same except on the question of who gets empowered by the election result.

In terms of both popular conceptions and most political science discussion what gets empowered is the government and the party forming the government. The idea of a median mandate is a new one, so far as we know being propounded systematically here for the first time. Accordingly we start with the traditional government-centred view of the mandate and only go on to the median version after showing that the conditions required by the government mandate are hardly met in practice even on a first simple test.

2.2 THEORETICAL CONDITIONS FOR A GOVERNMENT MANDATE

Government mandate theory can be characterized as saying that the policy preferences of a knowable and coherent majority of voters determine the winner of an election and that winner takes its turn at running government on the policy lines it had promised before the election. In its more detailed form, Table 2.1 summarizes the theory as comprehensively as possible.

Conditions 1 to 6 are explicitly spelled out by the various authorities listed in the table notes. They take somewhat different emphases depending on whether their focus is on the parties' role in offering choices or the voters' role in making them: however, the thrust of their argument is the same. Condition 1, *party distinctiveness*, says that for a mandate to operate parties have to offer a policy choice; otherwise there is no policy-based reason to prefer one party to another. Conditions 2 and 3, *voter information and motivation*, say that voters must be informed enough to recognize the party policy differences on offer and policy motivated enough to base their choices on the policy profile closest to their preferred position; otherwise their votes are not communicating policy information. With votes cast on the basis of policies, Condition 4, *voter majority*, requires that a majority preference for a particular party be clearly registered; otherwise one cannot know what the majority prefers. Condition 5, *electoral system translation*, says that adherence to all the preceding conditions would go for naught if the electoral system mistranslates the voter majority. Finally, Condition 6, *party policy commitment*, says that the party in government translates its policy proclamations into policy; otherwise voters would elect whom they (thought that they) wanted but would not get what they want.

To check whether the conditions for a government mandate are actually met in contemporary democratic practice, we do not need to look into each and every one of them. Each is necessary for a government mandate to operate. Thus failure with respect to any one condition indicates that a mandate is not present in the case in question. Given the conditions of the theory, it makes sense to concentrate on the electoral majority's endorsement of governments as it forms the essential mechanism postulated by the theory for creating a correspondence between popular preferences and public policy.

TABLE 2.1. *Conditions for a government mandate to emerge*

1. *Party distinctiveness*—at least two parties have policy profiles distinct from one another.
2. *Voter information*—voters recognize the policy profiles of each party.
3. *Voter motivation*—voters cast their ballots on the basis of the party policy profile they prefer to see implemented by a government.
4. *Voter majority*—a majority of voters are revealed to have the same preference, given the choices available.
5. *Electoral system translation*—the election outcome clearly designates the party with majority electoral support to form a government that will carry out its policy.
6. *Party policy commitment*—the party in government carries out its policies announced at the time of the election.

Sources: These conditions are a synthesis of statements made by various authors about conditions required by mandate theory, referred to variously as conditions for the 'responsible party model', the 'Westminster model', and popular control over public policy (Polsby and Wildavsky 1971; Sullivan and O'Connor 1972; Ranney 1975; Kavanagh 1981; Aldrich 1995).

2.3 PRELIMINARY EVIDENCE FOR THE PRESENCE OF A GOVERNMENT MANDATE

Our evidence on majorities comes from 21 democracies, covering 266 elections and 486 governments. These involve the first constitutionally authorized democratic election after 1949 through to the formation of any government in 1995. Seats and votes to 1990 rely on data reported by Volkens and her colleagues (1992), who themselves relied on compilations by Mackie and Rose (1991). After 1990, vote and seat data come from various annual political updates reported in the *European Journal of Political Research*. Designations of governments, parties in government, and durations of governments come from the compilation by Woldendorp, Keman, and Budge (2000). The American cases, thirteen governments and eleven elections, refer to presidential elections and presidential administrations.

Table 2.2 categorizes election results in six SMD countries. Support among the electorate and the status of ensuing government(s) are combined into five possibilities:

1. An electoral majority produces a majority government.
2. An electoral plurality manufactures a majority government.

TABLE 2.2. *Percentage of time in government and number of governments by majority six status of governments and electorates in six SMD systems, early 1950s to 1995*

	Government and electoral status									
Country	Government majority and electoral majority % time	no. of govts	Government majority and electoral plurality % time	no. of govts	Government majority and electoral minority % time	no. of govts	Government minority and electoral plurality % time	no. of govts	Government minority and electoral minority % time	no. of govts
Australia $n = 25$	11.5	2	60.9	15	27.4	7	0.0	0	0.2	1
Canada $n = 17$	19.6	2	59.7	8	0.0	0	17.3	5	3.5	2
France $n = 28$	32.4	7	46.2	14	0.0	0	15.4	4	6.1	3
New Zealand $n = 22$	6.5	1	82.1	19	11.4	2	0.0	0	0.0	0
United Kingdom $n = 18$	0.0	0	91.1	15	7.6	2	0.0	0	1.3	1
United States $n = 13$	72.1	9	27.9	4	0.0	0	0.0	0	0.0	0
Totals ($n = 123$)										
No. of govts	21		75		11		9		7	
% of govt	17.1		61.0		8.9		7.3		5.7	

3. An electoral minority produces a majority government, where an electoral minority refers to a party receiving fewer votes than the plurality party.
4. An electoral plurality produces a minority government.
5. An electoral minority produces a minority government, where an electoral minority refers to a party receiving fewer votes than the plurality party.

Only 17.1 per cent of the SMD elections have electoral majorities producing majority governments. The modal outcome under SMD rules is for a single party to win an electoral plurality and have majority control of government. This occurred for 61 per cent of the SMD elections. In another 8.9 per cent of SMD elections, most notably in Australia, we find an anomalous outcome where a party running second to the plurality party gains majority control of government. In 7.3 per cent of the SMD elections, a plurality party did not receive enough of the usual bonus to win a seat majority but did win enough seats to form a minority government. Finally, on seven occasions a party with an electoral minority held the largest number of parliamentary seats, formed a government, but fell short of majority control.

It is clear from these results that a necessary condition for a government mandate, the emergence of an identifiable majority-supported party, does not generally exist in these purportedly majoritarian, SMD-based, democracies. The plurality-supported governments that usually emerge do not meet the criteria for such a mandate, as there is no guarantee that they are not strongly opposed by the majority of electors who voted for other parties. Elections in these six democracies are thus often determining in the sense of deciding who wins but not majority-empowering, since often no electoral majority exists for any single party or for a particular grouping of parties. The winning party can claim a mandate, but it is not known that it has been given a mandate. Moreover, in the case of the USA we are only reporting on presidential elections, and there the President and Congress were under majority control by different parties more often than not.

How far do PR systems institutionalize the conditions for a government mandate? Table 2.3 shows, paradoxically, that they are far more likely than SMD systems to produce majority governments with groupings of parties that have garnered a majority of votes. This occurs in 53.4 per cent of the governments forming under PR systems, which is three times more frequently than in SMD systems (see Table 2.2). Given the duration of these governments, this condition amounts to majority-majority governance about 54 per cent of the time. However, only ten of these cases are single-party majority governments.[1]

---

[1] The ten governments resulted from eight elections: Austria 1971 (one government), Austria 1975 (1), Austria 1979 (1), Germany 1957 (1), Ireland 1977 (2), Portugal 1987 (1), Portugal 1991 (1), and Sweden 1968 (2).

TABLE 2.3. *Percentage of time in government and number of governments by majority status of governments and electorates in fifteen PR systems, early 1950s to 1995*

Country	Government and Electoral Status							
	Government majority and electoral majority % time	no. of govts	Government majority based on < 50% of electors % time	no. of govts	Government minority based on < 50% of electors % time	no. of govts	Caretaker or nonpartisan % time	no. of govts
Austria $n = 18$	87.2	16	9.3	1	3.5	1	0.0	0
Belgium $n = 29$	59.1	18	32.6	6	6.1	3	2.2	2
Denmark $n = 27$	15.1	3	3.5	1	81.4	23	0.0	0
Finland $n = 40$	67.7	20	8.8	4	11.3	8	12.2	8
Germany $n = 25$	82.7	18	15.7	3	0.0	0	1.5	4
Iceland $n = 18$	91.1	14	0.0	0	8.9	4	0.0	0
Ireland $n = 19$	12.8	3	42.6	6	44.6	10	0.0	0
Italy $n = 48$	49.7	21	10.7	5	35.4	17	4.2	5
Luxembourg $n = 18$	89.6	13	10.4	1	0.0	0	0.0	0
Netherlands $n = 18$	87.7	13	8.1	1	0.0	0	4.2	4
Norway $n = 21$	0.0	0	36.0	6	64.0	15	0.0	0
Portugal $n = 13$	48.1	4	14.8	3	31.3	3	5.8	3
Spain $n = 7$	19.4	1	17.9	1	62.8	5	0.0	0
Sweden $n = 21$	21.0	5	3.7	1	75.3	15	0.0	0
Switzerland $n = 45$	100.0	45	0.0	0	0.0	0	0.0	0
Totals ($n = 363$)								
no. of govts		194		39		104		26
% of govts	53.4		10.7		28.7		7.2	

On the face of it, this extensive majority-majority correspondence under PR rules meets the conditions for a government mandate. A fatal flaw exists however in the nature of the electoral majority manufactured in the process of putting together a majority coalition in the legislature. The electoral majority on which the government rests is top-down, not bottom-up, and thus is not one created by the voters' expressed preferences.

While perfectly good as a theory in itself, and omnipresent as a justification for democracy, the government mandate seems irrelevant to the practical workings of contemporary democracies. Its emphasis on empowering the majority is not met since a knowable and coherent electoral majority so seldom in fact creates a government.[2]

That does not imply that we ought to abandon totally the idea of a mandate from electorate to government. It is difficult, however, unless all parties converge on the median[3] to see any other mechanism whereby elections can translate popular preferences into policy under representative democracy. A temptation is to turn to direct democracy as the only way in which policy could be democratically determined. There is, however, the alternative already suggested. Alter the focus of the mandate from government to median party, and in so doing set up more realistic conditions for its conferment.

2.4 THEORETICAL CONDITIONS FOR A MEDIAN MANDATE

The key change in going from a government-centred to a median conception of the mandate is that instead of asking who governs, we ask from what policy position does governance emanate? When parties give a broadly unidimensional form to the policy space, and are motivated by the policy preferences that give rise to this alignment, the policy position in control is that of the party of the median parliamentarian. This is what van Roozendahl (1990, 1992) has identified as the 'central' party (see also Laver and Shepsle 1996 on the very strong party).

To see why, we can go back to Figure 1.1 again, where actors prefer any policy closer to their own preference on a Left-Right continuum. This puts C, at the median, in the most powerful position. Actors both on the left and right need C to form a majority. C can thus bargain for a public policy close to its own position, by threatening to join the alternative majority if C does not get its way. Compared to the policy positions of their rivals on the opposing wing, C's position will be preferred by partners on the other wing in whatever coalition it joins. Thus C's position will constitute the point towards which majority-based policy always tends.

---

[2] It could be argued that the situation is better than this because electoral alliances of parties often provide two alternatives to the electorate, one of which gets a majority (e.g. left and right in France). It is only rarely, however, that these agree on a common programme before the election. As electors generally do not know what policy package they are voting for, the conditions for a government mandate are still not being met.

[3] This implication derives from Downs' spatial model (1957: 118, 125). Even in his treatment, however, it is limited to two candidates or parties. His prediction that a multi-party system would be largely static in their policy offerings (Downs 1957: 125–7) applies to all democracies outside the USA and is upheld by the available comparative evidence (Budge et al. 2001: 19–50).

It is important to recognize that this standard 'power of the median' argument applies both to electors and to policy motivated parties (Black 1958). It is the reason why the median position is so often used as an indicator of majority preferences (Huber and Powell, 1994; Powell and Vanberg 2000; Powell 2000). Without the median voter, a knowable and coherent majority simply cannot be formed, by definition. Because the median position is so crucial, actors located there can bargain, implicitly or explicitly, to have the majority-supported position close to their own. Their trump is the credible threat to form an alternative majority with the people on the other wing. Thus majority preferences (under the conditions specified) must be at or near the median position.

The same logic must apply to parties if their internal discipline is tight enough for them to be regarded as unitary actors. Even if C is very small compared to the other parties these still need C's support to form a majority. Just as in the electorate, party C can bring the final policy close to its own preference by threatening defection to an opposing wing. Under majority voting rules in a legislature, C is the policy king (a position qualified of course by real-life practicalities such as party size, uncertainty, separated policy areas, and so on, which we consider later).

We spell out details of the necessary conditions for a median mandate in Table 2.4. They closely resemble those for the government mandate in Table 2.1. This is not surprising as the electoral majority on which a government mandate rests is a special case of the median mandate; where there is a single-party majority, the median position is by definition part of it. The reverse does not hold however; there can be a median position without the majority voting for a single party.

Under any mandate theory, parties have to present a choice to electors; otherwise there is no policy-based reason for voters to prefer one party over another. Thus once again we have Condition 1, *party distinctiveness*. Condi-

TABLE 2.4. *Conditions for a median mandate to emerge*

1. *Party distinctiveness*—at least two parties have policy positions that differ from one another.
2. *Voter information*—voters recognize the policy profiles of the parties.
3. *Voter motivation*—voters cast their ballots on the basis of the party policy position they prefer to see in control of policymaking.
4. *Shared party-voter alignment*—voters and parties arrange their public policy preferences within broadly the same policy space, probably a Left-Right dimension.
5. *Electoral system translation*—the election outcome makes the party supported by the median voter the party with which the median parliamentarian affiliates.
6. *Party policy commitment*—parties are motivated by a desire to see their own policy position control policymaking to the greatest extent possible.
7. *Power of the median*—the occupant of the median position is crucial to the creation of a majority in both the electorate and parliament.
   (*a*) Majority-endorsed preferences tend towards the median voter position, so this forms the best indicator of popular policy preferences in general.
   (*b*) Public policy tends towards the policy of the parliamentary median under legislative majority voting procedures.

tions 2 and 3, *voter information* and *motivation*, as for the government mandate, say that voters must be informed enough to recognize the party policy differences on offer and policy motivated enough to base their choices on the policy profile closest to their preferred position; otherwise their votes are not communicating policy information. Condition 4, *shared party-voter alignment*, requires that voters and parties communicate in largely the same political language, probably a Left-Right dimension, otherwise what the voters think they have expressed and what the parties think that they have heard will not connect. Condition 5, *electoral system translation*, says that the election outcome, in terms of the distribution of seats among parties in parliament, makes the party of the median parliamentarian the same as the party preferred by the median voter. Condition 6, *party policy commitment*, says that there must exist a self-motivation among parliamentarians to see their policy preferences converted so far as possible into actual policy; otherwise they would not empower the parliamentary median for policy purposes. A robust comparative finding on coalition governments is that over 80 per cent incorporate the legislative median party (van Roozendahl 1990; Laver and Budge 1992: 415–20: Muller and Strom 2000: 453–69). Where they do not, this is often under minority governments where the median can exercise control over legislative coalitions anyway. Finally, Condition 7 summarizes the standard *power of the median* reasoning previously discussed, and does not require detailed justification here. We can refer again to Figure 1.1 which demonstrates that, logically, actors with preferences located along a one-dimensional continuum who prefer nearer policy outcomes to ones further away will ally with the median actor, who can therefore swing the policy in its direction by the threat of changing allegiance to the other wing.

2.5 PRELIMINARY EVIDENCE OF A MEDIAN MANDATE

Using the same data with which we checked whether the majority condition for the government mandate operates in contemporary democracies, we can check also whether electoral system translation occurs in median mandate terms. Presenting the check in simpler language, we can see how far in contemporary democracies the party supported by the median voter is also the party with the median parliamentarian. Table 2.5 presents this information in a format similar to that of Tables 2.3 and 2.4 with SMD and PR systems shown separately.

Two clear conclusions emerge from Table 2.5. First, there is a quite extensive equivalence everywhere except Britain[4] between the median electoral party and the median legislative one. It is not perfect but at 80.5 per

[4] The discrepancy between less than a third of the British cases having corresponding electoral and parliamentary medians in Table 2.5 and the half of cases where they correspond in Table 1.1 is accounted for by the fact that the latter bends over backwards to make the equivalence and

TABLE 2.5. *Number and percentages of parliaments where the median legislative party was supported by the median elector, under SMD and PR systems, early 1950s to 1995*

	SMD			PR	
	Number of parliaments	Percentage of parliaments		Number of parliaments	Percentage of parliaments
Australia	14/18	77.8	Austria	11/13	84.6
Canada	11/14	78.6	Belgium	12/15	80.0
France	5/10	50.0	Denmark	18/19	94.7
New Zealand	11/15	73.3	Finland	11/13	84.6
United Kingdom	4/13	30.8	Germany	11/12	91.7
United States	11/11	100.0	Iceland	11/13	84.6
			Ireland	11/14	78.6
			Italy	8/11	72.7
			Luxembourg	8/10	80.0
			Netherlands	13/13	100.0
			Norway	8/11	72.7
			Portugal	7/8	87.5
			Spain	4/6	66.7
			Sweden	13/15	86.7
			Switzerland	12/12	100.0
Totals	56/81	69.1	Totals	158/185	85.4

cent—that is, four-fifths of all parliaments—it represents much more impressive support for the actual existence of median electoral system translation than for the government majority one.

Second, PR democracies achieve the equivalence more often than SMD democracies. Since PR is explicitly designed to reflect party vote shares in legislature seats, this is not a surprise. However, it is a confirmation of our expectations and a first indication that a median mandate may be more easily achieved under PR than SMD. This provides grounds for favouring PR in the design of democratic elections if we accept the median mandate approach to democracy. For that, however, we need much more theoretical and comparative analysis.

2.6 THE MEDIAN AND GOVERNMENT MANDATES: PRELIMINARY CONCLUSIONS

It is satisfying to have our conjecture, that the median mandate is a more relevant formulation of the processes of modern democracy than the government mandate, confirmed by a first empirical inquiry. The main focus of this chapter however has really been on drawing out the theoretical assumptions and implications behind these positions. The statements of government mandate theory (see Table 2.1) and of median mandate theory

---

hence takes coming near the median position as equivalent to occupying it. In the strictly numeric terms of Table 2.5 a party that is 2 or 3 points away from the median is simply not at the median.

(see Table 2.4) are to our knowledge the most complete and detailed made to date. As such they will guide the rest of this investigation, which we report in Parts II and III.

It is important to emphasize once more that the median mandate is a generalization and updating of the traditional mandate, which has given the winning party its legitimacy in Western democracies. In traditional mandate theory a winning party gains office because a majority approves its programme, which it then must carry through in government. Unfortunately such an electoral majority is seldom seen in practice, contributing to the idea that elections are a broken mechanism so far as controlling government goes. In fact, mandate theory has often been pressed into service to justify 'elective dictatorships' based on pluralities that sometimes seem to be opposed by a popular majority.

What our reconceptualization of elections does is to transfer the idea of the mandate from the governing party(ies) as such to the median party in parliament, provided its position corresponds closely to that of the median voter. A popular majority *can* be said to have endorsed that position and given a mandate to the party, which its centrality in legislative coalition building ensures it can carry out. If everything works out properly this is what *should* happen. The workings of elections and governments in twenty-one democracies over the post-war period indicate that in broad terms it *does* happen, despite procedural imperfections.

A major finding is that PR is better at bringing together median voter and party positions than single member plurality districts. Under the idea that elections were about winning, PR has seemed an inefficient anomaly, particularly in the Anglo-American world, since it matches votes and seats in ways that rarely allow a clear majority winner to emerge. A consistent voice protesting this notion has been Lijphart (1984, 1999) whose oft times heretical thesis has been that the resulting multiparty systems are better for negotiation and compromise—and ultimately popular satisfaction—than competitive two- or three-party systems.

The weakness of 'consensus democracy', however, has been the absence of any clear and necessary connection between electors' preferences and elite responses. One can well believe that a benevolent elite in certain countries can arrive at optimal political solutions. But the process is hardly democratic when divorced from the actual results of elections. What we propose is precisely a reinterpretation that makes the electoral connection necessary, through the strategic role of the central party in representing the preferences of the median voter in elite negotiations. In so doing it contributes to synthesizing 'two visions' of democracy that have often been taken as antithetical (Powell 2000) and hopefully also to the rehabilitation of elections as a practical policy device in which every vote counts for defining the median.

3

Communicating Preferences: The Public Policy Space

The central concepts driving the median mandate are empowerment and communication. We looked at empowerment in Chapter 2, in terms of the legislative median party being chosen by the median voter. A shared basis for communication is equally if not more important, however, for if the median is not known there can be no empowering it. Equally, if the overall structure and distribution of preferences is not clear, the true median party may not be able to assert itself and dominate policymaking. All this makes a shared party-voter alignment (Table 2.4, Condition 4) crucial. Parties and electors must see policy in broadly the same way and arrange their preferences comparably within a shared structure in order to match up their medians.

It is inevitable that this structure should be a space of some sort. The median is itself a spatial concept—the middle person in a distribution ordered along a line or within a complex of lines. This is not just a mathematical abstraction that lets us conceive of policy preferences as if they were ordered in some space! There is a large body of evidence that we all—electors, parties, politicians, reporters, and specialists—*do* think of policy in spatial terms, most generally along a continuum stretching from left to right, with party and personal preferences located along it.

Evidence for such agreement comes from the common characterization of parties as left, centre, or right—by political commentators and their audiences alike. Characterizations of parties as not simply being left or right but also *moving* leftwards and rightwards imply that there is a policy-line to move along. 'Seizing the centre ground'—regarded by most commentators as a prerequisite of electoral victory—implies that there *is* a centre defined by equidistance from both ends of the continuum.

Media commentators and reporters, avid coiners of such phrases, conduct the dialogue through which electors and politicians convey their positions to each other. The way these are represented by the communicators must help impose it on them, quite apart from the grounding of such terms in party ideologies and government records. From another point of view, these are the most prominent political referents that electors can use to orientate themselves in the public world of politics. At the very least they have an impression that their preferred party is to the right or left of the centre.

As remarked above (see Table 2.4, Condition 4) having policy summarized along a Left-Right scale facilitates a Median Mandate, hence it is much used in our analyses below. However, the Median Mandate thesis is not dependent on there being either a Left-Right or unidimensional policy space. More complex spaces with many policy dimensions might function as policy structures for some electors or parties, or impose themselves at some point in the political cycle. We examine these possibilities after first considering the most obvious candidate for a shared public space, the Left-Right single-line continuum itself.

3.1 EVIDENCE OF GENERAL USE OF THE LEFT-RIGHT FRAMEWORK BY ELECTORS

The classic account of political mobilization and alignment in the nineteenth and twentieth centuries (Lipset and Rokkan 1967) sees political leaders as organizing and mobilizing voters around a sequence of cleavages and political divisions. First came the rejection of old State regulations and hierarchies in the name of the free market—Conservatives versus Liberals. Then churches organized to take on free-thinking Liberals, particularly around the issue of State versus religious education—Liberals versus Christians. Then the countryside including peripheral regions fought for rights against the towns, stimulated by Agrarian parties. Finally the working class came to political consciousness under the impact of Socialist unions and parties fired by the writings of Marx and his followers.

These cleavages constitute historically salient issues which could be regarded as fundamental dimensions constituting the political space within which electorates operate. Two points should be noted about the account, however. The first is the central role of parties in constituting a 'cleavage' and hence a 'dimension'. Indeed as a cleavage has to be politically relevant (not red-haired versus brown-haired, for example) the evidence for its existence in one country versus another is often the presence or absence of a related party.

Second, the historical emergence of the cleavages is not as strictly sequential as implied above. In practice they might emerge concurrently. Duverger (1954) for example, regards Socialists and Christians as the great innovators, with their concurrent invention of mass party organizations, centralized but based on the local branch with an ability to mobilize and penetrate the neighbourhood.

A major use of the cleavage framework is to explain variations in number and type of parties between countries. Cleavage lines were not activated equally at every time and place. The multiparty systems of Scandinavia, for example, take their shape because all four cleavages provided a basis for mobilization there. But in mainland Britain only class and arguably religion became politically relevant. Of course the explanation is potentially tautological as parties were involved in creating a cleavage and indeed their presence is a proof they exist. So it is difficult to regard cleavages as independent factors accounting for the existence of the parties: rather, they coexist.

Be that as it may, the fact that cleavages are not everywhere or uniformly important means that investigations seeking a common frame of reference across countries have had to base themselves on the cleavage which is common to all of them—the class-based or Left-Right cleavage whose omnipresence is attested by the existence of Socialist or Labour parties everywhere. It is for this reason that the major follow-up to Rokkan's ideas on electoral mobilization conducts its analysis exclusively in terms of this one dimension, on the grounds of its centrality to electoral politics, generalizability, and stability (Bartolini and Mair 1990).

Of the four cleavages in the classic account, the Conservative-Liberal conflict in its nineteenth century form has been buried by history, while the urban-rural cleavage outside Scandinavia was largely subsumed under others. Regional cleavages, now generally involving minority nationalist parties against the rest, are largely insulated from mainstream national politics by the often deliberate inattention of the statewide media and parties. Only the religious cleavage had some claims to rival class in terms of generality and comparability. But it has been overtaken in most cases by the comprehensive separation of Church and State and settlement of the schools question—most famously in Belgium in 1958. The result is that Christians are now more commonly identified as a centre-right party on the Left-Right continuum rather than as a religious party per se.

These historical developments are reflected in survey findings from the 1960s onwards, most authoritatively summed up in the comprehensive review carried through by Converse and Pierce (1986) and more recently by Miller et al. (1999). Their analyses show that voters do have a strong sense of where they themselves and the parties stand on the broad contours of policy as indicated by the Left-Right dimension. Pierce (Miller et al. 1999: 30) summarizes the findings by saying:

The issue to which they [voters] are likely to give high priority...is the ideological 'super-issue'...: the Left-Right dimension on the European continent or the Liberal-Conservative dimension in the United States. Voter-party congruence on more specific issues, even those that are traditionally linked to the ideological dimension, is much more limited.

That implies that the Left-Right dimension is the most useful currency for information exchange between voters and parties. Its centrality and pervasiveness undermine objections to the possibility of rational policy-voting by electors. The availability of broadly construed information substitutes for more detailed policy information. The voters do not need to develop well-formed attitudes on each specific policy question because they are going to use broad constructions, which if supplemented by issue-by-issue attitudes could prove problematic due to multidimensionality. The parties encourage debate along a single dimension precisely because it is the most useful currency of information exchange with voters, as most famously suggested by Downs (1957: 96–105).

By simply casting a vote for the nearest party on this dimension, a voter can register his or her preference for a policy programme on shared criteria. The overall distribution of percentages based on everyone voting for their preferred party then designates the median voter position and the party closest to it.

So strong is the evidence for the necessity and sufficiency of Left-Right evaluation by electors across countries that one is tempted to adopt a hypothesis-testing approach to electors' policy space, as Budge et al. (2000: 62) do in regard to parties. The unidimensional Left-Right representation has so many advantages of parsimony, comparability and theoretical relevance, that there are strong presumptions in favour of its use. We should therefore model electors' policy thinking in these terms until strong evidence is brought against it. Its very success in generating plausible findings in the analyses reported below lends it additional support.

3.2 A GENERAL FRAMEWORK FOR THINKING ABOUT POLICY SPACES

As remarked above, electors' use of Left-Right evaluations facilitates the identification of median positions but is by no means necessary to it. A possibility that centrally affects our research is whether election-time policy space may not fragment during the interelection period (see Figure 3.2) as issues are divided between different legislative committees and ministries (Shepsle and Weingast 1981; Budge and Keman 1990: 142–58). More important than the dimensionality of the space are the possibilities for communication between electors and parties. We develop this argument by first considering the general way in which a public policy space develops out of private preferences (Figure 3.1).

Three kinds of positions feed into the public stances taken by electors and parties. Perhaps most important are electors' private aspirations for themselves and their family—more money, better schools and welfare, order and security, an end to irritating transport delays, clean environment: the list is potentially endless.

In fact there are probably as many dimensions to private preference space (see box 1) as there are electors and their aspirations. To vote or undertake

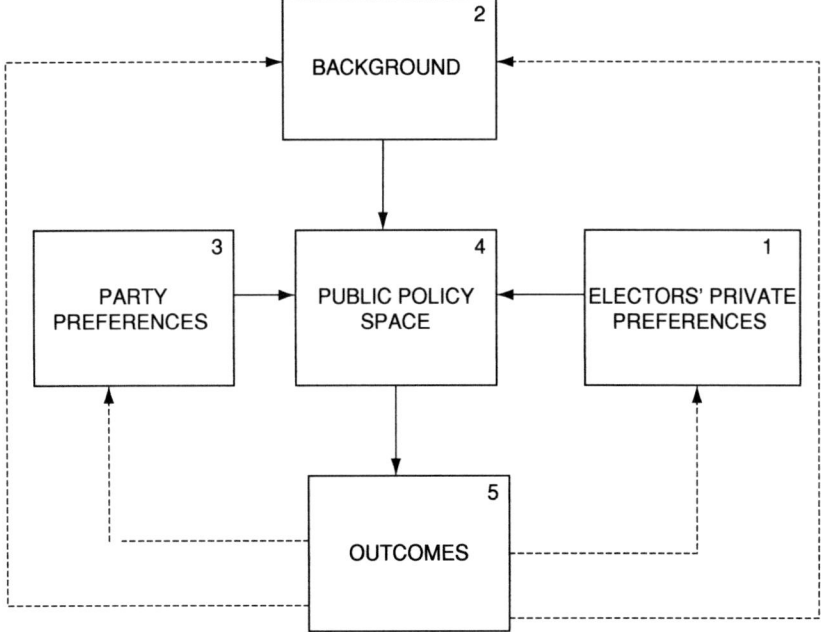

FIGURE 3.1. Relating public policy space to private preferences

other political action, however, electors have the difficult task of relating these to the public choices on offer, encapsulated under representative democracy in the party programmes at election time. How does a choice between spending more on welfare and promising to deliver it more efficiently (a typical opposition of left and right) relate to personal and family well-being, especially when these are combined with promises to lower taxes and increase personal security?

One can see that without some simplifying decision rule a final evaluation, especially one incorporating other personal preferences, is almost impossible. Hence the temptation for educated and uneducated alike to reason that the left is always more supportive of welfare and decide in these terms, distracted however by the consideration that the right is always better at providing law and order.

Putting things in this way underlines the importance of past record, traditional ideology, even the personal characteristics and class origins of candidates in deciding policy issues (Adams 2001). It is in this way that background (see box 2) affects and constrains the policy space. The importance of this to electors' decision processes underlines their importance for parties and the constraints on what leaderships can promise in terms of future policy (Downs 1957: 97–115).

These constraints help create a division between the party leaderships' private preferences (see box 3) and the way they present themselves in public (see box 4). Some parties may conceive and debate policies in public, thus blurring the boundaries between boxes 3 and 4. At the very least however parties will have preferences on issues not discussed for lack of time (or for strategic reasons) during the election campaign. How they present themselves in public will have a lot to do with credibility in maintaining links with the past and consistency in ideology and record. Again, therefore, their current policy will have strong links with their past (Budge, et al. 1987).

Political actors also have the difficult job of evaluating how policies actually link up with outcomes (see box 5). To eliminate unemployment, do we want to spend more money on public works or pursue a tough anti-inflation policy that will restore business confidence and create 'real' jobs? The answer is not obvious, and again it is likely that electors will fall back on Left-Right simplifications—the Left being more concerned about the problem and willing to do more about it. The actual outcome, however, may influence calculations next time, cause the party to consolidate or shift its policy position slightly, and certainly affect its record. These feedback loops are shown as dotted lines in the figure.

The millions of dimensions composing electoral policy space may make the question of whether they are simplified into one, two, or three public dimensions seem less important compared to the magnitude of the translation between private and public in the first place. It is clearly aided if not defined by the choices parties offer. In the next section we consider evidence on whether these are defined in the same Left-Right terms used by electors, before going on to multidimensionality and how it affects both median positioning and general political communication.

3.3 EVIDENCE FOR THE USE OF THE LEFT-RIGHT FRAMEWORK BY PARTIES

Within public space, electors have to choose between voting for one party or another. As a result parties both constrain and define the election choices voters make. It is very likely that the evidence presented on the use of the Left-Right continuum by electors reflects the way parties choose to present themselves and define their policies.

However, we do not need to rely solely on inferences from electors to parties since we already have much direct evidence, based primarily on the policy programmes (manifestoes or platforms) put forward by parties themselves at elections. These are supplemented by various surveys of party and country specialists who have been asked to order and comment on parties over the last twenty years. Most of these found no difficulty in using a Left-Right scale to place the parties, in line with what we said earlier about its general diffusion among political commentators and specialists (Castles and Mair 1984; Huber and Inglehart 1995). Even an 'expert survey' whose explicit aim was to extend the number of dimensions so that parties could be placed in multidimensional spaces (Laver and Hunt 1992) ended up with an almost exclusive reliance on Left-Right indicators, particularly a scale relating to economic intervention by government (Laver and Garry, 2000). Statistical analyses of the key documents through which parties locate themselves in public policy space at election time—their programmes—have similarly found a Left-Right dimension emerging as dominant within almost all countries (Budge et al. 1987). Moreover, it is the only one that occurs everywhere for comparative purposes (Gabel and Huber 2000).

These analyses were heavily inductive in their approach, applying factor analyses to the manifesto data and interpreting the correlated issue bundles that emerge as dimensions of the policy space. As noted, far and away the most important dimension has been the Left-Right one. Hearl (2001) actually used parallel factor analyses of the Manifesto data set as it first existed (1946–83) and the updated version up to 1998 (Budge et al. 2001) to check the reliability of estimates by seeing if he arrived at the same results. He did.

An alternative approach to dimensionality avoids the dependence of inductive inferences on correlations within the data set at a given time point (van der Brug 2000). The alternative utilizes frames of reference which are historically given to decision-makers and party strategists, and which provide an ideological framework to make sense of current developments and otherwise disparate events. The main ideologies of the democratic world are of course Marxism and its socialist descendants, on the one hand, and neo-liberalism and its associated free-market and individualist ideas on the other. Applying these ideological writings to the fifty-six policy categories within which programmatic sentences were originally coded we can pick out some as characteristic of the left and some as characteristic of the right. This forms the basis of a numeric scale which is made up by adding up percentage references to the categories grouped as left and right respectively (see Table 3.1) and subtracting the sum of the left percentages from the sum of right percentages.

The scale generally opposes peaceful internationalism, welfare, and government economic intervention on the left, to strong defence, free enterprise, and traditional morality on the right. These groupings, not logically entailed by any means, are nevertheless combined in the scale because the historical ideologies of the parties themselves put them together. Marxism, for example, emphasizes State intervention to enforce justice and secure welfare, a project which will be disrupted and threatened by capitalist wars from which workers have nothing to gain. Rightist ideologies see social order as a prerequisite for free markets (and for freedom more generally), which must be guaranteed against internal and external threats.

TABLE 3.1. *Creation of an additive Left-Right scale from coding of manifesto sentences*

Right emphases: sum of % for		Left emphases: sum of % for
Military: positive		Decolonisation
Freedom, human rights		Military: negative
Constitutionalism: positive		Peace
Effective authority		Internationalism: positive
Free enterprise		Democracy
Economic incentives		Regulate capitalism
Protectionism: negative	minus	Economic planning
Economic orthodoxy		Protectionism: positive
Social services limitation		Controlled economy
National way of life: positive		Nationalisation
Traditional morality: positive		Social services: expansion
Law and order		Education: expansion
Social harmony		Labour groups: positive

Source: Budge et al. (2001), pp. 21–4.

The Left-Right scale and the frame of reference it embodies have been checked for validity and reliability more widely and rigorously perhaps than any other policy measure, certainly as applied to political parties. Indeed an entire book (Budge et al. 2001) has been devoted to this task, along with substantial portions of another (Budge et al. 1987). The original estimates and the Left-Right scale to which they give rise both performed well. Of particular interest here is the ability of the scale to distinguish between the parties and to represent their movements plausibly over time, over a large number of countries (Budge 1994).

If party movements make sense in terms of received historical interpretations, this is strong evidence for the question that mainly concerns us here: How far do the parties use a Left-Right frame of reference themselves and seek to impose it on others? Perhaps the most relevant evidence comes from the substantive research that has sought to relate Left-Right policy positions to government formation and policy (Laver and Budge 1992), expenditures (Klingemann et al., 1994), and legislative proposals (McDonald et al. 1999). If Left-Right operates as a real frame of reference for parties, one would expect it to be used when deciding on action. The evidence is that parties do use it and for strategic electoral positioning as well (Budge 1994; Adams 2001). In some cases the postdictive capacity of Left-Right placements, in regard to subsequent policy, for example, has been checked out against a multidimensional representation of party positions (Laver and Budge 1992), The Left-Right scale has been shown to work equally well, if not better.

Much of the research we do below replicates and extends earlier work in using Left-Right positions to predict public expenditure patterns, for example, or other public policy measurements. So our analyses below, like all research using particular measures and assumptions, constitute a continuing check on their validity. We can proceed on the assumption that the Left-Right framework is appropriate, use it to identify the median, and then see if the estimated median party or elector has the attributes we expect. We may anticipate our results here by saying that they do. So, besides the impressive body of other research pointing to left and right as the major policy referents for parties, we can also base the case on our own subsequent results.

3.4 COMMUNICATION BETWEEN PARTIES AND ELECTORS

The opportunity for parties and electors to communicate policy preferences to each other is of course equally if not more important than establishing the median. As Miller and his associates (1999) observe, the Left-Right continuum is the prime framework for this. Electors do seem able to formulate their preferences along it in a stable and consistent way that they do not apply in specific policy domains or on individual issues. Thus messages from the parties seem to get through clearly in Left-Right terms where they become confused elsewhere.

The most direct comparative study of elector-party congruence is that by Klingemann (1995) who studied the correspondence between party Left-Right positions, as estimated by Manifesto data, and the ideological preferences of their supporters, from Eurobarometer survey data. The main party-family positions were well differentiated, a feature which may have helped produce the good correspondence with the ideological preferences of their supporters, which Klingemann also found. The theoretical potential for communication noted by Downs (1957: 114–22) within the Left-Right framework is thus matched by the available empirical results.

Again our own study makes assumptions about dialogue between electors and parties (see Tables 2.1 and 2.4, Proposition 2, voter information) that in combination with other assumptions generates implications tested with comparative data below. All forms of mandate theory of course depend on parties being able to communicate their positions to electors. The form in which we couch our operational assumptions is a Left-Right one.

3.5 THE DYNAMICS OF POLICY SPACE

None of what we have said claims that policy space necessarily remains the same over time. Under representative democracy it is important that parties and electors can communicate clearly during the election campaign. When the parties in parliament take over discussion of policy in the interelection period it becomes much more an internal legislative or government matter and is handled differently. This is partly because general Left-Right priorities have been stated by the election result. The need in parliament is to get down to detail in the particular policy area, which encourages the separation of discussion from other areas and concentration on its special features.

This separation is also—and possibly more powerfully—driven by institutional structures and the agendas they impose. Parliamentary and governmental business is divided up between specialist committees and ministries. Cabinet and parliamentary time is allocated in blocks to business sponsored by each ministry. Occasionally, as in budget debates, overall priorities may get raised again. But commonly transport or education bills drafted by the appropriate committee or ministry, are discussed in their own terms. At the cabinet level each minister leads discussion on the appropriate topic, so again business is divided on functional lines (Shepsle and Weingast 1981; Budge and Keman 1990; see Laver and Shepsle 1996, for an even stronger view of the autonomy of ministries within their own policy area).

All this means that the compression of political business into a single Left-Right dimension at election time and a short time afterwards, during the formation of the government, becomes superseded once ministries divide up the policy agenda. While parties may still strive to address electors in Left-Right terms, their audience is increasingly distracted by media coverage of the separate issue debates in parliament and cabinet. Electors who voted in Left-Right terms at the election may now react to each separate policy domain as it comes up and produce a policy median revealed by opinion polls that can influence the government and parliament. This has implications for our analyses below, with the result that we not only check the Left-Right median but also the median position on each of the separate policy domains we investigate.

Some indirect evidence for the switch in party attention after the election comes from the analysis of government declarations reported in Laver and Budge (1992). Government declarations are the statement of policy made by a prime minister designate at the beginning of the investiture debate in parliament. In coalition systems this may be crucial to the formation of the government, as the debates end with a vote of confidence that will decide its fate. In contrast with party programmes, the declarations talk a lot about the technical conduct of government business—up to thirty or forty per cent of their content in some cases. It is of course natural that parties in government, or heading for government, should concern themselves with such conduct and organization. The switch of focus does, however, support our argument that parties handle policies differently in the legislative compared to the electoral arena.

As the electoral arena becomes more relevant with the approach of the next election, however, parties, seconded by the media, are likely to address themselves increasingly to electors again, simplifying and combining separate issues into Left-Right choices between more or less interventionist government, more or less welfare, peaceful initiatives abroad versus a strong military stance. The election will be fought in these terms until the next government forms, when once more the Left-Right dimension will fragment into separate areas.

This cyclical process is illustrated in Figure 3.2. Some issues, ignored because of their technical or specialist nature, will never come up in political campaigns and hence are not spelled out in Left-Right terms at national elections. Questions involving specific regions of the country are a good example. These and other non-integrated issues are represented by the straight lines at the edges of the figure. Other issues show the concentration and fragmentation effect as they separate out during legislative terms and combine again at the election.

So far as we know, no one else has conceived of public policy spaces varying over time. It makes a great deal of sense to do so however, given evidence for the prevalence of a Left-Right framework at elections and the way we know parliamentary and governmental business is conducted. Over time variation also changes the terms in which the question of single dimensionality or multiple dimensions of issue space is debated by specialists. The question is not really unidimensionality versus multidimensionality. It is rather *when* is policy space packaged and discussed in unidimensional terms as opposed to being unpacked and discussed in separate, multidimensional terms.

3.6 SEPARABLE ISSUE DIMENSIONS

As we have just remarked, the multidimensional space illustrated for the interelection periods in Figure 3.2 is not a conventional Euclidean one, with linked dimensions at right angles to each other. The whole point is that official procedures separate and isolate policy domains from each other and force them to be discussed on their own. This has consequences both for the identification of a median position and for communication, which we consider here.

If each policy dimension is considered on its own there will always be a median position to be found on it (cf. Ordeshook 1986: 250). The problem for the median mandate is however that there may be many, different, median positions. At the extreme, each policy-specific median could be occupied by different electors and parties. This creates pluralism with a vengeance! Is each median party mandated to decide policy in its own area? If separate votes are taken will the different median parties each have de facto control in their own area, whatever the normative standing of their empowerment?

There are constraints on the potential confusion produced by separability. In the first place it is the party at the overall Left-Right median that has the major claim to democratic moral authority, since electoral discussion and decisions were made within its framework. Because Left-Right placements

Communicating Preferences 41

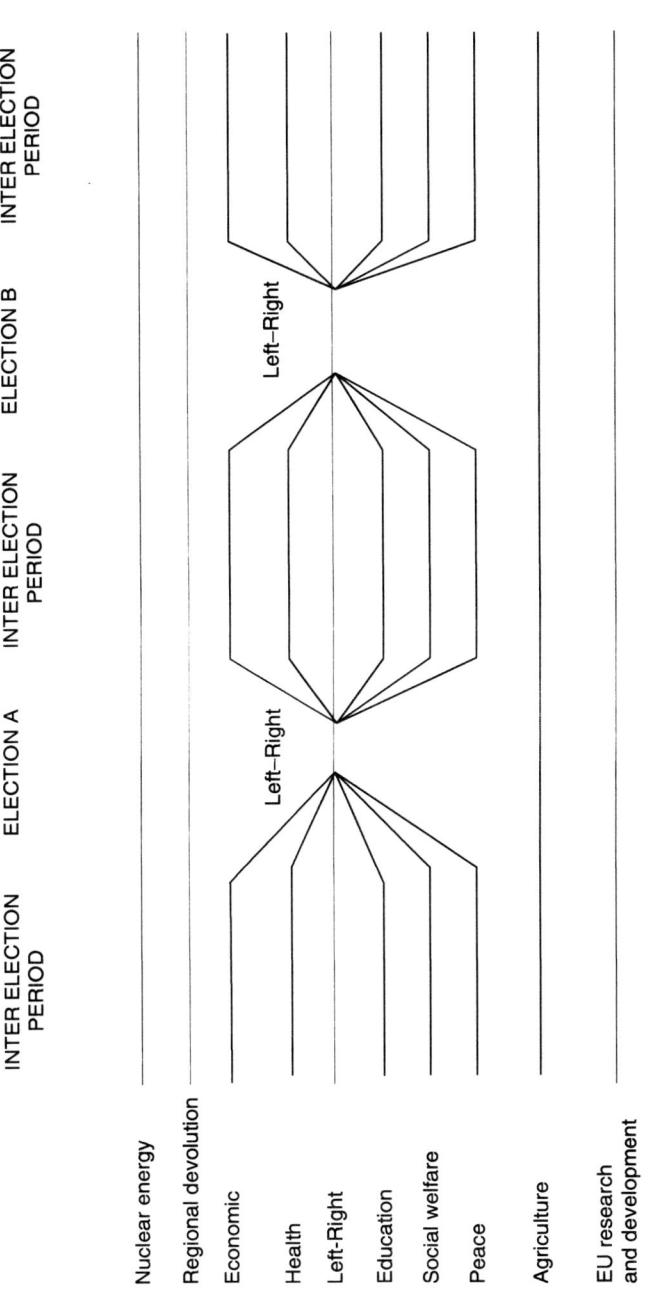

FIGURE 3.2. The dynamics of dimensionality

aggregate some of the most important issues, it is also likely that this party will be at the median in many of the separate issue areas. The larger it is the larger the number of its parliamentarians who are likely to be at the median in the various separate policy areas. Laver and Budge (1992) found it made little difference to their results if they used the Left-Right median party or the median party on the largest number of their twenty separate policy dimensions.

Despite these qualifications, it is clear that the possibility of fragmentation and separation makes it necessary to analyse policies separately, as well as combined in the Left-Right scale. Most of our analyses in Parts III and IV are therefore carried out in parallel, within a general Left-Right space and separate policy spaces.

The second problem introduced by separate issues is one of clear communication. As pointed out by Miller and his associates (1999), electors have a weaker and possibly non-party-mediated anchorage in specific issue areas. These are less discussed over time than general Left-Right distinctions, and at the same time involve a lot more detail. This accounts for the emergence of different medians on the different issues, but at the same time it suggests they may be less stable. These are all possibilities we consider below in our actual analyses.

3.7 LINKED MULTIPLE DIMENSIONS

Most theorists and analysts (an exception is Enelow and Hinich 1984) simply assume that dimensions are linked, implying that the implications of decisions in one policy area are considered for all the others before coming to a final resolution—a particularly strong statement to this effect is found in McLean (1989: 115–26). Not only that, but the implications for each area do not overlap, which means in spatial terms that the policy dimensions are at right angles to each other, indicating their mutual independence.

The relatively unreflective acceptance of these conventions as the norm has had major theoretical consequences. This is because McKelvey (1979) and Schofield (1985) have shown there is no guarantee of a median position being found and hence of majorities being created in spaces of two or more (Euclidean) dimensions.

This uncertainty about the very existence of any real democratic majority has been elevated into a major critique of mandate theories (e.g. Riker 1982). As no stable majority can be found to mandate governments, the only way a modicum of popular control can be enforced is to judge their record retrospectively and 'kick the rascals out' if they have not performed well. Schofield (1985: 292–9) points out however that stable majorities might not be found even to make retrospective judgments. (For an empirical analysis of the retrospective accountability of governments see Chapter 6).

The idea that policy spaces all consist of several related dimensions which are nevertheless independent of each other, which creates all these conceptual problems, has been heavily conditioned by the fact that these form the final outputs of factor analysis. Factor analysis is the analytic technique generally applied to produce reduced dimension spaces from large numbers of specific issue responses. On the assumption that a limited number of attitudes underlies the specific responses, it sorts out which of these go up and down more strongly together than any does with the members of other groups. Each grouping is then identified as a 'factor' or 'dimension' underlying the specific responses.

Almost all such dimensions are correlated with each other. For many mathematical and presentational purposes, however, it is more convenient to consider them as orthogonal, at right angles to each other. Computerized programmes obligingly deliver such spaces by rotating correlated dimensions to get the orthogonal space closest to the original, which then emerges as the final output for defining the space for positioning parties and electors and mapping their movements. The temptation for analysts is then to base all their inferences on this, forgetting that the original space with correlated dimensions has a better claim to accurate representation of policy and preferences.

This is important because Adams and Adams (2000) have shown that with even modestly correlated dimensions a median position is practically guaranteed within the resulting space. As the correlations become stronger the probabilities grow even higher. One can see why from Figure 3.3. As the vertical dimension correlates more and more highly with the leading horizontal one (always Left-Right in practice) simply projecting their positions on to the horizontal becomes a more and more acceptable representation. And a straight line always produces a median. In Figure 3B, if parties are relatively equal in terms of seats, the Christians are broadly at the median whether in the one or two-dimensional representation. In Figure 3A, if the dimensions have equal weights there is no overall median.

Correlated dimensions, the actual real-life case, thus promote a median. Even more important they aid communication, by allowing most parties to talk to electors in straight Left-Right terms and thereby put pressure on slightly deviant parties, such as the Christians, to conform to this mode or become irrelevant to the main debate. In practice we can see this as having happened to the European Christian Democrats over the last forty years as they have distanced themselves from the Church and stressed their moderating stance on economic and social issues.

Again this demonstration underlines the point that debates about the correct spatial representation of policy are not just about unidimensionality versus multidimensionality. They also involve crucial questions about what *kind* of dimensionality is involved—separable, linked-orthogonal, linked-correlated. Each has different implications for identifying and empowering the median and with the last we come back fairly quickly to unidimensionality or at least feasible approximations to it.

3.8 POLICY SPACE: EFFECTS OF POLITICAL PARTIES

In the preceding discussion parties appear as subjects rather than agents—they are located in a space that in some sense is defined independently of them. This of course is far from being the truth, since parties inevitably define the public space through their policy offerings as emphasized in the discussion of Figure 3.1. As pointed out there, there may be millions of potential policy dimensions—as many as electors and their preferences—but there are

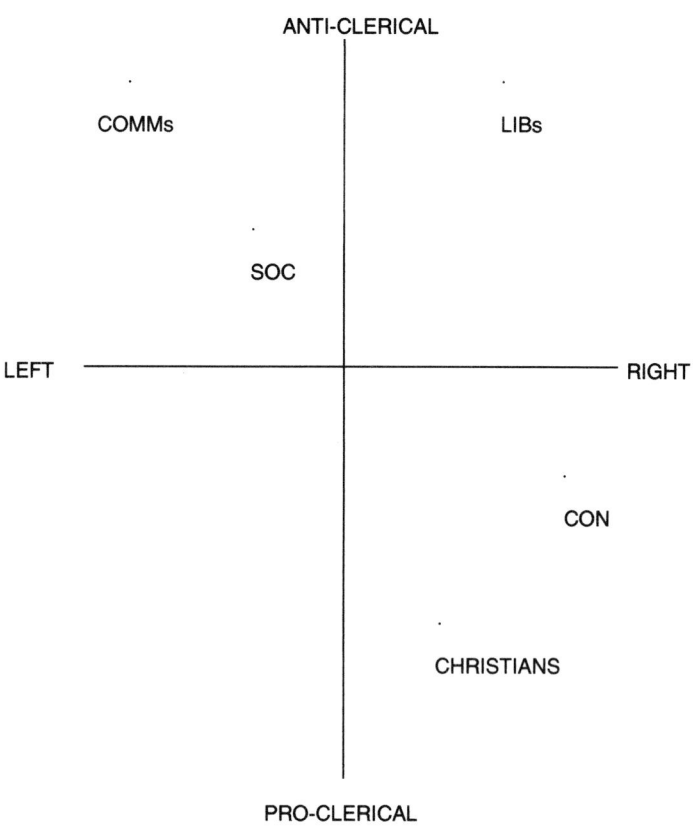

B) Correlated dimensions, showing party positions projected on to principal Left-Right dimension

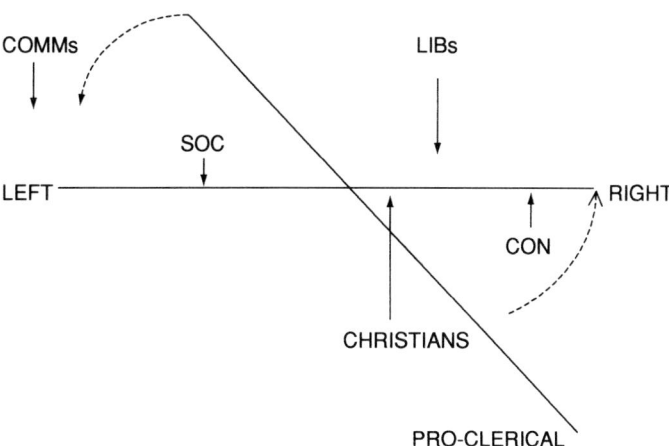

only a limited number of party programmes among which electors must choose. Inevitably this gives parties the major hand in defining public choices and hence easing difficulties of communication as well as identifying and empowering the median.

To fully evaluate the condition of a shared policy space, we need to start with its basic structure and move on to link it to shared communication in general and medians in particular. The important starting point is that the dimensionality of policy space depends less on the number of issues or policies involved than on the number of parties. While the policy space over k issues approaches something on the order of being k-dimensional, parties structure the k-dimensional space into a much smaller order of dimensionality by virtue of their limited numbers. That makes the conversation between voters and potential governors highly structured, where the structure comes principally from the parties on offer at election time. At the lower extreme of a two-party system, unidimensionality is true by definition. Three parties might require two dimensions, four parties three dimensions, and so on; so the hypothetically conceivable upper bound of the dimensionality of the policy space of an election as structured by P parties is $P - 1$. At the upper extreme, with a space of $P - 1$, each party is an entity unto itself, offering a programme incommensurable with the programme of every other party. This might be a description of a system organized by exclusively single-issue parties. One party takes a position on abortion and nothing else, another party takes a position on agricultural subsidies and nothing else, another takes up wetland preservation and nothing else, and so on. However, this is not a party system known to anyone. Rather, most parties take positions on a range of issues, and most observers, experts and citizens in the mass public alike, can characterize them along something like a single Left-Right dimension.

From this structured policy space of elections, the position of a median voter will emerge from the aggregate vote results and will be generally knowable provided that a unidimensionality of party alignment holds only roughly, only very roughly as it turns out. A sometimes overlooked contribution to the discussion of dimensionality and unstable majorities is Niemi's demonstration (1969, 1984) that there is only a small likelihood that the policy profiles of members of a collectivity, even randomly generated profiles, over N persons considering P parties would configure so as to produce instability—intransitivity in the collective preference profile and an absence of the median. Political parties campaigning in elections provide one of the hugely important instances of a structure-induced equilibrium that exists in democratic politics (Shepsle and Weingast 1981). If only two parties are on offer, a definite median has been induced. What Niemi's demonstration tells us, however, is that beyond two-party systems any number of parties within reasonable limits is likely to induce an equilibrium position. And, while this holds even at the extreme of randomly generated voter profiles, voters' policy profiles are not generated randomly. Numerous institutional devices, including the parties themselves[1] and the media, help to induce a dimensionalizing structure on political discussion and debate. Such an attitudinal structure makes it even less likely (i.e. less likely than a small chance) that electoral majorities will cycle.

There surely are policy profiles among electors, which when conjoined with a certain distribution of voter percentages, will produce majority cycles. However, it would be the height of incautious cautiousness to elevate the possibility that there may not be an equilibrium to something like a certainty that there will not be one.

[1] In essence, it is the parties that usually resolve the potential for Arrovian incoherence in mass elections They impose a structure on the elections that is, for any one election, in violation of Arrow's democratic condition (1963) that there be no restriction on the way policy bundles are put together. That is, while there is no restriction in the long run, in that parties with any type of policy profile can enter the electoral competition, for any one election the bundles are restricted to what the parties in that election are offering. Thus, when the number of parties, P, is less than the number of permutations of the ways policies could be put together into bundles, an Arrow condition is violated and the impossibility of purging incoherence is largely abated.

We can illustrate the point with an example using three alternatives, with Britain in mind. With three alternatives, there are six possible policy profiles: ABC; ACB; BAC; BCA; CAB; CBA. Imagine among 120 voters the vote splits exactly equally across the six profiles—20, 20, 20, 20, 20 and 20. This will create a situation in which the alternatives cycle. Change any one person's preference, however, say from profile No. 6 to No. 1, and there is no cycle. Worse for the proposition that there is some high probability of a cycle, the six profiles are probably not anything near to equally likely. For example, there are probably not too many Britons who have preference orders of (Con, Lab, Lib) or (Lab, Con, Lib); rather, most Britons probably have profiles of (Con, Lib, Lab), (Lab, Lib, Con), (Lib, Con, Lab), (Lib, Lab, Con). Niemi's point is that it would take an unlikely distribution across the four common profiles and the two uncommon ones to produce a cycle. In short, having multiple dimensions does not imply that there will not be a median voter; rather, multiple dimensions mean that you cannot guarantee with certainty that there will *always* be a median voter.

It is the parties, of course, that make some orderings of preference more likely and others less. This is not only a contribution to finding a median but also to ease of communication, as it simplifies discussion to have odd and generally inconsistent preferences removed. The ultimate example of this is the parties' tendency to align themselves in Left-Right terms and present this definition of policy-choices to the electorate.

3.9 OVERVIEW AND CONCLUSIONS

All that we have reviewed and discussed in this chapter implies that median mandate theory works within all the policy spaces one is likely to encounter in actual politics. A median position is nearly always identifiable both at electoral and legislative levels—much more so than a coherent government majority (for which having a median is indispensable of course).

Our review of policy multidimensionality underscores the point that though this is much discussed it is not necessarily well considered. Mostly it is identified with the kind of conventional Euclidean representation illustrated in Figure 3.3A. In practice, however, multi-dimensional spaces are likely to have either separate dimensions or correlated ones, with a good chance of simplifying to one dimension (the Left-Right one) without much distortion. This is a process vigorously aided and abetted by the political parties themselves.

The more formal analysis pursued in the second half of our discussion thus confirms the hunches of analysts (Miller et al. 1999; Bartolini and Mair 1990; Laver and Budge 1992) that a unidimensional Left-Right space is the best one for estimating policy preferences, both for parties and electors. On the basis of this conclusion we shall conduct our own analyses largely in Left-Right terms, always with the caveats that their success is not predicated on this choice alone and that any reasonable method of representing the public policy space would support broadly the same results.

4

Research Questions for Comparative Investigation

Most of the rest of this book is concerned with checking whether the conditions for a mandate are present in post-war democracies and, if so, whether they are the appropriate conditions for a government mandate or median mandate. From the evidence already considered we have reason to suspect that the median mandate holds but not the government one. However, any check into the (largely shared) mandate pre-conditions necessarily involves investigating both. So we can regard our comparative analyses of democratic functioning as a continuing check on mandate theory as a whole. As pointed out in Chapter 3 the analyses also form a check on our methodological assumptions (e.g. about policy spaces). Implausible results would spur us into querying these, and, so, in a sense, our comparative analyses also constitute a validity check on our measurements and estimates.

We have been careful to stress that mandate theories are from one point of view normative, telling us how we should organize democratic processes in order to make them truly democratic. In so far as they are normative and directive we cannot check their standing by seeing whether actual democracies put their recommendations to work. The aim of normative theory is to tell us how things should be, rather than how they are.

Nevertheless, mandate ideas come closer to applied empirical theory than most normative theories. Democracy is often justified in terms of making governments responsive to the popular majority along the lines of government mandate theory (see Table 2.1). In this way the mandate is brought into normative debate as a description of how democracies actually work. It seems fair to investigate the evidence further to see whether democracies really do function that way.

Conversely, if twenty-one post-war democracies of good standing fail to operate a mandate or to meet the conditions spelled out in Tables 2.1 or 2.4, this will give us pause to think about the general credibility of mandate theory in its normative as well as its descriptive aspects. If contemporary democracies can get along without the mandate is it really an essential aspect of representative democracy? We do not wish to exaggerate this point. However, we do feel that with a mixed descriptive-normative theory failure to give a good description of contemporary democracy casts some doubt on its standing as a whole. At this point, however, we do not feel that any knotty epistemological questions need to be confronted, as our expectation is that the evidence will uphold at least one version of mandate theory, namely, the median.

Evidence never speaks for itself however. It can only be used to answer the questions we put to it. Our previous chapters have discussed mandate approaches and their assumptions at an abstract, general level. The purpose of this chapter is to translate these into concerns that we can relate to our data, gathered from twenty-one democracies of thirty to fifty years' standing in Europe, North America, and Australasia. Before going into the questions we can pose, we need to consider the general nature of this information and the opportunities and constraints it imposes on the investigation.

4.1 COMPARATIVE EVIDENCE

Without going into details, which are in any case given later where appropriate, we can describe our data as falling into five main categories:

1. Aggregate voting results for post-war national elections over all twenty-one democracies with the resulting distribution of seats in parliaments and selected ministries in governments.
2. Policy preferences of all significant parties in each election in their published policy programme (their manifesto or platform). For statistical analysis the sentences of these texts have been counted into fifty-six policy categories, from which various general policy measures have been constructed (Budge et al. 2001).
3. By putting votes and party positions together, estimates of the median voter preference can be made. Similarly, the median party can be identified from policy scales and the distribution of seats (Kim and Fording, 1998, 2001).
4. Policy preferences of parties in government can be weighted according to each one's share of cabinet seats to form a measure of government policy intentions. A further insight into these can be derived from the Government Declarations (of policy intentions) generally issued by coalition governments before their investiture debate. This is a statement of how the partners intend to carry on government. It is not the same as the weighted 'wish list' derived from party manifestos, as the declaration already has to concern itself heavily with administrative and practical problems (Budge et al. 2001).
5. Of course the declarations continue to state policy intentions rather than actual policy. As estimates of actual policy we have largely expenditure-based measures—total government expenditures, welfare and social

expenditures, and foreign aid versus defence spending (Lijphart 1999). Expenditure is far from the whole of policy—for that we would need to have legislative and administrative enactments. These we have only with respect to welfare policy. Generally, such enactments are very difficult to get on a comparative basis. In the end however governments have to put their money where their policy aims are, and most enactments are likely to be ineffective if they do not have budgetary backing. Hence although they have their limitations, expenditures are a serious and central measure of what governments are doing.

All the information listed above relates to most stable democracies over the post-war period up to 1995 with the exception of the Government Declarations; those we have for ten countries prone to have coalition governments from the early 1950s to the early 1980s. In different analyses we may use differing sets of countries, as the questions and facts of the situations permit, but we expect our conclusions to extend to democracies in general rather than being limited to any one particular set of them. Our aim is to investigate how democracy works, not how it works in Europe or the West or in particular countries, even though our evidence may be limited to these.

The most general feature of our data is what could be regarded as a constraint but in the end has struck us as a major substantive finding about democratic policymaking in general—this is its slow moving quality. This is most evident in our spending data. It is of course true that budgets, with many entitlements and hence spending programmes fixed by law, forward contracts, and planning several years in advance, are notoriously incremental in nature (Davis et al. 1966 King and Laver 1993). It could certainly be argued that legislation and administrative directives change more sharply and certainly government intentions do, as evidence from at least one democracy, the USA, seems to indicate (McDonald et al. 1999). Even so, the policy and administrative framework is likely to look broadly the same over 10, 20, or 50 years.

Even party intentions as expressed through their election programmes are fairly consistent with past ideological positions (Downs 1957: 105–12). This is especially true in relation to their general policy stance. Opinions on specific issues may shift radically from one election to another. But of course this implies movement which is often in contrary directions, so the tendency is to balance out over a period of time to what would have been the case had there been no change! Median positions are by definition a form of averaging that tones down extreme shifts. This is accentuated by the general stability of votes and party support. It is difficult to beat past vote as a general predictor of present vote (Budge and Farlie 1983: 84–114), a persisting testimony to its stability over time. This, of course, has an entirely reasonable explanation in the relatively enduring social locations of voters and ideological continuity of parties (Downs 1957: 120).

What does stability imply? Most importantly it means that the variation in all our data is mostly between countries. Change over time, that is, between elections and governments, is limited to about 15 per cent of total change (Chapter 10). In turn this means that the policy initiatives of single governments or legislatures (Chapters 8 and 9), which media attention and indeed most political analysis generally focuses on, may be much less important than the general policy regime prevailing in a particular democracy. The policy regime is produced by the underlying balance of the political parties, reflected in median positions, rather than by an initiative of any one government or the political changes introduced by any one election.

Even when there is change, it may be balanced out by reactions and results at the next election. Indeed the method by which an average course is charted seems to differ between proportional representation and single district plurality systems. The latter are more prone to produce dramatic short-term changes, rendering politics more interesting and consequential. But as the changes balance out over the long term the result is an average over the long term which is not so much different from what might have been produced by overlapping governments and limited change under PR.

The actual analyses of Part III and particularly Part IV will bring out these points more clearly. They do form the general background however against which we will assess the government and median mandates. By downplaying change between governments and emphasizing the importance of average, centrist positions for policymaking, our evidence strengthens the case for the median mandate being the best description of how contemporary democracy works. After extensively considering the question we are convinced however that this is a substantive finding rather than a methodological artifact: policies in democracies do change relatively slowly.

4.2 GETTING DOWN TO SPECIFICS

The generally static rather than dynamic nature of all our estimates does not of course mean that we can ignore findings for specific elections. On the contrary, our general conclusions emerged from detailed analyses of these, starting with an overall examination of how far government and legislative policy (both intended and actual) correspond to electors' preferences in the shape of the median position. Clearly, if the conditions for a mandate are in place, correspondence should follow, though finding it does not guarantee there is a *necessary* correspondence of course. One check on this is to compare results under PR and SMD systems. So far as median mandate reasoning applies, correspondence should be better ensured under PR, which aims at matching vote and seat shares, than under SMD, which often mismatches them to form a manufactured legislative majority. As mentioned above, however, even this comparison of specific elections brings in the over time results as a modifying factor, since electoral victories under SMD often balance each other out.

Another check on the necessary correspondence of public policy with electoral preference is to see whether the individual conditions for a mandate, as spelled out in Tables 2.1 and 2.4, actually occur. The first three conditions are common to the Government and Median mandate, and probably preconditions of all mandate theories. The first, party distinctiveness, is the crucial condition differentiating a mandate situation, where electors shop around for the party offering they prefer, from a convergence situation where all party programmes focus on the median electoral position. Convergence would guarantee policy responsiveness to electoral preferences but not choice. The convergence hypothesis is of course the great rival to mandate ideas about how representative democracy works. Examining party positions, and seeing whether they come together or stay apart, is the crucial discriminating check between the two approaches. Fortunately our individual election time series enable us to carry through a fairly definitive analysis here.

The other two common conditions of the mandate concern voters. The first is their ability to recognize and distinguish party policy profiles, a necessity if they are then going to choose between them. The other voter condition is that they do choose between them on the basis of policy differences.

Our data resources do not allow us to check out mandate Conditions 2 and 3 (Table 2.4) directly. We will have to rely on the already cited extensive survey research that concludes that voters do distinguish between party positions on a continuum (Miller et al. 1999). In general, voters have been vindicated on a general review of survey evidence as more intelligent in terms of acquiring and processing information than has been credited them (Marcus and Hanson 1993). The assumption that they distinguish between profiles and vote for the one nearest to them is of course at the heart of most rational choice theorizing, starting with Downs (1957).

In general we can say that if our findings in the comparative analysis generally support mandate reasoning, the voter conditions gain credibility along with the others involved, as they are certainly crucial to its success.

Following through the other conditions for the median mandate there is the shared party and voter alignment (see Condition 4, Table 2.4) already discussed (see Chapter 3). We shall certainly be in a good position with our data to see if contradictions or anomalies occur in our use of the Left-Right dimension or specific policy scales that cast doubt on such an alignment. Condition 5 (See Table 2.4), the electoral system translation between the median voter and the median legislative party, has already been validated (see Table 2.5). Though present under SMD it is facilitated most by PR, as we would expect.

Obviously this link only works if parties *are* policy-pursuing in some sense, even if it is in an extended sense where primarily office-seeking parties realize they have to effect declared policy to maintain credibility with electors (Downs 1957: 105–9). We discuss this later. The power of the median, Condition 7 (see Table 2.4), follows from policy-motivated parties operating along a unidimensional continuum. The median is such a central concept that everything we do in the comparative analysis is a direct or indirect check on its presumed power and influence, which is again central to all mainstream rational choice thinking.

What happens if *several* median positions are relevant however—both a general median and specific policy ones? This is a major question that follows on the probable fragmentation of policy space (see Figure 3.2) in the legislature. Hence it needs to be considered on its own in the following section.

4.3 SEPARATE DIMENSIONS AND DIFFERENT MEDIANS: WHICH ARE IN CONTROL?

We have considered questions of dimensionality at some length in Chapter 3. The representation of public policy space and the median throughout our analysis provides a continuing check on its validity, since any failure to produce plausible results reflects first on this assumption. Plausible outcomes that fit our expectations will indicate that it functions as a reasonably accurate representation of policies and preferences.

The same consideration applies to the specific policy scales we have generated on economics, welfare and foreign policy. Their ability to distinguish between the parties and to pick out median positions with strong relationships to policy outputs will clearly indicate that they are measuring what we think they are measuring—that is, real voter preferences and policy positions.

The need to generate measures of preference on each specific policy stems from the fact that at certain points in the electoral-governing cycle we expect the policy space to fragment into separate dimensions or areas (see Figure 3.2). This is because of institutional features of both parliament and government which assign responsibility for separate areas to different bodies (committees and ministries) and which provide for separate discussion of each area.

The point that mostly affects our comparative research is that the median legislative party in each policy area may not coincide with the Left-Right median. In such cases, a different party may dominate discussion when each separate area comes up on the agenda. If each policy dimension is discussed separately, then, by the power of the median argument already applied (see Figure 1.1), the policy-relevant median party will determine the outcome rather than the overall Left-Right one. This is potentially serious for our argument since it is the latter that has been mandated by the election, when policy issues have been compressed into summary overall terms rather than divided into their separate areas.

In practice of course, precisely because overall positions do aggregate individual ones, we expect that the party occupying the overall parliamentary median will often emerge as the party at the median position in specific areas. Overlap is particularly likely where the median party is large and has a wide spread of parliamentary supporters. Nevertheless, when the overall and specific policy medians do differ, we should expect in terms of the median mandate that the former will be determining. If not, and particularly where the specific median party is in government, we may need to reconsider relationships between the two versions of mandate theory.

At this point we do not know how relationships may turn out. It is clearly a point to be kept in mind throughout the comparative analysis. Our regressions and tables will accordingly distinguish between specific and general median positions and indeed those of the government, enabling us to make a full examination of which mandate conditions prevail.

4.4 POLICY-PURSUING PARTIES?

Party policy commitment appears as a condition for the mandate under both its alternative forms (see Condition 6 in both Table 2.1 and 2.4). This is because we cannot expect parties to carry through mandated policies simply because they are obliged to, in moral terms. There are too many excuses and obstacles for them to act on obligation per se. They must be committed to their policies out of conviction, ideology, or even advancement of their own and their supporters' interests.

It is true as Downs (1957: 95–107) points out, that even office-seeking parties might be strongly committed to policy, as they see their credibility with electors and hopes of future re-election bound up with it. In actual practice, however, under conditions of great uncertainty there are so many strategies parties could adopt to blur responsibility that a personal commitment to policy on their own part is all but essential to ensure they carry through what they have said they would do. This is also important for ensuring that the median really gets empowered, as office-seeking parties even with some policy concerns might often have reason to bypass it.

The general ascription of policy-based motives to political parties supports the idea that they operate along a Left-Right and other policy continuums. Again one can say that theorizing about political parties has moved in general from assumptions based on office-seeking (Downs 1957; Riker

1966; de Swaan 1973) to assumptions based on policy-pursuit (Roozendahl 1990; Laver and Shepsle 1996; Muller and Strom, 2000). Thus we are hardly alone in postulating that policy is central to party concerns.

Major support for the ascription of policy-motivations to parties comes from the most established and widespread finding in the field of coalition research: that in over eighty per cent of cases the median party is represented in government (Muller and Strom 2000: 564–8; Laver and Budge 1992: 416). This coincides with our own observations from the data, examined later. If policy were not dominant, the median party would not have this obvious importance for government, as the median position would have no special relevance for purely office-seeking parties. This observation also supports the unidimensionality condition as the median has generally been identified in previous studies by being the central party on the Left-Right continuum.

Support from previous research for the conditions supporting a policy-directed approach can be supplemented by seeing below whether actual postwar elections function as if they were true. If there is a reasonable correspondence between actual results and what could be expected on our assumptions, we can take it as strong evidence of their validity.

We shall also be interested in seeing whether any deviations from what we might expect can be traced to Conditions 1 and 2—party policy alternatives being too sparse or too crowded together—as well as to election rules breaking the median party-voter link, Condition 5. This is what we would expect under a policy-directing approach to produce deviations from our reasoning. Two parties operating on the policy extremes may not provide a good match of policy with the preferences of a median voter located between them. Whichever wins the majority there will be some kind of hole in the middle, consequently providing a poor identification of the location of the median voter. Multiparty systems may be better at providing a policy-spread among parties, provided the alternatives they offer are not all overlapping.

4.5 PLAN OF DISCUSSION

These are possibilities we check out immediately. We begin our comparative investigation of how far mandate conditions hold in practice in Chapter 5. There we start off with our attention focused on the political parties, because they define the policy context of both elections and governments. The quality and distinctiveness of the choices they offer are thus critical to the whole mandate process, whether it involves medians or governments.

Single-party majority governments rarely emerge in practice (see Tables 2.2 and 2.3), so they can seldom be vehicles for effecting a future policy programme promised to the electorate. A watered down version of government mandate theory (e.g. Riker 1982) does however argue that governments can be held accountable for what they have done retrospectively. Can electors 'kick the rascals out'? Chapter 6 examines this possibility in the context of economic voting. Can governments be punished for bad economic performance and rewarded for good? Against the assumptions of most of the economic voting literature there is little evidence that they can. This finding clears the way to seeing how far governments and legislatures do succeed in reflecting the policy views of the median voter, more reliably under PR than SMD but with about equal long-run accuracy under both (see Chapter 7).

At this point we turn from the question of how voting affects policy (see Part II) to how policy gets made (see Part III). In Chapter 8 we look at policy declarations and then in Chapter 9 at actual policies to see how they are linked to individual government and parliamentary situations. We can anticipate our later discussion by saying the results for these specific cases are mixed and weak. It is difficult to see much policy control being exercised by particular governments or parliaments at a specific point in time.

This follows in large part from the fact that there is only limited over time variation in our data compared to cross-national variation. That implies that we should be looking for the determinants of policy regimes rather than those of individual policy shifts, which get smoothed out over time anyway. Voters, parliaments, governments and individual ministries mostly align with each other in a stable way over the long run and thereby define a general policy equilibrium rather than shifting specific ones (see Chapters 10 and 11).

On the crunch question of who ultimately determines the policy regime or general equilibrium, Chapter 12 concludes that it is the median parliamentary party as estimated in Left-Right terms. So far as we can tell, the conditions for a median mandate apply in actual post-war democracies.

This is an important finding both for the descriptive standing of the median mandate theory and justifications for contemporary democracy. Chapter 13 relates our comparative analyses to our starting theories and draws the appropriate conclusions. All rest on the central role of political parties in contemporary democracies, so it is appropriate that we begin our analysis with these in Chapter 5.

Part II

The Electoral Process

5

Choices Parties Offer

One of the most fascinating aspects of representative democracy is the nature of the exchange that goes on between voters, parliaments, governments, and ministries. Unlike markets, the currency of this exchange is soft, malleable, and open to continuous interpretation and reinterpretation. It is as if one is trying to explain activity in a barter economy where trades involve only promises and credits. Parties have different bundles of these on offer. Voters have to decide which has the most items of value, weighting items from an individual point of view. In the case of political representation not only do different people have different considerations in mind when they make a valuation, they are evaluating proposals to deliver largely intangible, non-divisible benefits.

Analyses of representative processes have to begin by assuming that we can understand what voters value in terms of some common yardstick, for example, by bundling issues up in a way describable by the Left-Right dimension. This assumption is certainly convenient. But it is more than that: it, or something like it, is essential to the functioning of representation. It follows from the institutional arrangements of electoral democracy, that is, from the idea that citizens can use elections to give direction to and retain control over what a government does.

Elections impose a highly restrictive structure on how a population communicates what it values. No single word—yes/no, Labour/Liberal/Conservative—can communicate effectively all that a person wants, prefers or values. The democratic aspiration of securing effective representation through elections has to rest on the assumption that the one word each elector is allowed has some knowable meaning, at least approximately and in the aggregate. Our analyses in this and following chapters are designed to tease out what this might be.

This first analysis of our comparative evidence therefore confronts some very central questions about party democracy—central to theoretical and normative as well as descriptive discussions. Given that parties have the major role in structuring choices and then in effecting them, do they perform the task well? What is the nature of the choice they offer to electors? In particular:

1. *Are* there choices?—a convergence on the median voter would not offer any
2. *Are* the choices gently graded or sharply polarized?
3. *Are* the policy alternatives on offer clear and distinct or ambiguous and overlapping?
4. *Are* the specific issues within the parties' bundle on a Left-Right continuum correlated with each other and with the overall party position?

In this chapter we shall be addressing such questions by seeing how parties line up on and move along a Left-Right dimension, and how this relates to their positions on three specific policy issues: peaceful internationalism, welfare, and economic planning. All derive from published codings of party programmes from 1950–95 in twenty-one post-war democracies (Budge et al. 2001).

5.1 CONVERGENCE OR DIFFERENTIATION? PATTERNS OF PARTY MOVEMENT OVER TIME

The unique feature of these estimates, which distinguishes them from static characterizations based essentially on ideological party 'families' (Castles and Mair 1984; Laver and Hunt 1992; Huber and Inglehart 1995), is that they exist for each significant party in each election of the post-war period. This enables us to 'map' movement from election to election, answering questions central to the party literature such as are parties consistent and reliable (Downs 1957: 105–11). Do they converge or not? Is there ideological differentiation? How far do parties leapfrog each others' positions? (Adams 2001). These are not questions we can answer with purely static characterizations of their positions.

The flexibility this gives us is illustrated by the party 'maps' for the USA, Germany, and Netherlands given in Figures 5.1, 5.2, and 5.3. All our subsequent analyses are based on figures like these summarized in various ways. The advantage of basing ourselves on party election programmes is that they allow the parties to speak to us directly, since the codings necessary for statistical analysis are basically inductive, driven by the clusterings of sentences in the text themselves (Robertson 1976).

In the maps, party movements are traced along the Left-Right scale (see Table 3.1; for details see Budge et al. 2001: 21–4). There are some surprises. Despite earlier characterization of them as pragmatic and prone to compromise (APSA 1950; Downs 1957: 114–17; Wright 1971), American parties appear quite as ideological in Left-Right terms as European parties, never taking over each others' policy positions ('leapfrogging') or indeed venturing much into the opposed right- or left-wing space. In this they resemble the two main German parties, the Christian Democrats

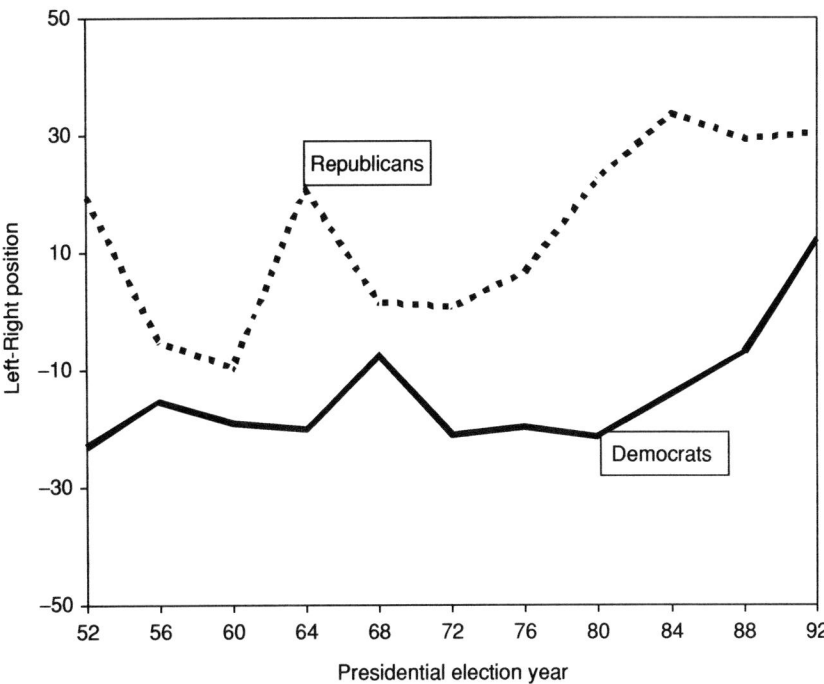

FIGURE 5.1. American party movements on a Left-Right scale, 1952–1992

(CDU-CSU) and the Social Democrats (SPD). The situation in Germany is blurred by the presence of third parties; the Free Democrats (FDP) in particular cross other parties' lines quite a lot though the Greens and Communists (PDS) are fairly distinctive.

Even in the multiparty Netherlands leapfrogging between the main parties—Christian Democrats (CDA), Liberals (VVD) and Socialists (PvdA)—is limited and in fact only occurs at one or two elections. Parties generally seem inclined to hold to their own policy positions from election to election, whether this is left, right or centre as the case may be.

There is a good deal of stability in party positioning over time, an observation which is important in light of our concerns about the extent and clarity of the choices parties offer to the electorate. Fascinating though these maps are in confirming or discrediting hunches about what parties did in particular elections (Clinton's spectacular change of 1992 in Democratic strategy shows up very clearly) they cover only three countries. To conduct a systematic analysis of dynamics over our twenty-one democracies we need to focus on particular aspects of the maps and summarize the

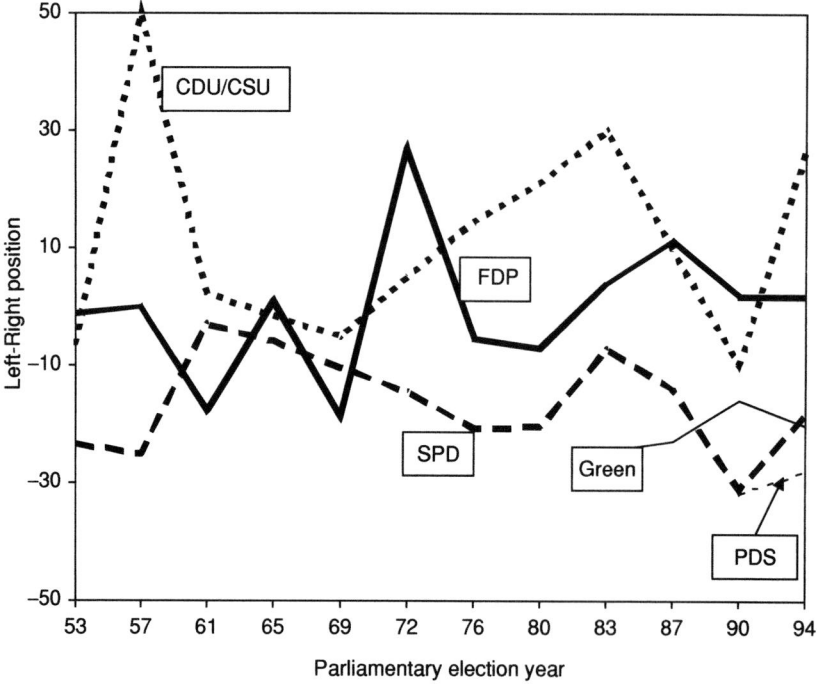

FIGURE 5.2. German party movements on a Left-Right scale, 1953–94

features that are relevant to answering our questions about the alternatives on offer. This is what all the following tables do in different ways.

Table 5.1 derives directly from published maps of party movement like those shown previously in Figures 5.1–5.3 (Budge et al. 2001: 29–46). For each pair of elections from 1950 to 1995 it looks at the policy moves made by the individual parties and asks: does it cross any other party's path (leapfrog)? If so, is the party it leapfrogs generally close to it and hence not too ideologically different (and perhaps sometimes allied) or very distinct? The latter would seem more likely to confuse electors' ideas about what the party stands for than would leaping over an already very similar neighbour. The third piece of information summarized in the table is whether in a particular election, the party stays in the ideological area it usually frequents (left, centre or right as the case may be) or often moves out of it? The more consistent a party's position is over time, the more distinctive it is and the easier it is for electors to see where it stands.

The converse of clear ideological and policy differentiation is, of course, convergence on some kind of centrist position. This has been expected theoretically as a result of strict two-party competition (Downs 1957:

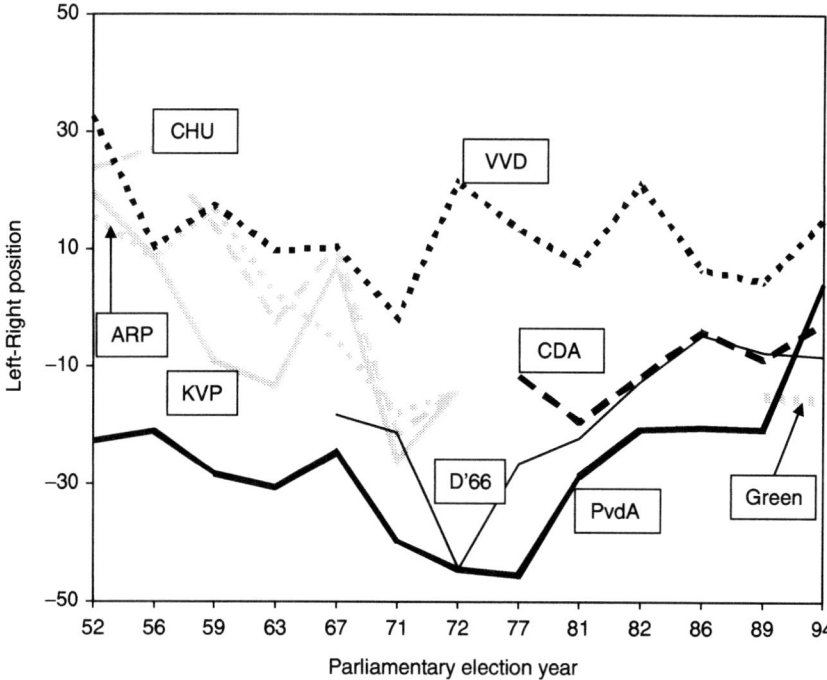

FIGURE 5.3. Dutch party movements on a Left-Right scale, 1952–94

114–17). The expectation in the case of multiparty systems is for stability and clear policy differentiation (Downs 1957: 118–25). This certainly appears in the case of the German and Dutch multiparty systems, but it applies, too, to the two-party USA. Further, differentiation appears to be the case in all the other published 'maps' we have. Table 5.1 summarizes the full evidence, providing information on convergence (or the absence of it).

We can go through the points in Table 5.1 with our first entry, the USA, referring back to the full Figure 5.1 which details the movements of the US parties. As we have noted, the Democrats and Republicans never cross each others' policy paths; one is always to the left or right of the other. This shows up as a zero score on leapfrogging, out of the ten shifts of positions each party made between presidential elections from 1952–1992 inclusive (we consider movements only up to 1995 as most of the rest of our data only goes up to that year).

The finding of no leapfrogging renders the question of whether it involves parties contiguous to each other on the policy scale irrelevant in this case. A further question about possible blurring of party positions comes from analysis of whether both parties occupy a distinct ideological area to left or

TABLE 5.1. *Policy moves initiated by parties over twenty-one democracies 1950–1995 which involve 'leapfrogging' other parties or moving out of their characteristic Left, Centre, or Right position*

		Leapfrogging[1]			Uncharacteristic policy area[2]	
		Number of party-initiated leapfrogs out of total moves	Percentage of party-initiated leapfrogs	Number of cases of leapfrogging involving contiguous party	Number of party-initiated moves outside own area out of total moves	Percentage of all party-initiated moves outside own area
USA	Democrats	0/10	0.0	—	1/10	10.0
	Republicans	0/10	0.0	—	2/10	20.0
Canada	New Democratic Party (NDP)	0/13	0.0	—	0/13	0.0
	Liberals	5/13	38.4	5	1/13	7.7
	Conservatives	4/13	30.7	4	3/13	23.0
	Social Credit (SOCRED)	3/6	50.0	3	1/6	16.6
Australia	Labour (ALP)	0/17	0.0	—	1/17	5.9
	Liberal-National Party Alliance	0/17	0.0	—	2/17	11.9
New Zealand	Labour	0/14	0.0	—	0/14	0.0
	National	0/14	0.0	—	1/14	7.0
	Social Credit	5/10	50.0	5	2/10	20.0
UK	Labour	2/12	16.6	2	0/12	0.0
	Liberals	5/12	41.6	5	5/12	41.6
	Conservatives	2/12	16.6	2	5/12	41.6
Ireland	Labour (ILP)	2/13	15.4	0	0/13	0.0
	Fianna Fail	10/13	76.9	10	6/13	46.1
	Progressive Dems (PDP)	0/2	0.0	0	0/2	0.0
	Fine Gael	6/13	46.1	4	7/13	53.8
Spain	Communists (PCE-IU)	0/5	0.0	—	0/5	0.0
	Socialists (PSDE)	2/5	40.0	2	0/5	0.0

Choices Parties Offer

Portugal[3]	Dem Centre (UCD)	0/2	0.0		0/2	0.0
	Centre Dems (CDS)	2/3	66.0	2	2/3	66.0
	Conservatives (AP, PP)	0/4	0.0		1/4	25.0
	Popular Dem Union (UDP)	1/6	16.6	1	0/6	0.0
	Communists (PCP)	5/8	62.5	2	0/8	0.0
	Socialists (PSP)	7/8	88.8	3	1/8	12.5
	Social Dems (PSD)	7/8	88.8	4	3/8	37.7
	Centre Soc Dems (CDS)	1/8	12.5	1	5/8	62.5
Italy (to 1992)	Communists	6/9	66.0	6	1/9	11.1
	Socialists (PSI)	6/9	66.0	5	1/9	11.1
	Liberals (PLI)	6/9	66.0	4	4/9	44.4
	Christian Dems (DC)	5/9	55.5	2	0/9	0.0
	National Alliance (AN)	3/9	33.0	2	2/9	22.2
France (V Republic)	Communists (PCF)	3/9	33.0	3	0/9	0.0
	Socialists	3/9	33.0	3	0/9	0.0
	Radical Soc (RRS)	1/7	50.0	2	0/2	0.0
	Popular Rep (MRP)	1/4	25.0	1	0/14	0.0
	Gaullists	1/9	11.1	1	0/9	0.0
	Front National (FN)	0/2	0.0		0/2	0.0
Germany	Party of Dem Socialism (PDS)	0/1	0.0		0/3	0.0
	Greens	1/3	33.0	1	0/3	0.0
	Social Dems (SPD)	3/11	27.3	3	0/11	0.0
	Free Dems (FDP)	8/11	72.7	8	3/11	27.7
	Christian Dems (CDU-CSU)	4/11	36.3	4	3/11	27.7
Austria	Greens (GA)	1/2	50.0	1	0/2	0.0
	Socialists (SPO)	2/12	16.6	1	0/12	0.0
	Freedom party (FPD)	4/12	33.3	4	7/12	58.3
	Christian Dems (OVP)	3/12	25.0	2	3/12	25.0

(continued)

TABLE 5.1. *Policy moves initiated by parties over twenty-one democracies 1950–1995 which involve 'leapfrogging' other parties or moving out of their characteristic Left, Centre, or Right position—Cont'd*

		Leapfrogging[1]			Uncharacteristic policy area[2]	
		Number of party-initiated leapfrogs out of total moves	Percentage of party-initiated leapfrogs	Number of cases of leapfrogging involving contiguous party	Number of party-initiated moves outside own area out of total moves	Percentage of all party-initiated moves outside own area
Luxembourg	Communists (PCL,KPL)	3/9	33.3	2	0/9	0.0
	Social Dems (PDSL,LSAP)	2/9	22.2	2	0/9	0.0
	Liberal Dems (PD,DP)	3/9	33.3	3	2/9	22.2
	Christian Social (PCS,CSU)	2/9	22.2	2	4/9	44.4
Belgium[4]	Socialists (PSB,BSB)	2/14	14.2	0	1/14	7.1
	Christian Social (PSC, CVP)	9/14	64.4	8	5/14	35.7
	People's Union (VU)	3/13	23.0	0	8/13	61.5
	French Speaking Front (FDF)	2/9	22.2	2	0/9	0.0
Netherlands[5]	Liberals (PUU, PRL)	3/14	21.4	3	3/14	21.4
	Greens	1/1	100.0	1	0/1	0.0
	Labour (PvdA)	1/12	8.3	0	1/12	8.3
	Progressive Liberals (D'66)	5/8	62.5	5	2/8	25.0
	Market Liberals (VVD)	2/12	16.6	2	0/12	0.0
	Christian Democrats (KVP, CDA)	4/12	33.3	4	3/12	25.0

Choices Parties Offer

Country	Party				
Switzerland	Greens	1/2	50.0	1	0/2	0.0
	Social Dems (SPS-PSS)	0/11	0.0	—	0/11	0.0
	Independents (LdU-ADI)	0/4	0.0	—	0/4	0.0
	Radical Dems (FDP-PRD)	7/11	63.6	7	0/11	0.0
	Christian Dems (CVP-PDC)	7/11	63.6	7	3/11	27.3
	People's (SVP-UDC)	8/11	72.7	8	2/11	18.2
Denmark	Socialist People's Party (SF)	2/7	28.6	2	0/7	0.0
	Social Democrats	8/9	88.8	8	1/9	11.1
	Radicals (RV)	7/9	77.7	7	2/9	22.2
	Liberals (V)	7/9	77.7	7	0/9	0.0
	Conservatives	4/9	44.4	4	0/9	0.0
Norway	Left Socialists (SV) (earlier Communists)	2/10	20.0	2	0/10	0.0
	Labour (DNA)	2/10	10.0	2	0/11	0.0
	Liberals (V)	2/10	20.0	2	8/10	80.0
	Centre Party (SP)	2/10	20.0	2	1/10	10.0
	Conservatives	2/10	20.0	2	3/10	30.0
Sweden	Greens	1/2	50.0	1	1/2	50.0
	Communists (VK)	0/14	0.0	—	0/14	0.0
	Social Democrats (SSA)	3/14	21.4	3	0/14	0.0
	Liberals (FL)	13/14	92.9	8	10/14	71.4
	Centre party (CP)	9/14	64.4	6	3/14	21.4
	Conservatives (MS)	1/14	7.1	1	0/14	0.0
Finland	Greens (SVL)	1/2	50.0	1	0/2	0.0
	Communists (SKDL)	5/12	41.6	4	1/12	8.3
	Social Dem (SSDP)	9/12	75.0	7	4/12	33.3
	Centre party (SK)	8/12	66.6	6	5/12	41.6
	Conservatives (KK)	8/12	66.6	2	7/12	58.3

(continued)

TABLE 5.1. Policy moves initiated by parties over twenty-one democracies 1950–1995 which involve 'leapfrogging' other parties or moving out of their characteristic Left, Centre, or Right position—Cont'd

		Leapfrogging[1]			Uncharacteristic policy area[2]	
		Number of party-initiated leapfrogs out of total moves	Percentage of party-initiated leapfrogs	Number of cases of leapfrogging involving contiguous party	Number of party-initiated moves outside own area out of total moves	Percentage of all party-initiated moves outside own area
Iceland[3]	Communists (AB)	0/13	0.0	—	1/13	7.7
	Social Dems (A)	7/13	53.8	3	1/13	7.7
	Progressives (Ff)	7/13	53.8	0	5/13	38.4
	Independence (Sj)	6/13	46.1	6	4/13	30.7
TOTAL		311/888	35.0	251	164/888	18.5

Notes:
1. Leapfrogging is a slippery concept, since it involves a deliberate move to cross another party's policy path. Both parties involved may converge to do this. But one party only may serve to do so while the other continues on its accustomed way. In the first case both parties are counted as leapfrogging while in the second case only the initiator is.
2. Characteristic policy area is counted as Left (all negative scores) Right (all positive scores) and Centre −10 to +10.
3. Modified Left-Right scorings are used for Portugal and Iceland as explained in the data-appendix.
4. The two linguistic branches of the main Belgian parties are combined 1970–95.
5. Leapfrogging between the Catholic Party (KV) and its future partners on the CDA is not counted 1950–74

right, or whether they frequently change from being one to the other. The answer for the USA is that this is limited to Republicans accepting the New Deal in the 1950s and to Clinton repositioning Democrats to the right in 1992 (and 1996). Otherwise the parties keep fairly consistently to Left and Right.

These findings about the American case more or less generalize to the other 'Anglo-Saxon' systems based on SMD. Leapfrogging is limited, particularly as involves the two major parties in competition. They rarely or never leapfrog each other except in the case of the Liberals and Progressive Conservatives in Canada—both broad middle of the road parties, the real alternative to which is provided by the NDP. Fianna Fail and Fine Gael in Ireland are also prone to leapfrog each other. In the other countries it is the minority party or parties that leapfrog, though even they stick broadly to their own ideological area. The British Conservatives, like the US Republicans, affirmed their acceptance of the Welfare State in the 1950s but then put 'clear blue water' between themselves and Labour. Otherwise the major parties in this group of countries stick firmly to their own ideological ground.

Figure 5.2 shows this is also true for Germany. Social Democrats and Christians, the main political contenders, never cross each other in policy terms (despite the publicity given to the SPD's renunciation of Marxism at Bad Godesburg in 1959). Left Socialists (PDS), Greens, and SPD with more developed ideologies, never venture into other ground. The Christians are certainly more eclectic. The wild card is the FDP, the third party for most of the post-war period that leapfrogs extensively but mostly with the Christians. Even the FDP however sticks to the centre ground in three-quarters of its moves.

What is true of Germany holds also for other countries like Spain, Austria, and France. The Spanish Conservatives (Popular Party) do not leapfrog. The Socialists do but not with their Conservative rival as the dominant government party. Centre parties are again more prone to cross policy paths with others, though usually neighbours. These generalizations even hold for the spectacularly multiparty Netherlands (see Figure 5.3) even though the Christians, linchpin of almost all post-war coalitions, blur the picture a bit by leapfrogging and leaving the centre from time to time (in common with their Italian counterparts). Many-way party competition in the Netherlands has pitted Labour (PvdA) against free-market Liberals (VVD). They are the ideological poles of the system and do not overlap—a pattern which repeats itself generally in neighbouring Belgium and Luxembourg, Switzerland, Italy, and Scandinavia.

Small parties in the Centre are most likely to leapfrog and move from their restricted ideological area. As the number of parties grows we expect more leapfrogging almost as a mechanical effect though it is surprising how many parties still succeed in holding to their ideological ground.

On the other hand, parties with an ambiguous ideology have little to anchor them to a fixed point. We have already noted the lack of distinctiveness of the two main Canadian parties, Conservatives and Liberals. This is echoed in the behaviour of Fianna Fail and Fine Gael in Ireland, Progressives and Independents in Iceland, and many of the Finnish parties. In the latter case this may reflect influences outside normal electoral politics. Up to 1988 all Finnish politicians were acutely aware of the need not to offend the Soviet Union lurking large next door. For a similar reason, competition in Portugal was muted under the oversight of the military-dominated Council and residually the presidency, installed after the revolution of 1974. Excessive criticism of the original radical reforms was avoided, pushing party politics as a whole to the left.

It is essential in reading Table 5.1 to take into account all the information reported there, as focussing on one aspect of a figure to the exclusion of others makes for an unbalanced assessment of what it is actually telling you. Thus leapfrogging blurs policy clarity less where it involves a party very similar in ideology to the one that leaps, meaning the party does not quit its own ideological area to do so.

The overall impression from Table 5.1 is that leapfrogging is limited to one-third of the cases overall. Eighty per cent of these cases involve contiguous parties however (251/311). Leaving one's characteristic policy area occurs even less, in less than one fifth of the cases (18.5 per cent).

Aggregating over the whole set of figures can be misleading however, as so many of the examples of parties not being firmly anchored in policy involve small, transitory parties often in densely packed systems, where they have difficulty in avoiding policy stands taken by other parties.

In terms of our initial questions to the comparative evidence we can say from Table 5.1:

1. There *are* choices. Parties do not consistently converge, and the choices they offer are consistent with the party's record, thus overcoming some of the barriers to acquiring relevant information on the voters' part.
2. Choices are *both* gently graded, in systems with many parties, and sharply polarized in systems with few parties. Each situation may present problems, particularly in identifying the median position. A gentle gradation with much leapfrogging may render it harder for voters to choose, particularly between centre parties. Indeed parties on the wings may offer clear choices while only overlapping ones are available in the centre. We shall pursue this point below with Table 5.2.
3. Point 2 is linked with point 3—are the policy alternatives on offer clear and distinct, or ambiguous and overlapping? Given the time series data on

which Table 5.1 is based, one could say 'sometimes, but sometimes not'. Overall the tendency is to offer clear choices. We shall have better ideas about this when we look at the average party positions in Table 5.2.
4. The point about specific issues fitting into Left-Right bundles cannot be answered here but it will be below. What we can say is that Left-Right characterizations do seem to catch the main features of post-war party competition rather well and to conform to the broad contours of historical accounts. This is just as well since most of the tables examined in this chapter derive from party maps for each country like those in Figures 5.1–5.3. These have all been published and their validity extensively and intensively assessed (Budge et al. 2001). We can thus proceed with some confidence to the complementary analyses of these data reported below.

5.2 DISTINCTIVENESS OR OVERLAP? PARTY POSITIONING ON THE LEFT-RIGHT CONTINUUM

We have examined party movement, taking advantage of the dynamic nature of the Manifesto data. The analysis showed that party policy is characterized by continuity rather than change, by differentiation rather than convergence. This provides a necessary basis for the analysis here where we look at the average positions of parties over the post-war period to see how far they truly differentiate themselves and thus provide clear guidance for electors. To draw firm conclusions from such averages, however, we have to be sure that they are reasonably representative of the specific positions parties take up and are not, for example, putting them at the centre when in practice they alternate violently between Left and Right. Table 5.1 shows this is not the case. With reasonably stable position taking in specific situations, the overall averages should provide a fair representation of overall tendencies.

The averages are presented pictorially, along the Left-Right continuum, in Figure 5.4. Printed names or initials indicate parties for which we have a reasonable number of specific election scores and which can thus be averaged with some confidence.

As is clear from the figure, average party positions may be quite clearly distinguished as in the USA or appear very close to some others, as in the extremely fragmented multiparty system of the Netherlands. This reflects closeness in party positioning and variations in leapfrogging already discussed. In some of these cases the policy differences between parties are not statistically significant. Boxes around sets of parties indicate unreliable differences. The number of policy alternatives available for choice in the country (shown in the next to last column, at the side of the figure) is reckoned on the basis of these clusters—plus of course the number of parties that stand on

74　　　　　　　　　　　　*The Electoral Process*

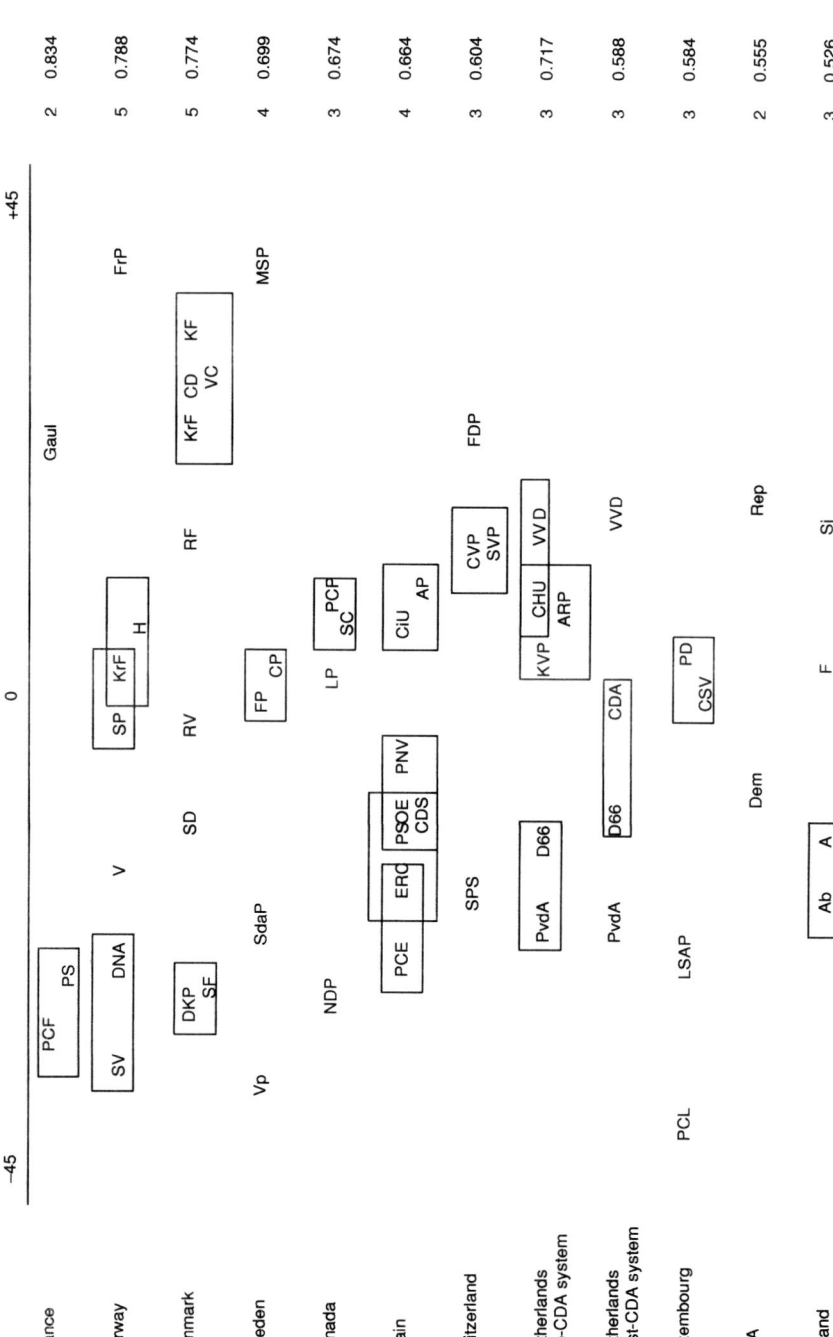

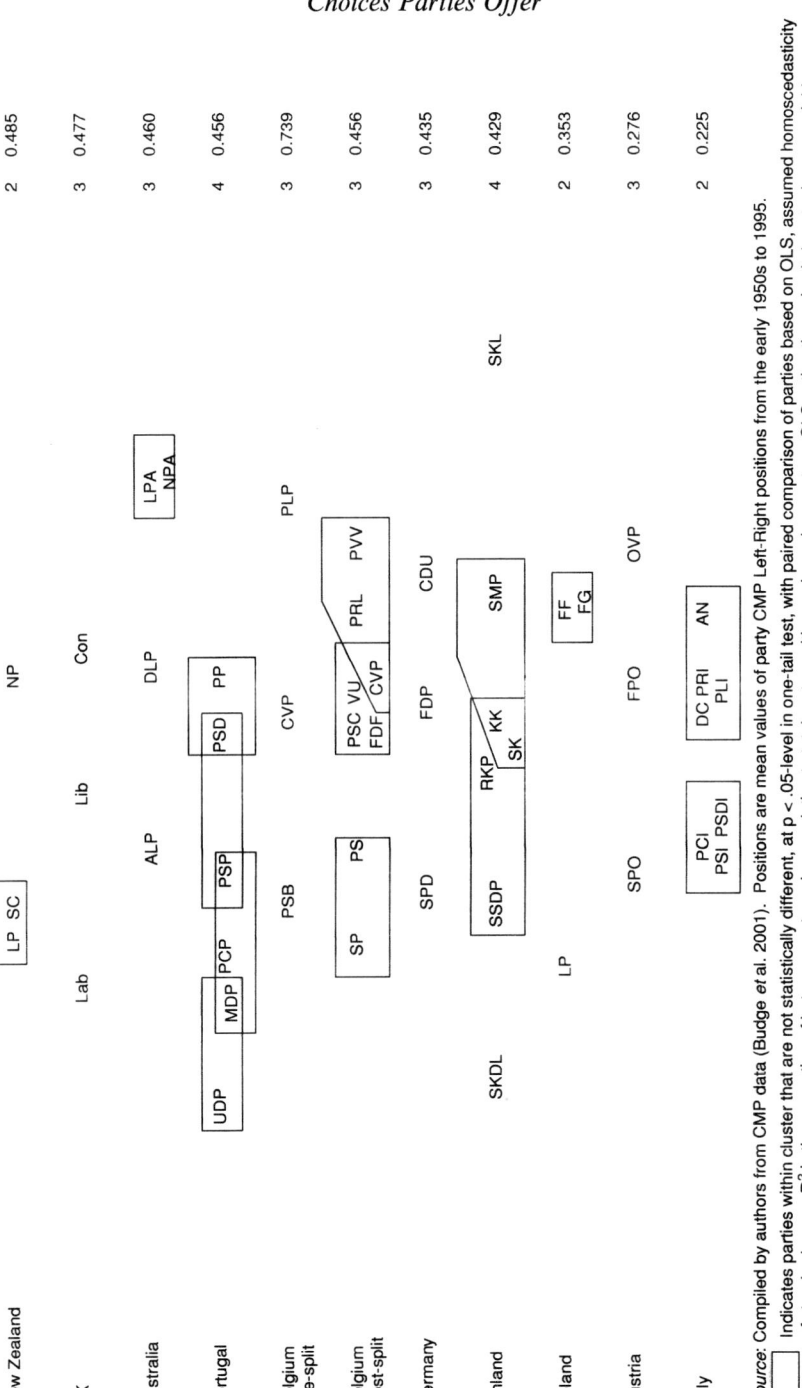

FIGURE 5.4. Distinctiveness of choices offered by parties along the Left-Right dimension, by country, 1950–95

Source: Compiled by authors from CMP data (Budge *et al.* 2001). Positions are mean values of party CMP Left-Right positions from the early 1950s to 1995.

☐ Indicates parties within cluster that are not statistically different, at $p < .05$-level in one-tail test, with paired comparison of parties based on OLS, assumed homoscedasticity of standard errors. R^2 is the proportion of between-party variance relative to total party position variance in a system, OLS estimation using k-1 party dummy variables.

their own. Thus the USA offers voters two distinct policy positions but so does multiparty Italy where the parties fall into only two clusters—Left and Right. Denmark on the other hand offers five alternatives even though many parties on the right overlap.

The last column at the side of Figure 5.4 is the squared multiple correlation coefficient, R^2, from an equation linking all the parties (scored as dichotomous variables) to the individual post-war policy scores. The numbers in the column thus represent the proportion of variation in these scores explained by differences between the parties. Where parties differentiate themselves more in policy terms this improves the range and quality of the choice voters are asked to make. Thus Norway and Denmark offer a wide choice between quite different party policies and Italy a limited choice between not very distinct policies for the most part. This indicates that choice depends on the behaviour of the parties as well as on the numbers in the system. SMD countries are quite dispersed. Canada, rather surprisingly in terms of the leapfrogging between its major parties (see Table 5.1), shows a lot of between-party differentiation in policy terms, principally due to the distinctiveness of the NDP.

Not surprisingly the extent to which parties differentiate themselves corresponds fairly well with the number of clusters they fall into, though not perfectly. One could therefore deduce that the closer countries come to having a two-party system (facilitated by SMD) the less choice they offer to electors, although the choices they do offer are distinctive ones. In the case of the USA, along with New Zealand and Australia to some extent, the choice seems reasonably sharp.

A clear mark of distinction between the PR and SMD systems in Figure 5.4 is indeed that the former seem to offer a finer gradation of choice to electors, with parties spreading out between Left and Right at frequent intervals, while SMD systems (and their run-off relative in France) frequently leave a hole in the middle. Voters are thus forced to vote for the one of two opposed alternatives that is slightly more preferable to them, whereas many might much prefer a centre alternative that is closer but alas does not exist. Whether this distortion between median voter and parliamentary median positions is due to the effect of SMD on the evolution of the party system in these countries or to its internal mechanics is a point we take up in Chapter 7.

A hint that it may derive from the mechanics of the system comes from the fact that in Britain, for example, a centre party exists and is the one frequently chosen by the median voter. However the aggregation of votes into seats under SMD rules has the effect of pushing the parliamentary median away from the choice of the median voter. The only SMD system where distortion of one kind or the other does not take place is Canada. There we see a choice and, owing to the fact that the two main parties take up positions close to each other near the centre, the median voter endorses one of them.

The system, owing to the particular balance and stance of the parties, is then likely to provide a reasonably close correspondence between the electoral and parliamentary medians.

The last thing PR systems do is to depopulate the centre—or as it happens, the left. It could be argued that Norway, until the FrP came on the scene in the 1970s, and Luxembourg, leave a hole on the political right. However, to then misidentify the position of the median voter we would need to envisage both countries having large concentrations of unrepresented voters on the right. This does not seem to be the case. Norway has seen attempts to set up right-wing parties that have not gained enormous support. Luxembourg has had the same party system since the war with none of the changes that have occurred in neighbouring Belgium and the Netherlands. This indicates popular support or at least acceptance of the present range of alternatives.

The comparative evidence presented in Figure 5.4 thus has a considerable bearing on the questions about choice that underlie the general discussion of this chapter and which were also posed in regard to the party movements reported in Table 5.1. The first of these concerned the question of whether there is choice. Figure 5.4 shows that parties, on average, offer a statistically significant choice in all twenty-one nations, sometimes between a graded range of alternatives and sometimes just between two, but always a choice.

Gradation versus polarization we have already touched on. A majority of countries offer a reasonably nuanced gradation but some produce polarized choices. This is generally associated with a contrast between their election systems—PR versus SMD. Graduated choices offer better opportunities for electoral preferences to express themselves more accurately, as is the case with Denmark for example. On the other hand they may often create overlapping and ambiguity between alternatives, as is evident in Belgium and the Netherlands. SMD systems score by providing clear-cut alternatives but on a take-it-or-leave-it basis that leaves little room for subtleties of electoral expression.

5.3 PARTY POSITIONING ON SPECIFIC ISSUES

Specific issues are relevant because of the likelihood that the public space fragments between elections into separate policy segments defined by the institutional arrangements of governments and legislatures (see Figure 3.2). If the median parliamentary party in one of these areas differs from that in one of the others, or in the overall Left-Right continuum, there is a possibility that decision-making will be dominated by a party without a mandate no matter how well the election system translates votes cast on a Left-Right basis into parliamentary seats. In the following section we examine the correspondence between party Left-Right positions and their positions on specific issues. First, however, we have to look at the actual distributions of positions in each area. It is always possible that some well-informed electors with strong issue-focussed concerns may cast their votes with reference to one of the specific areas. So we have also to ask, as with the overall Left-Right space, what kinds of choice parties offer to them.

The areas we focus on are those picked out by previous investigators as particularly important. Indeed two of our choices—support for welfare and support for peace first as opposed to strong defence—are suggested by an earlier comparative study of democratic policymaking (Lijphart 1999) from which we take our 'output measures' of welfare and foreign aid (see Chapters 9 and 12). The third 'output' we are concerned with is government size, itself an indicator of overall state intervention in society. That takes us into considering the role of the state versus the market in organizing an economy.

What we examine as party policy indicators for our three policy areas are indices of opposition to welfare provision minus support for it, support for military alliances minus peaceful internationalism, and support for free-market measures minus government planning. All of these are pro and con measures combined from original codings of party electoral programmes. In later chapters we will examine how far these relate to the way government spends its money in the various areas. Here we are concerned to see, as with Left-Right positioning, how far parties distinguish themselves from each other in the way they respond to these issues, and how far they offer electors clear choices.

We start with the question of strong defences versus building peaceful international relationships. As the latter is generally a 'leftish' position we give it a negative score, and assign positive scores to the 'right-wing' alternative of a strong military posture. Of course this leaves open the possibility that positions do not exactly correlate with the overall Left-Right scale.

Looking in detail at Figure 5.5 however the Socialist and Radical parties do seem to line up in support for peace, while the conventionally right-wing parties either take a 'balanced view' or opt outright for a military perspective. We will check the exact degree of correspondence with the overall Left-Right positions of these parties below (see Table 5.2). Looking here at party differences and the number of choices on offer, these seem slightly, but only slightly, less than those for overall Left-Right differences in Figure 5.4. Between-party differences (R^2) go down more rapidly in value over the various countries and the choices on offer are more often two in number. In general, party positions spread out less than they do in Left-Right terms, naturally enough since these also incorporate other issues. An extreme case is Ireland, where all parties uphold the policy of neutrality followed since the foundation of the State. In terms of clustering however (whether in one direction or another) other countries are not much, if at all, behind (cf. New Zealand and Austria).

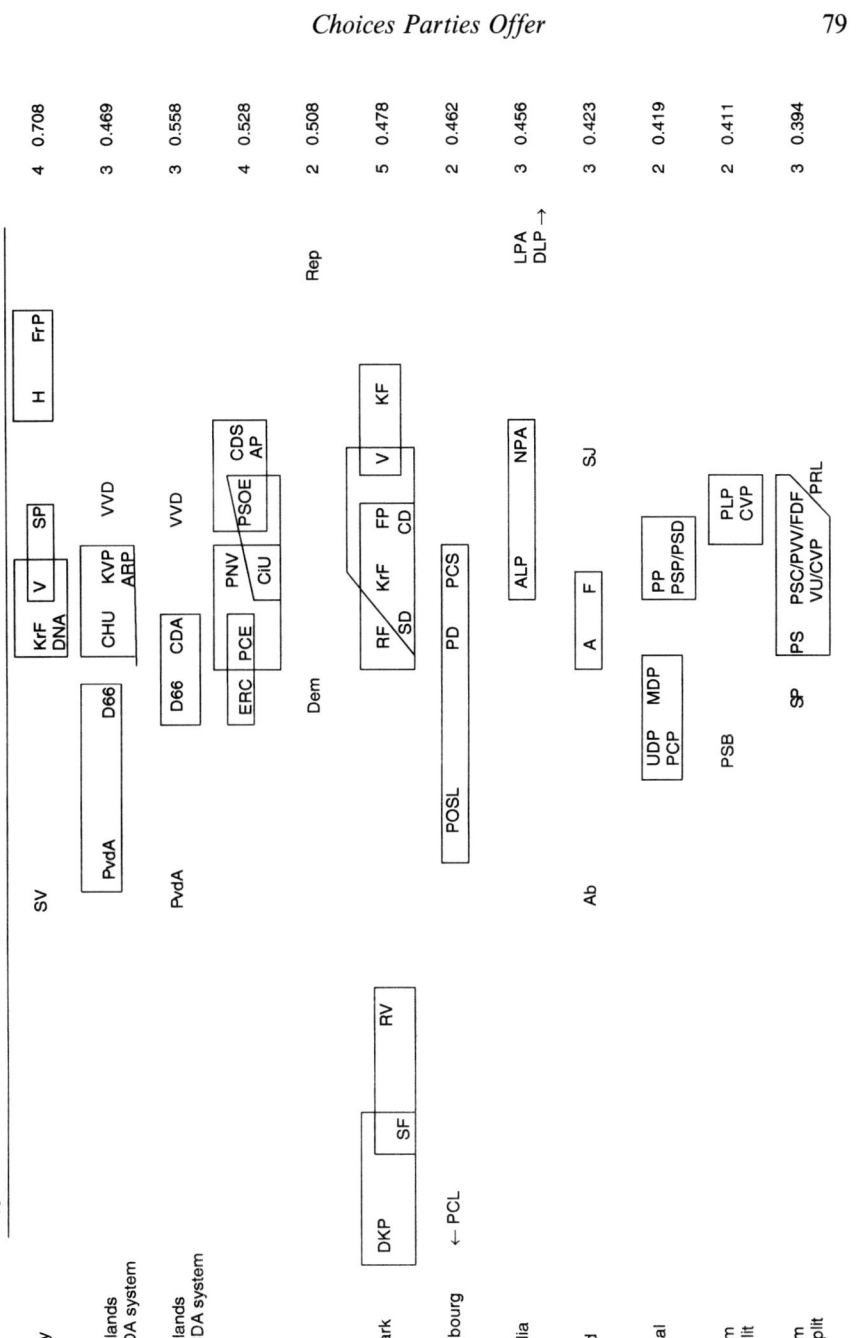

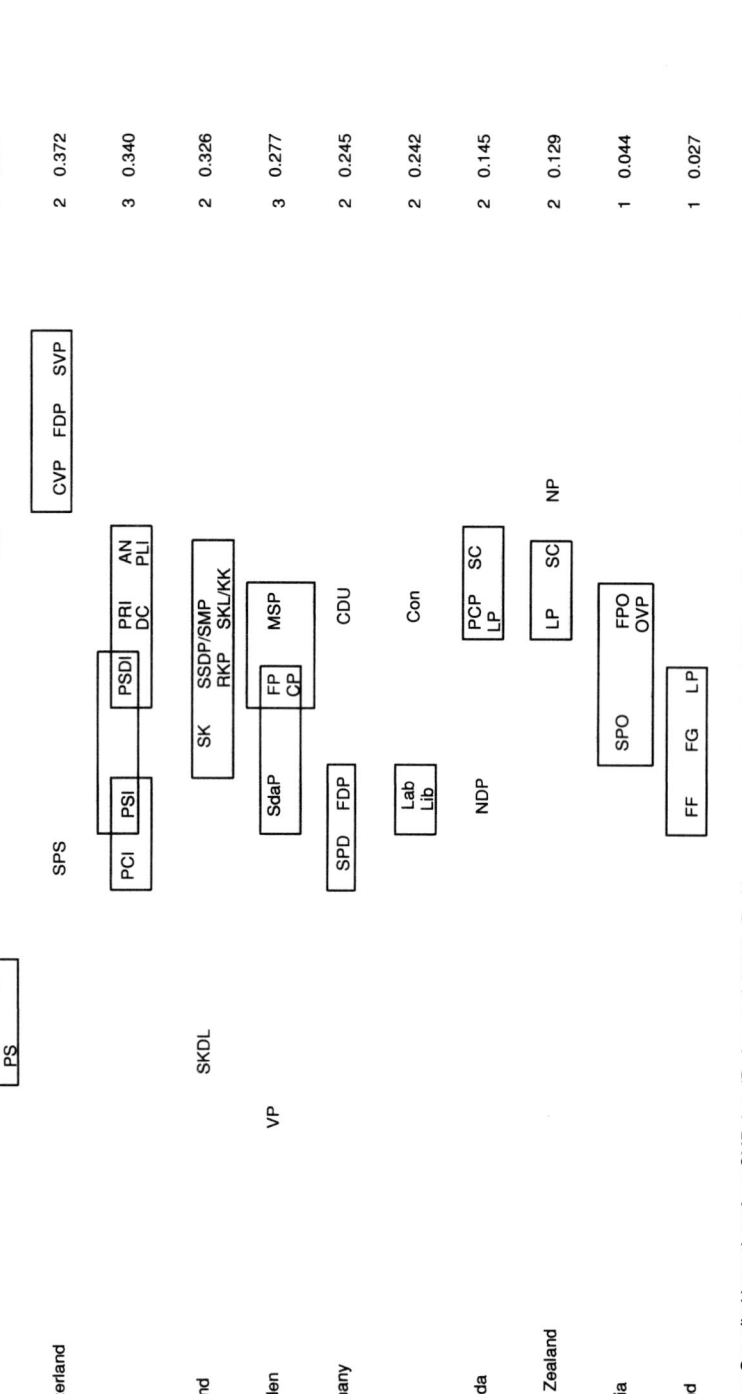

FIGURE 5.5. Distinctiveness of policy options offered by parties on military alliances minus peaceful internationalism, by country, 1950–95

It is also of some interest to look at the substantive choices being offered to electors, since as noted these run over a more restricted segment of the continuum than they do with Left-Right. In Australia and New Zealand for example the choices are between higher and lower levels of military preparedness: purely peaceful internationalism is not an option with South-East Asia on their doorstep. In contrast, Finland, Sweden, Germany, Luxembourg, Portugal, and the UK offer choices between varieties of peaceful internationalism. Ireland and Austria, as we have seen, offer no choice between them at all! Only a slight majority of countries—Belgium, Canada, Denmark, France, Iceland, Italy, Netherlands, Norway, Spain, Switzerland, and the USA—offer a more consequential choice between peaceful cooperation and military strength. We shall investigate the nature of these substantive choices further (see Table 5.3).

In the meantime, however, we turn to choices on domestic issues, starting with welfare (Figure 5.6). Here the range of choices is even more restricted; virtually every party supports some sort of social provision for their population. The only question is how much. The American, Australian, and Italian systems offer a choice between modest and weak support for the welfare state. Belgium, Denmark, Germany, Iceland, Portugal, and Sweden impose on the electorate a more strongly differentiated alternative between strong and weak support for welfare. The main opposition is a more graduated one, between modest and very strong support in Austria, Canada, Finland, France, Iceland, Luxembourg, Netherlands, New Zealand, Norway, Spain, Switzerland, and the UK. Every country does offer a choice, however, and about half the countries have parties that are quite strongly differentiated on the issue ($R^2 > 0.3$).

Clearly there is much more of a consensus on welfare than there is on the direction of the economy (Figure 5.7). Here parties are more sharply differentiated from each other in terms of between-party variance (R^2). The systems offer more 4- and 3-alternative choices. And in all countries there is a real split between planning and free-market measures, compared with the relative consensus on welfare and defence. From the distributions it seems to be the economic issue that is at the root of active Left-Right differences.

5.4 THE EQUIVALENCE BETWEEN LEFT-RIGHT AND SPECIFIC ISSUE POSITIONS

It remains a moot point of course whether in this area as in the others it is parties' positions on the specific issue-related scales or their general Left-Right stances that most closely correlate with actual public decisions in the area. This question remains to be settled later (see Part IV). We can get a handle on it here by examining the extent to which party Left-Right orderings correspond to those on each of the specific issues.

82   *The Electoral Process*

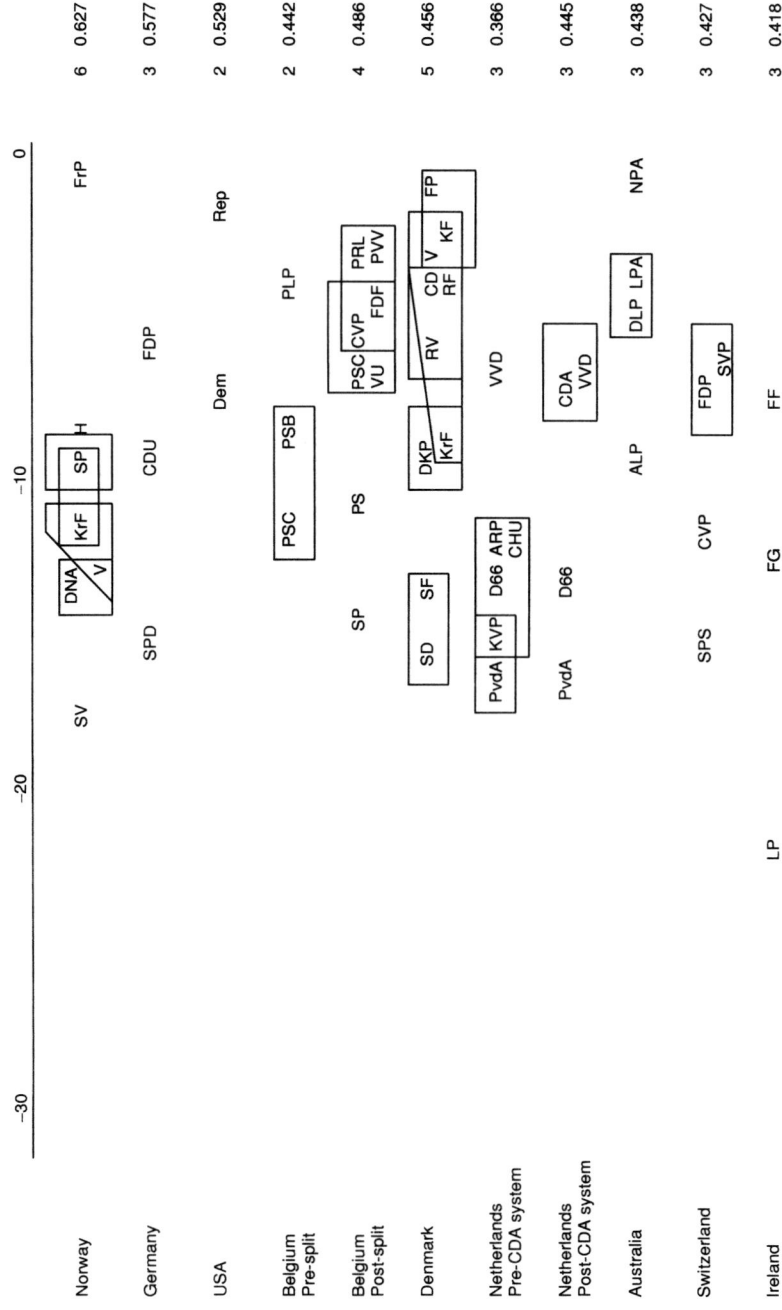

Choices Parties Offer

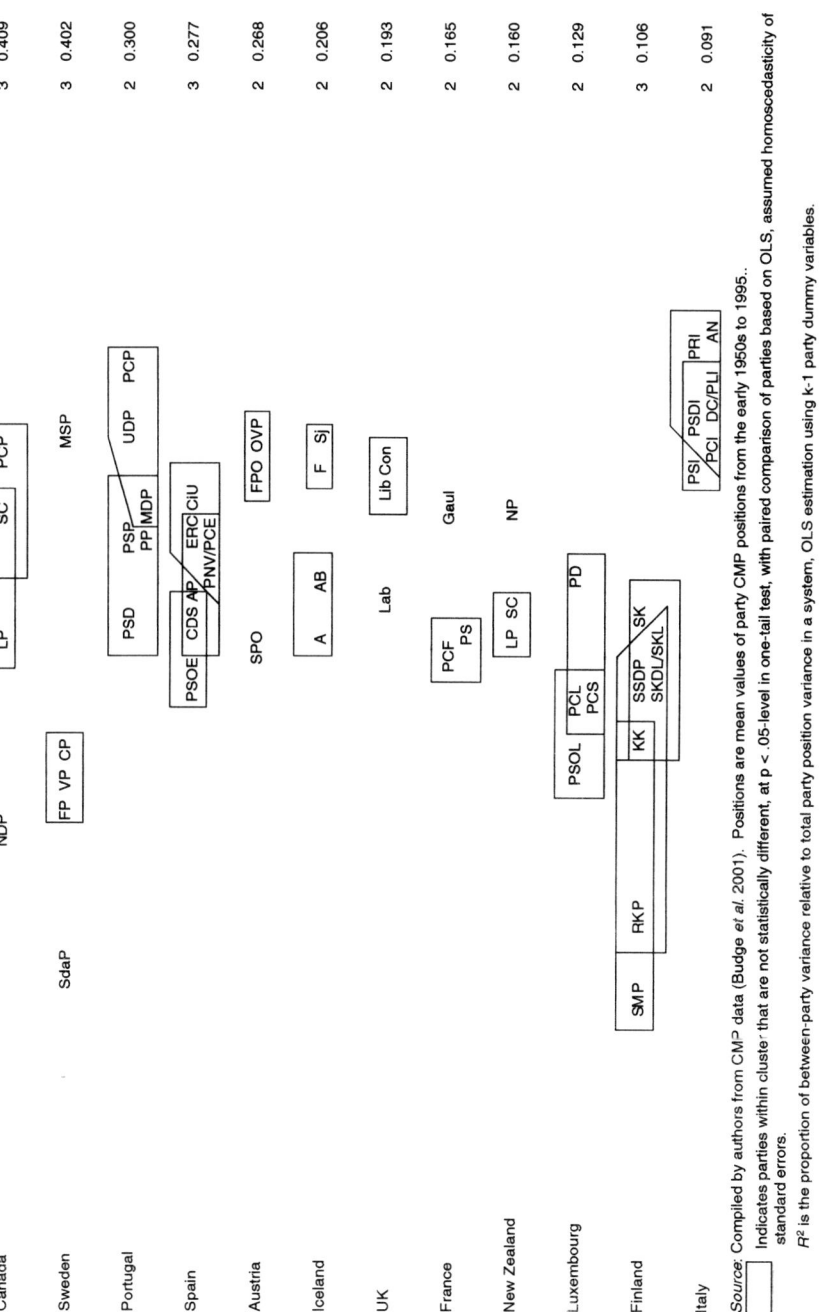

FIGURE 5.6. Distinctiveness of policy options offered by parties on opposition to welfare minus support for it, by country over post-war period

Source: Compiled by authors from CMP data (Budge *et al*. 2001). Positions are mean values of party CMP positions from the early 1950s to 1995.

☐ Indicates parties within cluster that are not statistically different, at p < .05-level in one-tail test, with paired comparison of parties based on OLS, assumed homoscedasticity of standard errors.

R^2 is the proportion of between-party variance relative to total party position variance in a system, OLS estimation using k-1 party dummy variables.

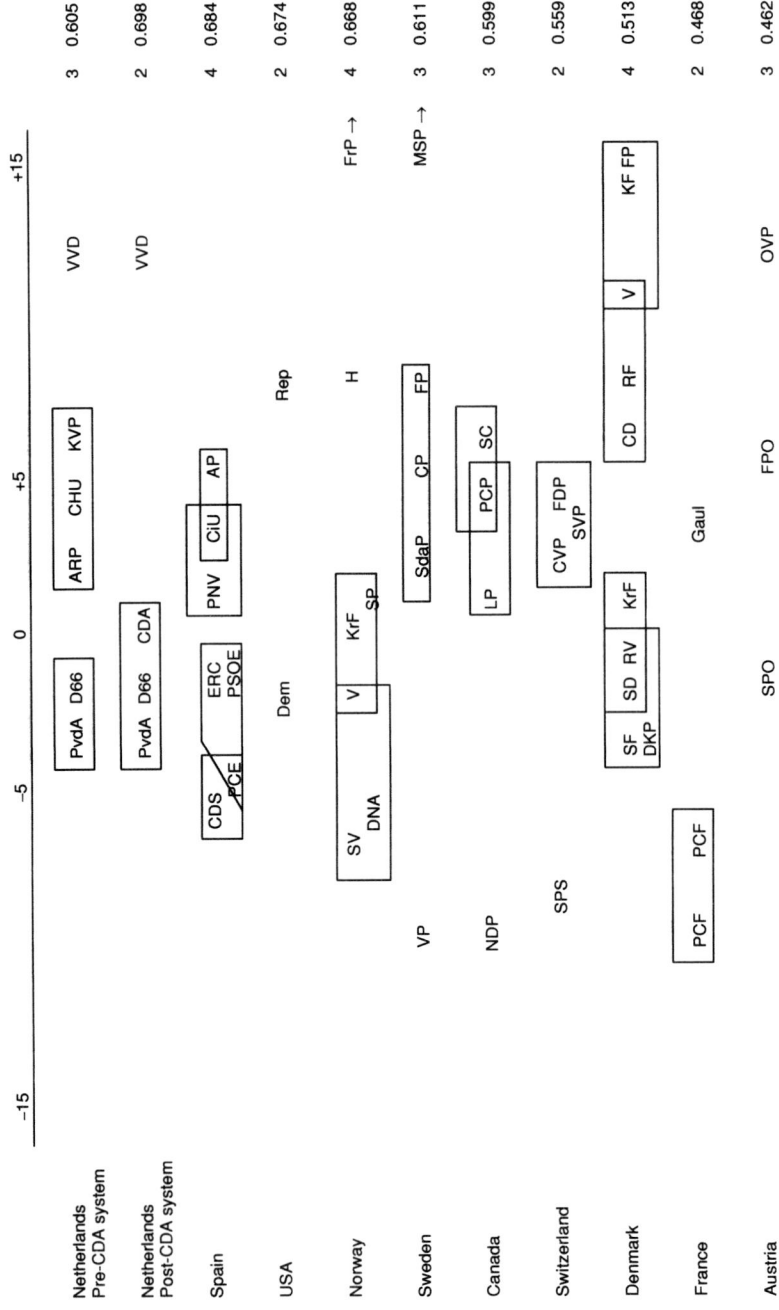

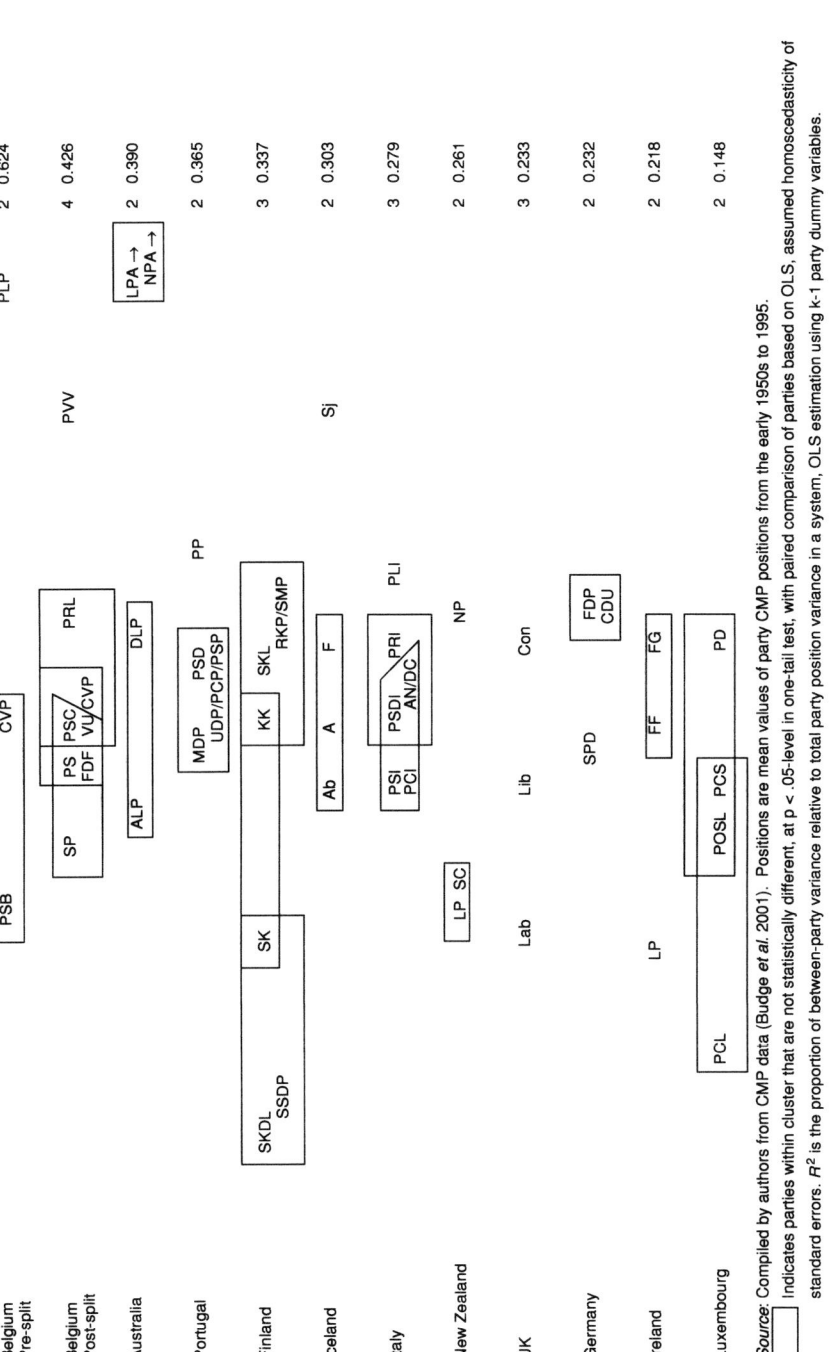

FIGURE 5.7. Distinctiveness of policy options offered by parties on support for free market minus economic planning, by country over post-war period

This analysis is not in any sense causal, as Left-Right positions form an aggregation of the three individual ones. The question is rather how well the aggregation performs as indicator of attitudes on the specific issues. Given a party's Left-Right position how reasonable is it to infer how supportive it will be relative to other parties in regard to peace, welfare and planning? This is central to considering how far a mandate interpretation applies to political processes in our democracies, given that voting and party direction-giving proceeds in largely Left-Right terms. If these do not mesh well with specific issue-preferences, the decisions made within each area will not be well-anchored in the general mandate, and no 'necessary' connection can be established with popular preferences in the area. Conversely, if they do mesh well, then the Left-Right mandate will inform specific decisions in particular areas and popular preferences will be reflected, however crudely, in public policy-outputs. Table 5.2, showing the general correspondence between the party Left-Right line-up and their line-up on specific issues is thus quite central to all mandate arguments—government as well as median—since it is difficult to see how a general mandate could be formed over all the specific issue areas without going through some process of aggregation, most likely a Left-Right one.

Table 5.2 examines the extent to which the Left-Right rankings of parties in each country correspond to their rank-order on each of the specific issues. It does this by pairwise comparisons as explained in the notes to Table 5.2. Basically all individual parties and clusters of parties are compared with each other to see if they are in the same relative positions on one scale as on the other. The message from Table 5.2 is that they overwhelmingly are, with only a few very specific exceptions (Finnish, Spanish, and Portuguese Communists on welfare).

This is a striking and powerful finding for the reasons emphasized earlier. Above all it means that the median party picked out by the election on a Left-Right basis is also likely to be the median party on all its component issues. Although these may be discussed and voted on separately in parliament, the fact that the same party is pivotal on all of them and is also the party legitimized to be so by the election result, means that the transmission mechanism for reflecting the popular will is working at this disaggregated issue level (see also Chapter 12).

Going back to the discussion of Chapter 3, the high level of correspondence also means that the Left-Right ordering of parties does offer a good guide to where the parties stand in individual issue areas, so it is not unreasonable that it should provide the setting for the policy debate during elections, or the terms for the policy directive to parties which emerges from the election.

TABLE 5.2. *Correspondence of party policy positions on specific issues with their general Left-Right positions*

	# of possible pairs	Percentage corresponding to Left-Right positions on		
		Peace/Milt	Welfare	Plan/Market
Australia	5	60	100	100
Austria	3	Not applicable*	100	100
Belgium pre/post 1972	3/23	100/100	100/100	100/100
Canada	5	100	100	100
Denmark	34	94	91	97
Finland	17	100	24	100
France	1	100	100	100
Germany	3	100	67	100
Iceland	5	100	100	100
Ireland	2	Not applicable*	100	100
Italy	12	100	100	100
Luxembourg	5	100	100	100
Netherlands pre/post 1974	13/5	100/100	92/100	100/100
New Zealand	2	100	100	100
Norway	20	75	95	100
Portugal	15	100	33	100
Spain	19	100	74	89
Sweden	9	100	89	100
Switzerland	5	100	100	100
UK	3	100	100	100
USA	1	100	100	100
TOTAL	210*	95%	83%	99%

* The Irish and Austrian parties offer no reliable choice on a peace vs. military posture. On peace-military there are thus 205 possible pairs.

Notes: Aligning Policy Areas by Left-Right (Discordant Pairs)

We have taken the gradation of choices in each country and rank-ordered the parties. The number of Left-Right ranks in a country is determined by the number of clusters plus the ranking information we can infer from the overlaps. For example, in Norway we have five clusters. We also know that the Christians are not reliably distinguishable from the Agrarian party (Centre, SP) nor are they distinguishable from the Conservative party (Hoyre); however, we know that the SP is distinguishable from Hoyre. By inference, therefore, we can say that the Christians must sit at a position between the SP and Hoyre. In all, therefore, Norway has five ranks, from left to right.

For the seven Norwegian parties, two of which occupy the same rank, there are 14 pairwise comparisons that could be in discordant order (i.e. SV versus the four ranks below + DNA versus four ranks below—Ven versus three ranks below + SP versus two ranks below + KF versus one rank below. Thus $4 + 4 + 3 + 2 + 1 = 14$).

Across the three policy areas, only 8.7 per cent of all pairs are out of order. Most of these, 35 of the 48 discordant pairs, occur in the welfare area. Many of these welfare discordant pairs involve communist parties in Finland, Spain and Portugal who are less supportive of welfarism than their left-wing position might suggest.

5.5 ISSUE BUNDLES ON OFFER: A COMPARATIVE SURVEY OF CHOICES

We began this chapter by talking about the 'policy market' as one that traded in bundles of policy promises. These can be summarized by positions on the general Left-Right scale. Now that we have uncovered the strong equivalence between these and policy on specific issues we can talk more concretely about what is in the bundles. We can thus examine the policy alternatives on offer in each country at a specific level—always with the proviso that this is the result of an overall averaging process that irons out subtle shades of differentiation. However, if the previous analyses of the chapter have shown us anything it is that parties by and large stick to the same kinds of policy over time, and differentiate themselves from their rivals by doing so. Thus, characterizing countries in terms of fairly fixed alternatives on offer is not too misleading.

Each alternative is characterized by three positions on each of the three issues we have examined. The Leftist position of modest to strong support for peace, welfare and planning is symbolized by L: a neutral position is M: and support for military preparations and the free market is R, for Rightist. In theory parties can offer any bundle of positions from LLL through MMM to RRR. But as we have noted there are constraints, and certain positions on one issue tend to go with certain ones on the others.

Table 5.3 is arranged so that the sharpest political oppositions occur at the left-hand corner and diminish in intensity as one moves East and South. Only in the USA, Denmark, and Italy is there a stark Left versus Right choice—with the caveats that (*a*) we consider a weak acceptance of welfare to be on the Right, and (*b*) we ignore the fact that the USA and Italy do not offer a wide choice within specific policy areas, especially welfare.

TABLE 5.3. *The policy choices offered by parties in twenty-one post-war democracies*

L L L versus M R R	**L L R versus L R R**	**L M L versus L R R**
Denmark, USA, Italy	Netherlands, Luxembourg	New Zealand
L L R versus M R R	**L L L versus L M R**	**MMM versus MMM**
Sweden	Austria, Spain, UK	Italy
L L L versus L R R	**L M R versus L M R**	
Belgium, France, Germany, Norway	Portugal	
L L L versus L L R	**L R R versus L R R**	
Finland, Ireland	Canada	
L L R versus M R R	**L R L versus M R R**	
Iceland	Australia	

Notes: The entries in Table 5.3 are formed by the two most prominent party alternatives in each nation and characterized as what an electorate would get from one versus from the other. Judgements are made on the basis of Figures 5.5–5.7 above. They are characterized as follows:
1. Modest to strong welfarism = L weak welfarism = M anti-welfarism not applicable
2. Modest to strong peace = L neutral = M military = R
3. Modest to strong planning = L neutral = M market = R

Generally parties offer fairly mixed bundles, to the left on welfare and opposing each other particularly on planning versus the free market. Fifteen countries offer no choice on welfare, the major parties all endorsing modest to strong positions of support. The six exceptions to this are again the USA, Denmark, and Italy, joined by Sweden, Iceland, and Australia. Portugal, Canada, and the Netherlands and Luxembourg in contrast hardly offer issue alternatives at all—rather gradations within the limits of an overall consensus.

In the end electors can vote for no more than what the parties offer. Parties structure the electoral debate and define the alternatives being voted on. The way parties set the political agenda for the nation is thus likely to tell a lot about the policy choices being made there. From what we have seen, these differ relatively little over time but quite a lot between countries (cf. USA and Finland). In turn, this suggests that what we ought to be looking at are not so much the policy outcomes of specific elections but the pattern of outcomes over a series of elections—perhaps even for the whole post-war period—which will be powerfully shaped by the stable choices offered by parties. This is a point we will be taking up with the policy regimes we identify in Part IV.

5.6 CHOICE: PRECONDITION FOR A MANDATE

Two rival mechanisms for translating popular preferences into public policy have been postulated in contemporary debate. One is the (government) mandate, whereby the party elected to government has received a popular endorsement of its programme which it then carries through. This implies that parties offer alternative programmes that the electorate choose between. The alternative to this is party convergence on policy as each tries to get the median elector to vote for them. This implies that parties end up with the same programme—the one preferred by the median voter—rather than offering choice.

Both views are to be found in the *Economic Theory of Democracy* (Downs 1957: 20–41, 96–110), which pursues a kind of dialectic, starting off from a mandate point of view that then leads on to convergence under certain conditions. These are straight two-party competition or approximations to it (Downs 1957: 114–20) that is favoured by any SMD plurality system of election. A further twist to Downs' argument is to point out that where parties *do* provide stable choices, under PR with multiparty systems where there is little prospect of gaining a majority of the vote, and therefore no inducement for convergence, mandate theory does not work anyway. Voters have no way of knowing what a government formed by party negotiations after the election will look like, or what it will do (Downs 1957: 120–44: an extension to the argument is that there is no way of holding it accountable either, Powell and Whitten 1993).

Our suggested revision of mandate theory draws on both sides of the debate. We can certainly agree that a government mandate rarely emerges in practice, without abandoning mandate ideas entirely. And we can base ourselves on the power of the median without subscribing to the view that it produces party convergence. Indeed our evidence shows that even in the strictest existing conditions of pure two-party competition (USA) parties do not converge in policy terms.

Downs' critique of multiparty situations falls short because he does not pursue the power of the median argument to the legislative and governmental level. The median party is essential to majorities there just as the median elector is at her or his level. If the two can be linked by the rules for aggregating votes then popular preferences can be reflected in decision-making whatever the number of parties. Among other things, this argument deflects the critique—incipient in Downs' reasoning—of PR as reducing the potential for electoral direction of policymaking.

The findings of this chapter tell decisively in favour of mandate theory against convergence. There simply is no consistent convergence over the party systems and time period examined. Parties offer reasonably stable policy-packages to electors, a feature which simplifies information-gathering and rational decision-making by the latter. Sometimes the choices offered by parties are wider and sometimes more restricted. Presumably the relative absence of challenges from new parties in most of the democracies indicates that the existing alternatives offer an acceptable choice, though this is speculation. What we do know is that parties differentiate themselves in the packages they put before electors, and this offers the latter the policy choices that are a necessary precondition for a mandate (see Tables 2.1 and 2.4). Whether other, equally necessary conditions are present will emerge from the following chapters.

APPENDIX

The policy preference measurements were constructed using the following coding categories, as described in CMP98 (Budge et al. 2001).

Variable	Coding categories
Left–Right	26 item CMP Left-Right scoring (Budge *et al.* 2001: 22, 228)
Planning–Market	Free enterprise (401) + economic orthodoxy (414)
	Minus
	Market regulation (403) + economic planning (404) + controlled economy (412)
Welfare	Welfare state limitation (505)
	Minus
	Social justice (503) + welfare state expansion (504)
Peace–Military	Military, positive (104)
	Minus
	Foreign special relations, negative (102) + military, negative (105) + peace (106)

References are to the names (numbers) of one of the 56 policy categories used by CMP98 (Budge et al. 2001).

6

Mandates Without Obvious Majorities?

6.1 INTRODUCTION

The findings on choice, based on the clearly differentiated policy packages offered by each party, clearly meet the parties' responsibility for the electoral phase of a mandate—any mandate, including a government mandate. What do voters do with these choices? That is an equally important question. What we have seen is that they do not normally come together as single-party majorities to vote a government into office on the basis of a future programme.

Can the mandate idea survive without clear majorities? The answer is perhaps, in one of two different ways. The first is a scaled down version of the government mandate. Following on reasoning articulated by Riker (1982), who thought that voting cycles made true majorities close to impossible, political scientists have taken up his suggestion that electors could hold governments to account retrospectively by judging them on what they had done in office (see also Fiorina 1981). As parties might anticipate these electoral reactions, the prospect of such an appraisal could also exert a restraining influence on their current actions. Parties could be voted *out* by a majority, even if a majority cannot be mustered to vote them *in*.

A second possibility is a median mandate. It sees elections as pointing governments in directions the voters would like to see policies move. The communication comes principally from the position occupied by the median voter. As the median voter moves left or right, so too does the distribution of preferences among their representatives. Self-evident majorities, as such, are not the operative force coming from elections under this thesis; rather, it is information about the policy preference of the median voter.

In this chapter, we ask whether either of these two alternatives can stand in the face of evidence. We look first for evidence of a negative majority, which we see as a minimalist version of a government mandate. Evidence that could make one look with favour on that version is almost non-existent. We turn next to analyses that could support or discredit a median mandate thesis; after confronting it with the evidence, we find it looks rather promising.

6.2 A MINIMALIST MANDATE

The idea of 'kicking the rascals out' is as old as representative democracy itself. It is quite compatible with Burkean ideas of representatives using their own judgement rather than being 'mandated' or constrained in any way by their constituents. Constituents would have the right to judge the actions of their representative retrospectively and not to re-elect him or her. That in its original form was what representative democracy was all about.

Although hardly a full-blown mandate theory, retrospective voting does have mandate ideas embedded in it. It involves some judgement that the alternative set of rascals is better than the current set, otherwise one would not want to kick them out even though they had done badly. In turn, however, this relative judgement rests on expectations about what the different parties would do in government. If reconfirmed or voted in on that basis, parties are likely to draw inferences about what they are supposed to do and then to act accordingly, either on their own policy volition or to avoid future electoral punishment. It is difficult therefore to wholly separate the past from the future in voting. Even in reacting to the existing government, the majority voting for or against it has to make *some* projections. On this basis we can say that holding governments to account is a minimalist version of government mandate theory.

A sticking point is that this account is performance based. We have to ask, therefore, performance with respect to what? If the answer were 'performance with respect to anything and everything', the minimalist mandate would hardly differ from its heartier counterpart. Over the past three decades the almost unchallenged assumption has been that performance is judged by governments' economic policies and records. This is partly because the economy is centrally important to well-being and prosperity, placing it at the centre of party policy differences. The economy is also recognized by electors as central; from 1970, inflation and employment have vied for public nomination everywhere as the most important problem facing the country (McDonald et al., 2004). Moreover, there is a fairly direct link between economic conditions and individual welfare, making it easier for electors to attribute responsibility for the economic situation, in a way that is difficult with foreign affairs, for example.

All of this makes economic voting a good field within which to pursue our analysis of retrospective assignment of credit and blame by electors. It is largely focussed on the question of what conditions favour pro-government voting, with explanations heavily based on the incidence of unemployment, inflation, and economic growth during its term of office. When the economy has done well, do electors reward governments with their votes? Or at least, as a minimal mandate might imply, do they turn against them when the economy does badly?

Evidence is very mixed on these points (for reviews of a large literature, see Nannestad and Paldam 1994; Lewis-Beck and Paldam 2000; Dorussen and Palmer 2002). There are few consistent or stable findings on economic voting across time or across countries. This might be due to differing political circumstances which make it easier to attribute retrospective responsibility where there is a single-party majority government (usually associated with plurality voting in constituencies—SMD—as opposed to a multiparty coalition usually associated with proportional representation—PR). In the latter case some coalition partners are almost bound to form part of the next government. However electors decide to vote in the case of incumbent coalitions, they cannot punish party culprits very effectively and this would attenuate anti-government voting (Powell and Whitten 1993, 398).

We can set this possibility against the one consistent, stable, and generalizable finding that does emerge from studies of comparative voting—governments everywhere seem consistently to lose votes in the current as opposed to the previous election, at an average of about 2.3 per cent (Paldam 1991; Nannestad and Paldam 2002). A crucial methodological question thus becomes—How and against what baseline are vote losses and gains to be assessed? As this forms a basis for all the conclusions one can draw about retrospective economic voting from comparative data, it is the first point we consider in the next section.

6.3 ASSESSING VOTE MOVEMENTS AGAINST DIFFERENT BASELINES

The starting point in all analyses of economic voting is indeed the baseline by which to evaluate what otherwise would have happened but for the good or bad performance of the economy. The baseline plays two important roles. The more obvious is to create a standard by which to see how the expressed preferences of an electorate are changing. A second comes from using the baseline to draw a preliminary inference about where conditions for economic voting exist. Differences in volatility around a baseline are a sign that the opportunity for purposeful and directed economic voting is there (Palmer and Whitten 2002).

In most economic voting studies, the baseline has been vote support in the preceding election for the party or parties standing as incumbents in the current election. This creates serious analytical and conceptual problems, however. First, an incumbent's previous vote often has us looking at unusually favourable vote support for the parties concerned—it is after all usually the election that propelled them into government in the first place. As a result, we have to expect voter support to erode almost mechanically as it moves back towards its normal level. Failure to take this reversion to the norm into account can play havoc with what we think we are learning about electoral dynamics. In other words, relying on just the previous vote to establish a baseline leaves the normal level of the vote unspecified, and that carries with it the undesirable implicit assumption that all parties everywhere are heading towards exactly the same level. This form of a dynamic equation implies that the party votes being analysed have a single equilibrium value.[1] That is impossible. It would mean the American Democrats and Republicans, the Swiss Socialists, Liberals, and Christians, the Austrian SPÖ, FPÖ, ÖVP, separately and the SPÖ and ÖVP jointly when they are an incumbent coalition, are all expected, eventually, to move to the same vote percentage—a substantive concept that is implausible and, simply put, a numerical consequence that is impossible.[2]

An alternative baseline for assessing incumbent vote dynamics, in addition to the incumbent vote level in the previous election, is the average vote a party received over the post-war period, aggregated as need be in the case of multiparty coalitions. This stands as a sort of normal expectation (Converse 1966; Tufte 1978). When we look at changes in incumbent vote percentages between the current and previous election, they are almost always negative and average -2.33 (statistically significant, $p < 0.01$). This confirms findings from the general literature (Paldam 1991; Nannestad and Paldam 2002). Differences between the current vote and the normally expected percentages (averaged over the post-war period) are not uniformly negative, however, and their small average, -0.26, is not statistically significant.

At the very least this indicates we need to specify carefully how we analyse vote dynamics. Using the vote in the previous election as the single baseline vote will bias the results towards stability, because long-term stability will become incorporated into the estimated short-term dynamics. The obvious solution is to incorporate both baselines and thereby to be able to know something about both the short- and long-term dynamics. This can be achieved with the following equation:

---

[1] An equation of the form

$$IV\%_{it} = \alpha + \beta\ IV\%_{it-1} + \mu_{it}$$

tells us that the long-term expected vote value for the incumbent party or coalition i equals the intercept value of the equation divided by one minus the slope (i.e. $\alpha/1 - \beta$)—see this chapter appendix for an explanation of why this is so. Both α and β are constants. Therefore, the resulting value is a constant, meaning there is a single long term expected value for each incumbent party or coalition.

[2] The Austrian SPÖ and ÖVP situation reveals the impossibility straightforwardly. We start with the fact that the estimation tells us that the long-run equilibrium vote for both parties is in the neighbourhood of 16 per cent, based on 215 elections analysed below. On its face that does not make sense for the two largest Austrian parties—E(SPÖ%) = 16 and E(ÖVP%) = 16. Implausibility turns to impossibility, however, when one considers the implication for an incumbent SPÖ and ÖVP coalition. The incumbent coalition has the same expected equilibrium value; so E(SPÖ%) + E(ÖVP%)} = 16, but that is contradicted by the fact that $16 + 16 \neq 16$.

1. $IV\%_{it} = \alpha + \beta$ *Trend Adj Norm* $IV\%_{it} + \lambda$ $(IV\%_{it-1} -$ *trend adj normIV*$\%_{it}) + \mu_{it}$

where

- $IV\%_{it}$ is the incumbent party or parties' vote percentage in nation i at election year t,
- *Trend Adj Norm* $IV\%_{it}$ is a trend-adjusted post-war normal vote percentage in the respective nation-year, where the trend adjustment takes account of the long-term decline in support that some established parties have sustained, and otherwise it is the simple post-war mean value.
- $IV\%_{it-1}$—*trend adj normIV*$\%_{it}$ is the discrepancy between the incumbent party or parties' election result in the previous election (t-1) and the long-term norm; this provides an estimate of short-term change as opposed to the long-term baseline provided by the trend adjusted norm itself.
- α is the intercept, which should equal zero because it represents the expected vote percentage for incumbents *after* taking into account their long-run expected level and short-run dynamics.
- β is the effect of the long-run expected level, which should equal 1.0 because if we have measured the long-run expectation accurately that is the level towards which vote percentages should tend to move.
- λ is the short-run vote dynamic, which should range between 0 and 1, the exact value of which indicates the speed of adjustment towards the normal vote from the deviation in the last election.

The results from applying this equation under three electoral circumstances are reported in Table 6.1. The left-most column shows results for the clearest case of accountability, where two parties compete to form single governments. We see that the SMD electoral situation brings with it a strong short run dynamic; λ is near zero and thereby indicates that whatever deviation from the incumbent vote norm occurred at the previous election it is immediately withdrawn at the current election. There are, in Stokes and Iversen's (1962) apt phrase, 'forces restoring party competition' under these circumstances. Single-party governments also occur in elections under PR. Their dynamic analysis results, reported in the middle column, show very much the same sort of short-run dynamics that we can see under SMD elections.

Finally, elections that in general offer less clarity of responsibility are those involving multiparty coalitions. Their lesser short-run dynamics are given in the last column of the table. The estimated λ in this case, 0.33, is statistically distinguishable from zero, indicating some drag on the reversion to normal conditions. It generally takes two elections to return 90 per cent of the way towards their respective long-term averages (0.33, and $1-0.33^2$ is approximately 0.90, or 90 per cent). The seemingly greater voting stability

TABLE 6.1. *Vote dynamics measured against baselines for long-term average vote as well as previous election vote, by differing types of electoral systems and governments*

	Single incumbent party and SMD system	Single incumbent party and PR system	Multiple incumbent parties and PR systems
λ (Short-term Incumbent Vote%$_{t-1}$ minus Long-term Incumbent Adjusted mean vote %)	−0.02 (0.16)	0.04 (0.16)	0.33 (0.10)
β (Long-term Incumbent Adjusted mean vote %)	1.04 (0.17)	0.97 (0.06)	0.98 (0.03)
α, Intercept	−1.24 (7.45)	1.54 (2.35)	−0.20 (1.77)
Summary statistics			
R^2	0.379	0.872	0.927
S_e	5.69	2.93	4.25
N	71	47	97

or *immobilisme* under coalitions could, however, mask vote transfers between government parties.

What are the substantive consequences of these conclusions? They offer support, though in weak terms, for the proposition that the difference in the volatility of incumbent vote comes from clearer and less clear party alternatives. Besides that, the results support the positive inference that there are more opportunities for purposeful and directed retrospective voting than had been thought previously, even under coalition arrangements. That is, evaluated against the two proper baselines, all electoral situations have faster moving dynamics than previous analyses would lead us to believe.

6.4 DYNAMICS PLUS ECONOMIC CONDITIONS

The simple fact of incumbent vote loss dominates much of what we can say about voters holding governments accountable. Incumbent governments usually suffer vote losses. The question therefore becomes: are incumbent vote losses larger when the economy is performing poorly compared to when it is doing well? 'Poorly' and 'well' are relative terms, evaluative judgements in the minds of electors. The judgements might be made relative to economic circumstances in the rest of the Western world (Powell and Whitten 1993), relative to a year before the election in each country (e.g. Anderson 1995), or relative to rational expectations in each country (Palmer and Whitten 1999). Palmer and Whitten have mustered some of the most favourable cross-national evidence of economic voting effects on the basis of a relative-to-expectations construction. Thus, to give economic voting the optimal chance of showing itself, we use the Palmer Whitten economic data for 16 nations covering 118 elections from the late 1960s into the mid-1990s. The economic indicators include inflation, unemployment, and GDP growth, each measured as deviations from what should be expected in the quarter during which an election took place. Data and measurement details are described in the chapter Appendix.

In evaluating voter responses to the economy we must as indicated by our previous discussion, take proper account of the political context particularly of clarity of responsibility. And we must also allow for who was in government—Leftist, Centrist, or Rightist parties—each with their particular claims to economic competence.

All these considerations are incorporated in Table 6.2. The first column reports an analysis for all 118 elections in our set. To the long- and short-run vote dynamics from the analyses reported above (see Table 6.1) we have added variables to reflect unexpected levels of inflation, unemployment, and growth. The vote dynamics themselves are much the same as we saw in the analyses based on the larger set of elections, going back before the late 1960s to the early 1950s, a period for which we do not have Palmer and Whitten's economic data. In addition to the vote dynamics, however, we see a statistically significant negative effect of unexpectedly high inflation on incumbent party votes. Unemployment is improperly signed and, in any case, unreliably estimated. The growth effect is properly signed but small and statistically insignificant. A potentially important result is that we now see evidence of economic effects in the case of inflation.

The equation in column 2 allows us to consider the possibility that the impact of inflation is conditional upon the type of government, providing a test for whether left-leaning and right-leaning incumbents are affected to different degrees by unexpected inflation (or unexpected unemployment for that matter). We see no evidence of this. The coefficient on the interactive variable is essentially zero, telling us that inflationary effects are the same for governments of either ideological colouration.

We subdivide our investigation to take account of varying clarity of responsibility in columns 3 to 8. These, too, comport with some limited retrospective voting reactions. The inflation effect is largest and most reliably recorded when responsibility is clearest, under SMD systems. It is also relatively large, though not statistically significant, under PR systems with a single party standing as the incumbent. It is smallest, and statistically insignificant, under PR with a multiparty coalition standing as incumbents. All of this holds whether the effects include or exclude consideration of differential effects depending on the left-versus right-leanings of the incumbents.

With these positive, if limited, economic voting results in hand, what political importance can we attribute to 'kicking the rascals out'? Not very much, we have to say. If we take the evidence at face value, the estimated effect is reliably recorded among SMD elections. That is only 38 of the 118

TABLE 6.2. *Incumbent vote related to economic expectations under different electoral systems and government types: sixteen nations late-1960s to mid-1990s*

	All systems #1	#2	SMD #1	#2	PR, with single-party incumbent #1	#2	PR, with incumbent coalition #1	#2
Incumbents' Normal Vote	0.96** (0.04)	0.96** (0.04)	1.16** (0.23)	1.13** (0.24)	0.94** (0.10)	0.93** (0.12)	0.95** (0.05)	0.95** (0.05)
Deviation from Norm at Last Election	0.07 (0.12)	0.07 (0.12)	−0.13 (0.23)	−0.16 (0.24)	0.12 (0.26)	0.13 (0.27)	0.40** (0.18)	0.40** (0.18)
Inflation	−1.14** (0.45)	−1.23** (0.48)	−1.61* (0.78)	−1.79* (0.85)	−1.28 (0.79)	−1.21 (0.90)	−0.27 (0.82)	−0.26 (0.84)
Unemployment	0.83 (1.60)	0.94 (1.67)	−1.92 (3.76)	−2.30 (4.23)	−1.68 (2.71)	−1.63 (2.89)	4.19 (2.42)	4.21 (2.53)
Growth	0.11 (0.32)	0.14 (0.33)	−0.17 (0.74)	−0.15 (0.76)	−0.10 (0.90)	−0.05 (0.96)	0.42 (0.41)	0.53 (0.44)
Inflation* L-R Incumbent Government	~~~	−0.02 (0.03)	~~~	−0.03 (0.05)	~~~	0.01 (0.05)	~~~	−0.03 (0.06)
Unemployment* L-R Incumbent Government	~~~	−0.002 (0.08)	~~~	−0.04 (0.21)	~~~	0.03 (0.12)	~~~	−0.07 (0.12)
Intercept	1.48 (1.87)	1.40 (1.89)	−7.56 (9.94)	−6.28 (10.55)	2.50 (3.83)	2.93 (4.44)	0.73 (3.16)	0.98 (3.22)
Summary Statistics								
R^2	0.853	0.854	0.529	0.537	0.875	0.875	0.878	0.879
s_e	4.8	4.9	5.7	5.8	3.5	3.7	4.7	4.8
N	118		38		27		53	

*=statistical stability of error is below 0.05
**=statistical probablity of error is below 0.01

elections (32 per cent). Taking a very favourable view we could say that a unit increase in unexpected inflation leads to something like a one and a half percentage point vote loss for, perhaps, over half of the elections (38 SMD elections and 27 single-party incumbent PR elections). A point and a half could be a heavy 'kick' at incumbents. In fact, only on eleven occasions in our data is inflation running more than one point above expectations at the time of the election. In ten out of eleven of those inflationary worst-case elections, incumbents do lose support. But that is no surprise; incumbents generally lose votes. The average loss across the eleven elections is 4.4 percentage points. That is about two points worse than the overall average of 2.3 for all elections over the post-war period and 1.5 points worse than the average for the set of 118 elections for which we have economic data. What is equally or perhaps even more important when considering the economic voting thesis as a general effect is that unexpected inflation in the Palmer-Whitten data averages zero. It almost has to by definition (deviations from what is expected, as in the form of a mean value, are defined as summing to and therefore averaging zero). That means inflation can help not at all, on average, in the long run, to explain what Peter Nannestad and Martin Paldam refer to as the one *robust fact* in all the economic voting literature, that is, incumbents tend to lose about 2–2.5 percentage points in the current election relative to the last election (Nannestad and Paldam 2002).

Might an additional loss of a point and a half, beyond what is normally expected, be enough to turn the electoral tables? Of the eleven instances of especially high, unexpected inflation, nine involved single-party incumbents. Four of those nine elections saw the single-party return to government after the next election, though in four of the five cases involving SMD systems the incumbent was replaced. In the two coalition-incumbent situations, half to three-quarters of the coalition partners came back into office. These findings suggest that elections are not important accountability devices as far as the economy is concerned. Staying versus going is hardly better than a chance outcome, even in the worst of times.

Why should this be so? The basic explanation it seems to us can be found in the fact that economic conditions, like other issues, impinge differently on different voters. They are not unproblematic—not even when everything is going well. This is illustrated in Table 6.3. Whatever the situation, there is always an (entirely rational) argument for voting against the government. While there is also a rational argument for voting pro-government, the cons are likely to convince some previous supporters. As the government by definition maximized its vote in the last election in order to become the government, the pro-argument is likely to draw in less support than the government loses to the ever-present con-argument. This accounts for consistent government vote losses relative to the previous election, the only stable statistical finding in the field.

Table 6.3 shows why clear majorities will not emerge round any particular retrospective judgement of the government—there are always different

TABLE 6.3. *Why retrospective voting is never unproblematic: the case of the economy*

(A) Possible Political Situations

	Left or Left-Centre control unemployment			Right or Right-Centre control unemployment	
	Better	Worse		Better	Worse
Better Inflation Worse	I	II	Better Inflation Worse	I	III
	III	IV		II	IV

(Continued)

TABLE 6.3 *Why retrospective voting is never unproblematic: the case of the economy—cont'd*

(B) Arguments For and Against Voting for Incumbents of the Left or Right under the Different Situations

Situation I Any Government, Unemployment and Inflation Better, Sustained Growth	Situation II Left, Unemployment Worse and inflation Better	Situation III Left, Unemployment Better and Inflation Worse	Situation IV Left, Both Unemployment and Inflation Worse
Argument 1: Government is doing very well so leave it in office to carry on Argument 2: Economic problems have been solved so it is time to bring another party in to tackle other problems (e.g. terrorism)	Argument 1: unemployment is running higher than it should, but the Left is most inclined to deal with this problem. Further, inflation is fine, and that makes it unnecessary to empower parties of the Right. Argument 2: unemployment is running higher than it should, and the parties of the Right could do just as well, maybe better.	Argument 1: unemployment is better than expected, and that is just what is to be expected from the parties of the Left. Argument 2: the parties of the Right are needed to bring inflation in line with what is expected.	Argument 1: Unemployment is worse than expected and so is inflation; maybe it is time to give the parties of the Right a chance. But that is risky because under Right influence unemployment could get even worse. Argument 2: unemployment is worse than expected and so is inflation, we might as well give the Right parties a chance.
	Right, Unemployment Better & Inflation Worse	Right, Unemployment Worse & Inflation Better	Right, Both Unemployment & Inflation Worse
	Argument 1: inflation is running higher than it should, but the Right is most inclined to deal with this problem. Further, unemployment is fine, and that makes it unnecessary to empower the parties of the Left. Argument 2: inflation is running higher than it should, and the parties of the Left could do just as well, maybe better.	Argument 1: inflation is better than expected, and that is just what one would anticipate from the parties of the Right. Argument 2: the parties of the Left are needed to bring unemployment in line with what is to be expected.	Argument 1: Unemployment is worse than expected, and so is inflation; maybe it is time to give the parties of the Left a chance. But that is risky because under Left influence inflation could get even worse. Argument 2: Unemployment is worse than expected and so is inflation; we might as well give the parties of the Left a chance.

opinions that a rational voter might come to. Table 6.2 has summarized the statistical evidence which supports this view.

The idea of different electors coming to different conclusions about how to vote, even under the same conditions, is not an unfamiliar one however. We do not generally expect a majority of electors to come to the same view or to decide on the same vote in regard *to any* issue, especially when there are a diversity of party options to choose from. This after all is the situation we started off with in Chapter 2, where we showed that the absence of clear cut spontaneous majorities discredited the idea of a prospective government mandate. In this chapter we have shown that the idea of a retrospective, negative, minimalist mandate is also unworkable, and for the same reasons— even in the economic field where it has been thought to have its best chance of success.

This leaves us, as before, with the alternative of a median mandate. In the absence of a clearly countable majority, shifts in the median position still point governments in the direction electors would like to see policy move. They point up this message by changing the balance of power among parties in parliament and in government. Where the median mandate differs from a retrospective minimalist one, however, is that we are not able to say definitely in what direction the median voter will move under a given set of circumstances. That remains a matter for specific predictions. But then we do not need to anticipate a specific direction of change to see a median mandate working. We detail this argument in the next Section.

6.5 A MEDIAN ELECTORAL MANDATE

If elections cannot be counted on to create government mandates through majority votes, which they do not, and if electorates cannot be counted on to create minimalist government mandates by retaining incumbents for good performance and turning them out for poor performance, which they do not (at least with respect to the economy), just what can they do? Our answer is that elections are communication devices. Electorates signal, implicitly, to anyone and everyone who cares to hear what they are saying, that governance is to emanate from the position of the median voter along something like the Left-Right dimension. What happens thereafter is for parliament to sort out. The party of the median parliamentarian has been placed in a powerful position. If that party has the will and political skill to do what it said it wanted to do during the electoral campaign, the policy process should unfold fairly much in line with the position of the median voter.

The details of this unfolding are left for consideration in later chapters. Here the questions are (*a*) where do we find median voters situated within the various countries, and (*b*) do the Left-Right positions of governments correspond to the Left-Right positions of median voters?

6.5.1 Where are the median voters?

Our analysis of vote dynamics (see Table 6.1) told us that party electoral support, in and among the nations under investigation here, is in something like an equilibrium state. In any one election, support swings in favour of a party or set of parties, and in the next election it is likely to revert to (or at least approach in the case of coalitions) its more normal level for incumbents. That is what Stokes and Iversen (1962) meant when they observed 'forces restoring party competition' in the USA (see also Spafford 1971). If the dynamics were otherwise, such that incumbent support did not revert quickly to its norm, democracies would be creating electoral competition that would become quickly unbalanced. Changes at the last election would become incorporated into the party vote percentage distribution (Stokes and Iversen's 'random walk'), running the risk of something like permanent winners.

With forces restoring party competition, an expected starting point for each new election is the long-run vote distribution. A deviation from that normal situation at the previous election is expected to evaporate so that the starting point for a new election is the competitive balance that has been established over the long run. This implies that there is enough uncertainty about the next election result to make one wonder which party or parties might be empowered after the votes are counted. Prognosticators are loathe to give odds on precise predictions but would likely do so if their predictions had only to be in the range of ± 5 to 10 per cent. From our analysis (see Table 6.1), the range in predictions is revealed by the standard errors of estimate, about 95 per cent of all outcomes being in this range. Party vote support operates with something akin to equilibriums over the long run, does not change much even in the short run, but does change enough, in ways not easily predictable, to keep people wondering and parties competitive.

Given that the parties themselves have identifiable Left-Right positions, from which they deviate only modestly—not so much as to blur their positions so that one would confuse them each with the other—and given that parties can be reasonably characterized along a Left-Right dimension, the vote dynamics should carry with them something like equilibrium positions for the middle of a vote distribution characterized as being along a Left-Right dimension. That is the long way round to saying that national electorates should be marked by stable, long-run, Left-Right positions of their median voters. Are they?

We have measured the Left-Right positions of median voters using an approach developed by Kim and Fording (1998, 2001). Details are given in the appendix to this chapter. With these scores we can take our model of incumbent vote dynamics and apply it to the dynamics of Left-Right median voter positions. In equation form, the median voter dynamics can be estimated through:

2. $MV\ L\text{-}R\%_{it} = \alpha + \beta\ Norm\ MV\ L\text{-}R\%_{it} + \lambda(MV\ L\text{-}R_{it\text{-}1} - Norm\ MV\ L\text{-}R_{it}) + \mu_{it}$

where

- $MV\ L\text{-}R_{it}$ is the median voter Left-Right position in nation i at election year t,
- $Norm\ MV\ L\text{-}R_{it}$ is an estimated normal Left-Right position in the respective nation-year, where the normal expectation is based on average median voter Left-Right position over the post-war period.[3]
- $MV\ L\text{-}R_{it\text{-}1} - Norm\ MV\ L\text{-}R_{it}$ is the discrepancy between the median voter Left-Right position in the previous election ($t\text{-}1$) and the long-term norm; this provides an estimate of short-term change as opposed to the long-term baseline provided by the norm itself.[4]
- α is the intercept, which should equal zero because it represents the expected median voter Left-Right position *after* taking into account their long-run expected level and short-run dynamics.
- β is the effect of the long-run expected level, which should equal 1.0 because, if there is a long-run median voter position and if we have measured it accurately via the post-war mean values for each country, the long-run expectation is the position towards which each national median voter position should tend.
- λ is the short-run vote dynamic, which should have a value between 0 and 1, the exact value of which indicates the speed of adjustment towards the equilibrium position—the speed itself is given by 1-λ. A value of 1.0 for λ says the deviation at the previous election will forever be incorporated into the norm (no adjustment); a value of 0.5 says that the median voter deviation at the previous election reverts halfway to the norm at the next election; and a value of 0 says the deviation at the previous election is removed totally and immediately, at the next election.

---

[3] In this equation, we could use a set of nation dummy variables in place of the normal vote construction (which we could not do for the incumbent vote analyses because the norm in those analyses are party- and coalition-specific, not nation-specific). In the absence of control variables, the normal vote and nation dummy variable equations are equivalent (i.e., $\Sigma\beta_I\{1\} = 1\{\Sigma\beta_I\}$, where β_I is a mean for nation i). Our construction, however, allows us to explicitly test whether the nation means are operating as the equilibrium values we have hypothesized. If they are, then the coefficient on the normal vote variable will equal 1.0. We actually do write and estimate the equation using nation dummy variables in Chapter 10. The near-equivalence will be apparent (where near- rather than exact-equivalence is the result of a control variable and the inclusion of a few more countries).

[4] The averages are given in Table 7.1, except for the USA. The USA average median voter position is 2.59, and its average government position is 5.02.

The results of estimating the equation are much as expected. With numerical values attached, the equation is:

3. $MV\ L - R\%_{it} = -0.15 + 0.99\ Norm\ MV\ L - R\%_{it}$
   $(0.86)\ (0.09)$
   $+ 0.32\ (MV\ L - R_{it-1} - Norm\ MV\ L - R_{it}) + \mu_{it}$
   (0.07)

with $R^2 = 0.408; s_e = 10.3; N = 203$

There are nation-specific equilibrium positions for median voters, estimated reasonably well by the post-war means. Given an intercept value of essentially zero, that is what the 0.99 coefficient on the normal vote variable indicates. The post-war mean median voter Left-Right position is the position, within a nation, towards which the Left-Right position of the median voter moves at the next election, if it is not at that position currently. As for the speed with which it moves towards its equilibrium, we see from the short-run dynamic estimate, 0.32, that it is rapid. From one election to the next, a median voter that has deviated from his or her normal position at the previous election is expected to move more than two-thirds of the way back towards the norm at the next election $(1 - 0.32 = 0.68)$ and about 90 per cent of the way back towards the norm over the next two elections $(1 - 0.32^2 = 0.90)$.[5]

Along with the theoretically important information our equation gives us about equilibriums and the speed of adjustment towards them, we can also derive detailed information about the electorates in each country. That is, we can use the information from the equations to say where the median voter position is in each. These are reported in Table 6.4. The results have a good deal of face validity. Norway, Sweden, and Finland are reported to have the most left-leaning median voter equilibriums, while Australia, Switzerland, Ireland, and the USA have the most-right leaning median voter equilibriums. Canada and Germany, among others, are in-between.

For any given nation the equilibrium estimate varies to some degree depending on what has occurred in recent elections, typically varying by about 3 units (the within-nation standard deviation of estimated values; that is the British median voter appears to have moved right when electing Thatcher-Major governments; so too did the American electorate during the Reagan-Bush years; and so too did Austria and Italy as they moved into the 1990s). And, of course, the observed median voter positions for any one or

---

[5] We saw in Table 6.2 that vote redistributions for incumbent parties move even more rapidly than we are now reporting for the speed of movements of median voter positions. That is because some movements involving redistribution of vote percentages cancel one another in marking the centre of a distribution. Indeed, neither all the median voter movement nor all of its speed is attributable to voters redistributing their votes across parties from one election to the next. Some of both come from parties taking up different Left-Right positions over a series of elections.

TABLE 6.4. *Estimated Left-Right equilibrium positions of median voters by nation: early 1950s to mid-1990s*

	Estimated Left-Right equilibrium	Standard deviation
Australia	+5.2	3.3
Austria	−4.9	4.4
Belgium	−4.1	2.7
Canada	−3.1	1.9
Denmark	−4.9	3.2
Finland	−13.4	4.0
Germany	+1.3	3.6
Ireland	+4.4	5.1
Italy	−5.5	2.4
Netherlands	−7.4	4.2
New Zealand	−8.2	2.7
Norway	−24.4	2.2
Sweden	−18.6	3.9
Switzerland	+4.2	2.7
UK	−10.0	4.1
USA	+2.5	1.2

another election varies around their equilibrium values. The standard error of estimate tells us that the standard deviation around what we can predict median voter positions to be, based on the dynamics as we understand them, is 10.3. That degree of predictability does not permit us to say with any certainty where median voters will be for a particular election, even when we know which particular country we are observing and thereby have a reasonably good idea of what its equilibrium positions is. But the absence of predictability has its rewards. It keeps democratic electoral competition fresh and prospects of winning the next policy argument vital.

6.5.2 Does the Position of Government Move with the Position of the Median Voter?

That we as political scientists can know approximately where a median voter is located means that politicians can know it too. But, then, it is one thing to be able to read election results as we have; it is another to actually read them as we have; and it is still another for them to have consequences in line with the reading. As a final step in coming to understand the electoral process as it might relate to mandates we need to inquire whether median voter positions have the power our thesis would assign to them. In order to answer this we relate the positions of median votes to the weighted mean positions of parties in government before and after elections.[6]

---

[6] We have extended the analyses we are about to report to all governments, not just incumbent governments and those taking office immediately after an election. The results are similar to those we report.

The translation from electorate to government is a crucial one, for there are a number of reasons why an electorate's voice might not become translated into something similar in governments. Pluralities manufacture majorities most of the time in SMD systems. Movements, especially in an SMD system, of an electorate to the left so as to support a minor left party may redound to the benefit of parties on the right as the left vote is fractured. Party policy offerings may be so polarized as to leave any government position distant from its median voter. Party negotiation may take governments in any number of directions, independent of the distribution of electoral support across parties. And, of course, the meaning and importance we have placed on the Left-Right dimension may be irrelevant to parties negotiating the spoils of office.

Our analysis of government policy position dynamics is set up in much the same way as our analysis of incumbent vote dynamics and median voter dynamics. We start with an equation containing an independent variable that indicates each nation's long-term government Left-Right position[7] plus a second term that indicates the short-run government Left-Right dynamics, from one government to the next in situations when an election has intervened as a potential agent of change. In equation form we have:

4. $Govt\ L - R\%_{it} = \alpha + \beta\ Norm\ Govt\ L - R\%_{it}$
$+ \lambda(GovtL - R_{it-1} - Norm\ Govt\ L - R_{it}) + \mu_{it}$

where

- $Govt\ L - R_{it}$ is the weighted government Left-Right position in nation i immediately after an election year t.
- $Norm\ Govt\ L - R_{it}$ is an estimated normal Left-Right position of a nation's government in the respective nation-year, where the normal expectation is based on average time weighted average of weighted government Left-Right positions over the post-war period.
- $Govt\ L - R_{it-1} - Norm\ Govt\ L - R_{it}$ is the discrepancy between the weighted government Left-Right position for the incumbent government at the time of the election $(t - 1)$ and the long-term norm; this provides for an estimate of short-term change as opposed to the long-term baseline provided by the norm itself.
- α is the intercept, which should equal zero because it represents the expected government Left-Right position *after* taking into account their long-run expected level and short-run dynamics.
- β is the effect of the long-run expected level, which should equal 1.0 because, if there is a long-run government position and if we have

[7] We are again grateful to Kim and Fording (2001) for suggesting a technique for measuring government policy intentions from those of the parties making them up. Details of these are given in the Appendix.

measured it accurately via the post-war mean values for each country, the long-run expectation is the position towards which each national government position should tend.

- λ is the short-run vote dynamic, which should be a value between 0 and 1, the exact value of which indicates the speed of adjustment towards the equilibrium position—the speed itself is given by $1 - \lambda$. A value of 1.0 for λ says the deviation last time will for evermore be incorporated into the norm (no adjustment); a value of 0.5 says that the median voter deviation at the previous election reverts halfway to the norm at the next election; and a value of 0 says the deviation at the previous election is removed totally and immediately, at the next election.

The estimated equation reveals dynamics similar to those we previously reported for median voter positions. The results are:

5. $Govt\ L - R\%_{it} = -0.75 + 0.85\ Norm\ Govt\ L - R\%_{it} + 0.32(Govt\ L - R_i$
   $\phantom{5.\ Govt\ L - R\%_{it} = }(1.24)\ \ (0.13)\phantom{\ Norm\ Govt\ L - R\%_{it} + }(0.07)$
   $\phantom{5.\ Govt\ L - R\%_{it} = }- Norm\ Govt\ L - R_{it}) + \mu_{it}$

with $R^2 = 0.249$; $s_e = 16.7$; $N = 200$

There are (seemingly) nation-specific equilibrium positions for governments, estimated reasonably well by the post-war means. The slope, 0.85, is not (statistically) significantly different from 1.0. Also, given an intercept value statistically indistinguishable from zero, there is no Left-Right bias in government positions once we take account of the long-run values. Finally, to the extent a government is not at the position of its long-term tendency, the deviation from the tendency is likely to be reduced by two-thirds $(1 - 0.32)$ at the next election and by just less than 90 per cent after two elections.

How do these governments come to have long-term equilibrium values? The hypothesis following from the median mandate is that they come principally from the median voters in their countries. Indeed, the specific hypothesis asserts that government equilibriums, as such, do not exist; rather, to the extent that the positions of the median voters are finding their way through parliaments into governments they set the positions of governments. We can test this directly by adding the position of the median voter to the government dynamics equation.[8] If median voter positions operate as a controlling force, making the seeming long-term equilibrium irrelevant, then the coefficient on the median voter should equal 1.0 and the coefficient on the normal, or long-term, Left-Right government variable should equal 0. The results are

---

[8] Three Finnish cases are missing, compared to the analysis estimating median voter dynamics. These are the result of non-partisan governments immediately preceding the 1958 and 1975 elections and a non-partisan government taking office immediately after the 1970 election.

6. $GovtL - R\%_{it} = 1.54 + 0.15\,NormGovt\,L - R\%_{it}$
   $\quad\quad\quad\quad\quad\;(1.05)\;(0.13)$
   $\quad\quad\quad + 0.20\,(GovtL - R_{it-1}\,NormGovt\,L - R_{it}) + 0.88\,MV\,LR_{it} + \mu$
   $\quad\quad\quad\;\;(0.06)\quad\quad\quad\quad\quad\quad\quad\quad\quad\quad\quad\;(0.09)$

   with $R^2 = 0.503$; $s_e = 13.6$; $N = 200$

Several inferences are possible. Importantly, we find (*a*) long-term government equilibriums do not exist once we account for the position of the median voter at the current election, (*b*) the weighted Left-Right positions of governments are set in near to one-to-one relationship with the position of median voters in an election, and (*c*) the short-run adjustment of government positions to something close to the position of the median voter is rapid. The median voter coefficient is a little below 1.0, but not to a statistically reliable extent. The 0.15 coefficient on the long-term Left-Right national tendencies of governments is statistically indistinguishable from zero and therefore tells us there is no real long-term government equilibrium position independent of whatever the position of the median voter is at the current election. Finally, the speed of adjustment, $(1 - 0.20)$ or 0.80, indicates that when governments are not at the position of the median voter, they will tend to adjust towards it but not precisely to it at the next election. For example, a nation with a median voter located at 0 (i.e. in the centre) of the Left-Right dimension at successive elections and with a government at -10 (on the left) after the first election, is expected to find its government at about -2.0 after the second election. That does not imply that the second election will produce a government at -2.0; it says that is the expected value. That expectation could be the consequence, on average, of a slightly greater tendency to re-elect a party or coalition at -10 than one at $+10$. It might also be the consequence of an opposition party or parties moving towards the centre, say from $+10$ to $+8.0$, and getting itself elected but with the implication that it will govern from a position of 8.0. Over the set of elections that would make the expected governing position -2.0 rather than zero. And there are other possibilities. The general point, however, is that governments will move close to the position of a median voter if they are not already at that position but in the process there is some small drag in approaching that position if the government is not there already.

6.6 ONE FINAL LOOK AT RETROSPECTIVE ECONOMIC VOTING

We have seen that median voters have equilibrium positions within nations and that their positions move around from one election to the next. Could it be that their movements are in response to economic conditions more and less favourably associated with parties of the left and the right? We doubt it because, as we have argued, it does not make a lot of sense for electors to be single-issue voters, nor does it make a lot of sense to say that there exists a single form of rational calculation that would predictably move voters in one direction or the other as a result of good or bad economic conditions. Nevertheless, our doubts can be subjected to tests just as well as those hypotheses our reasoning leads us to believe with more conviction.

To provide this test we return now to the 118 elections for which we have economic data and investigate Left-Right median voter movements in response to unexpected changes in inflation and unemployment. This test is performed by adding the economic variables to the equation we developed in order to estimate median voter dynamics. Given the understanding that parties of the left are thought to be better prepared to deal with unemployment and parties of the right are better prepared to deal with inflation, the hypothesis suggests that unexpected unemployment will move a vote distribution to the left and unexpected inflation will move a vote distribution to the right. Our estimates offer no support for either proposition. We find:

7. $MV\ L - R\%_{it} = 0.19 + 0.99\ Norm\ MV\ L - R\%_{it}$
   $\quad\quad\quad\quad\quad\ \ (1.08)\ \ (0.12)$
   $\quad\quad\quad\quad\quad + 0.17\ (MVL{-}R_{it-1} - Norm\ MVL - R_{it})$
   $\quad\quad\quad\quad\quad\ \ (0.10)$

$- 0.63\ Unexp\ Unemploy - 0.59\ Unexp\ Infl + \mu_{it}$
$\ \ \ (3.06) \quad\quad\quad\quad\quad\quad\quad (0.89)$

with $R^2 = 0.396$; $s_e = 9.7$; $N = 118$.

Neither economic variable is anywhere close to being statistically significant, and the vote dynamics among these 118 elections are much the same as we reported for our larger set of 212 elections. Median voters have equilibriums identifiable as long-term national mean positions and rapidly moving short-run dynamics that draw a deviating median voter towards its equilibrium at the next election by more than 80% of any previous deviation.

6.7 WHERE DOES THIS LEAVE MANDATE THEORY?

Government mandates in their full form are undermined by the absence of electoral majorities. Government mandates in their minimalist form are undermined by difficulties, in fact and even in rational calculation, encountered when trying to hold governments to account for good and bad circumstances during their tenure. It is of course true that from time to time electors may vote retrospectively in quite a unified way and hold governments responsible for bad leadership, corruption scandals, unpopular wars, and even on occasion for bad economic management. However, this is no more than to say that occasionally a majority will form to vote a party in on its prospective programme (see Table 2.2).

However, both retrospective and prospective majority voting for governments happen so occasionally and erratically that we cannot base a general account of the mandate on it. Economic circumstances are the most obvious and general issues, electors could base vote decisions on. If they are found to exert only erratic and occasional effects this is even more likely to hold for more transient sets of circumstances which are only likely to occur in some elections. Difficulties with the government mandate in either its full or minimalist forms push us towards the conclusion that elections are not about winning and losing. Or, if they are, they do a poor job identifying clear-cut winners and losers.

Alternatively, they may be about communicating what voters want in Left-Right terms. This they do with some degree of dynamic fickleness. Fickleness or not, we are able to identify equilibrium positions for median voters by nation, and to observe that, in some way, those equilibriums get themselves lined-up with governments' policy intentions. How do they do this? That is a question for the next chapter. At this point what we know is that parties (see Chapter 5) and electorates (this chapter) are doing enough to make the median mandate plausible.

APPENDIX

In this appendix we first describe the data used in Chapter 6, their sources, and timeframes. In section two we describe and discuss our measurements of several key variables mainly Left-Right median voter positions and weighted government Left-Right positions.

6.A.1 Data

The data used in this chapter come from sixteen nations. Elsewhere we usually analyse data on twenty-one nations. The five nations omitted are France, Iceland, Luxembourg, Portugal, and Spain. France is missing because it is sometimes difficult to determine which party or parties are incumbents (e.g. Palmer and Whitten (1999) excluded some French elections on this basis) and because the various relationships between French Independents and other 'parties' make it difficult to arrive at unequivocal estimates of party normal votes. Rather than report our results and interpretations conditional upon the choices made about French parties, we decided it would be more straightforward to remove France from analyses in this chapter. Iceland, Luxembourg, and Portugal are excluded because the Palmer-Whitten economic data do not cover them. Spain is excluded because we are not confident we could arrive at normal party votes, given the short series of elections since becoming a constitutional democracy.

The vote percentages to 1990 are based on party votes and valid votes reported in Volkens et al. (1992), which relied heavily on Mackie and Rose (1991). These were updated to 1995, except in Italy where the series stops after 1992, on the basis of annual election and government reports in various issues of the *European Journal of Political Research*. The identification of incumbent parties at the time of an election, ignoring caretaker governments and one Australian transition government, is based on the compilation by Woldendorp, Keman, and Budge (2000). In the case of the USA, voting data are for presidential elections.

Harvey Palmer and Guy Whitten generously provided us with their economic data. These are quarterly estimates of inflation, unemployment, and growth rates, by nation, from about the mid-1960s to the mid-1990s.

Among the sixteen countries, there were 219 elections between 1950 to 1995. For analyses of incumbent vote we were able to record, except in Finland, incumbent votes for a nation's election before the first one in the 1950s. In addition, however, the altered party system in Italy before the 1994 election required that we remove that election from our analyses of incumbent votes; two Finnish non-partisan governments also required removal. That leaves 215 cases for analyses involving incumbent votes. When analysing median voter dynamics, we lose one additional case per nation (except in Finland) by lagging a variable, but we reclaim the 1994 Italian election case and the two Finnish cases lost due to non-partisan governments. Thus there are 203 cases in our median voter analysis. Those same 203 cases minus three due to Finnish non-partisan governments (two incumbent non-partisan governments plus a post-election non-partisan government) are used in the government dynamic analyses ($N = 200$).

When we analyse economic voting, the Palmer-Whitten data cover a shorter period and the number of elections drops to 118. Nearly all the dropped cases come from the period between 1950 and the mid-to late 1960s, but in a few countries the economic series (in the version of their data set we use) stop before 1995—Belgium 1987, Finland 1991, Germany 1990, Ireland 1989, Italy 1992, New Zealand 1993, and Switzerland 1991.

6.A.2 Measurement

6.A.2.1 Incumbent votes

Party voting percentages are calculated from party votes as a ratio of valid votes. Incumbent coalition vote percentages are simply the sum of the percentages of all parties in the coalition. Normally, incumbent status is determined according to the government in office at the time of the election, based on governments reported in Woldendorp et al. (2000). Exceptions are where (*a*) we have skipped over caretaker governments, also as reported by Woldendorp et al. (2000), (*b*) we dropped non-partisan governments, and (c) we treated the Australian transition government preceding the 1975 election as if it were a caretaker.

6.A.2.2 Normal vote

A party's normal vote is an expectation based on its long-term electoral performance. This could be measured simply as each party's mean post-war vote percentage, but that runs into two complications. First, it ignores the possibility that support for certain parties could be changing across time (see Spafford 1971). Second, it ignores the possibility that a party's mean support might be affected by incumbent status.

We estimated whether there have been trends in individual party vote percentages for each of 88 party series, those parties contesting more than half of a nation's post-war elections. The time variable is scored: 1950 = 0; each year thereafter adds 1.0; and months add fractions calculated by scoring January = 0.5 ... December = 11.5 and computing (month/12). A dummy variable was added to control for a party's incumbency status

Half of the eighty-eight party series, forty-four, showed statistically significant trends. There are twelve positive trends and thirty-two negative trends. Seven of the twelve positive trends are for parties in the liberal family. Another five party series in the liberal family show statistically significant negative trends. Included among the thirty-two party series showing declining trends are Christian parties in six out of ten countries. The only positive trend among Christian parties is that of the Norwegian Christian People's Party (KF). Eight of the twenty-four social democratic party series have statistically significant negative trends. Just one, the mid-1960s upstart Democrats '66 (D66) in the Netherlands, shows a statistically significant positive trend.

We find also that only sixty-seven of the seventy-two series for parties that variably were and were not incumbents show no statistically significant negative effect from being an incumbent. The five parties with significant negative incumbency effects include Austria's Christians (ÖVP), Belgium's Flemish Socialists (BSP), Irish Labour (ILP), Ireland's Fianna Fáil (FF), and New Zealand's National Party (NAT). Germany's Social Democrat Party (SPD) and Denmark's Conservatives (KF) have a significant positive effect from being an incumbent. This supplies additional confirmation that an incumbent's vote loss should usually be considered little more than reversion to its norm. Virtually the same results obtain when we estimate party dynamics singularly with a partial adjustment model applied to each party series.

The dynamic qualities of the forty-four trending parties were incorporated into measurement of their normal vote by taking each statistically significant party trend into account. The adjustments ignore the coefficients on the incumbency variable, of course. Measurements proceeded in three steps. First, we determined the mean time for each party. Next, we scored the party at its mean vote percentage at exactly that mean time point. Third, we adjusted a party mean according to the magnitude of each statistically significant party trend. All parties for which we had no indication of a statistically significant trend were scored at their respective post-war mean vote percentage throughout.

6.A.3 Economic Conditions

The economic data come from Harvey Palmer and Guy Whitten (see Palmer and Whitten 1999; Whitten and Palmer 1999; Palmer and Whitten 2002). They refer to unexpected levels of inflation, unemployment, and GDP growth rates. The expectations are based on iteratively predicted values using a series of quarterly based autoregressive equations, per indicator, from the mid-1960s to the quarter during which a election occurred. An unexpected value is the difference between the value observed and the value predicted. For greater detail, see Palmer and Whitten (1999) and Whitten and Palmer (1999).

6.A.4 Median Voter

Our measurement of a median voter's position relies on the procedure developed by Kim and Fording, with two adjustments discussed below (1997, 2001).

The formula used by Kim and Fording is

$$M = L + [\{(50 - C)/F\}^* W].$$

where

M = median voter position, Left-Right.
L = lower end on the Left-Right dimension of the interval containing the median.
C = the cumulative vote percentage frequency up to but not including the interval containing the median.
F = the vote percentage of the party in the interval containing the median.
W = the width of the interval containing the median.

In a three party system, with parties at P, Q, and R at Left-Right positions of -12, $+2$, and $+8$ and vote percentages of 47, 12, and 41, the median voter position is,

$$M = (-5) + [\{(50 - 47)/12)\}^* 10];$$
$$M = -2.5$$

The one adjustment we made to their measurement strategy involved situations when the farthest left or farthest right party in a system is involved in the formulation of either L or W. In those cases, Kim and Fording allow the extreme score of -100 or $+100$ to mark the endpoint where voters of that party are located. We find this implausible and its effect on the calculation undesirable. In particular, the -100 and $+100$ endpoints can artificially stretch the distribution of voters around a party's position. Rather than assume the party's voters are so widely dispersed, we assume they are distributed in a symmetrical interval around the party's position. For example, for a leftmost party at -15 and a 0 midpoint between it and an adjacent party on the right, we assume the left boundary of that party's voters is -30. With this marginal modification, the measure produces cross-national characterizations of considerable plausibility (see the national median voter positions in Table 6.4) as well as passing several reliability checks such as correlations between the country placements over time, all of which add to the extensive series of checks reported by Kim and Fording themselves.

One strength of the median measure, as with the Manifesto data themselves, is its ability to catch cross-national differences and overtime movements. Static expert judgements about party positions and infrequent survey data on citizen self-placements would not allow this. A second strength is that we are able to measure voters, parliaments, governments, and ministries on the same metric, an essential quality for the study of representation (Achen 1977, 1978).

On an intuitive level, survey data might seem preferable to the Kim and Fording approach. For the following reasons, they are not. First, surveys asking respondents to locate themselves on a Left-Right scale often do not permit the identification of the party for whom a respondent had voted in an earlier national election. That requires the survey-based measure to refer to a median citizen rather than a median voter. Second, and more important, surveys that ask a Left-Right self-placement question are infrequently available and hence are not applicable to time series analyses. Third, and most important, even if surveys did distinguish a median citizen from a median voter and even if they were more frequently available, they would not be up to the task of providing a good match to the party-position data. The party-position data are designed to have meaningful cross-national variation—that is if Norwegian parties locate themselves on average to the left of Australian parties of the same family (e.g. social democrats and conservatives), this can be taken as indicating that the Norwegian Left-Right space is left of the Left-Right space in Australia. This feature holds for the CMP data as well as for the 'expert' survey data. Mass survey data on respondents' Left-Right positions, on the contrary, appear to have no such cross-national variation.

In nearly all countries the median voter positions identified by mass surveys are quite similar (see Powell 2000: 162, 180–85). For example, the median citizen in Norway is recorded by surveys to be at the same Left-Right position as the median citizen in Australia, and even as the median citizen in the USA. This is implausible when one thinks of the general differences between these countries' politics, Norway by almost any account being well to the left of Australia or the USA. One consequence is that, but for three countries that stand three to four standard deviations to the left of all the others (viz., France, Italy, and Spain), the cross-national correlation between median citizen positions identified by surveys in the 1980s with those in the 1990s is almost non-existent and, worse, negative, that is $r = -0.14$. It appears, therefore, that voters in surveys report they are on the left, in the centre, or on the right within the context of their own country's political space, rendering their self-placements suspect for any comparative analysis and, more damning for present purposes, for matching to the party position data that do contain valid cross-national differences along the Left-Right dimension. The overtime $r = +0.44$ for the Kim-Fording measure applied to same elections for which we have data on the nations Powell's data cover.

6.A.5 Government Left-Right Positions

We follow Powell's lead and calculate the Left-Right position of a government as the weighted mean position of the parties in government, where the weights are the parliamentary seat percentages among parties in government (Powell 2000: 173; see also Huber and Powell 1994). Using parliamentary seats as the weights is justified on the repeated findings that government ministries are usually allocated to government parties in proportion to the seats they hold in parliament among the parties in government (Browne and Franklin 1973). Using a weighted average to indicate a government's Left-Right position is based on the assumption that parties in government influence policy in proportion to the cabinet posts they occupy. When there is just one party in government, that party's Left-Right position is the government's position; the party holds 100 per cent of the weight of the parties in government. When there are two parties in government, one with 75 seats and the other with 25 seats, then the position of the party with 75 seats has three times as much weight in the calculation of the government's position compared to the party with 25 seats.

The 'normal' or long-term government Left-Right position is calculated as the time-weighted average weighted government Left-Right position in each nation, not including caretakers. We weighted by time in order that governments of longer duration would receive greater weight in the calculations (see Chapter 7).

7

Representing the Median Voter

Our conclusion through the first six chapters is that if contemporary democracies do operate by a mandate, it must be a median one. Table 2.5 showed that in most countries the median parliamentary party is usually the one the median voter supports. Chapter 5 showed that party systems do offer a reasonable and stable range of choices to electors. Chapter 6 showed little evidence of elections as accountability devices but firm evidence that Left-Right movements of governments correspond to Left-Right movements of median voters over time. Median mandate ideas have thus passed the first checks on whether they are actualized in democratic practice.

In this chapter we go to the heart of political representation and ask how, through what means and processes, do government positions become connected to median voter positions? An important subsidiary question is whether representation is more distorted under SMD than under PR. Having over-time estimates of policy positions for electorates, parliaments, and governments in each country, we can ask across which steps in the process distortions enter—party system offerings, electoral mistranslations, and negotiations over which party or parties enter government. Importantly, we can also see whether distortions cumulate—creating a long-term representational bias—or whether they counterbalance over a series of elections to create a system that works to represent electors in the long run despite short-term distortions.

7.1 REPRESENTATION—STAGES AND STEPS

Under the government mandate in parliamentary systems a majority selects the government, with parliament rubber-stamping its decision. Under the median mandate, things are more complex. For one thing, the government that emerges will often be the outcome of legislative bargaining, rather than predetermined by the election. Indeed, the translation from median preference to government inclination is even more complicated than that. The process unfolds in three steps across four stages.

1. Elections accurately reveal the will of the voters.
2. Electoral systems translate the people's will so that it is accurately represented in parliament.

3. Governments are selected so that they accurately reflect the ideological inclination of parliament.

Viewed from the bottom-up the process can be pictured as follows—ideally proceeding along the paths of the solid arrows.

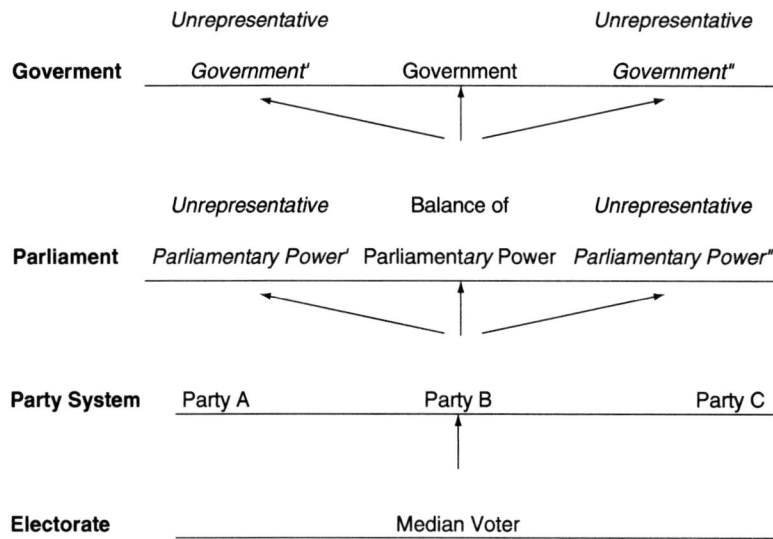

In this stylized set-up, the party system makes available three choices—Party A, Party B, and Party C. If everything works well, then from the available choices the median voter's position is revealed. Thereafter, the position of the median voter, in the form of Party B, holds the balance of power in parliament. Finally, given its powerful position in parliament, Party B enters government.

7.1.1 Distortions

How might this accurate representation of the median voter become distorted? We have three possibilities in mind. One form of distortion could arise from the activity of parties in elections. Another form could arise from the electoral system. And a third could arise from the parties in parliament.

A party system that leaves a gap between the positions of Party A and C, because perhaps there is no Party B or because Party B is located to the left of Party A or to the right of Party C, can end up translating the position of the median voter into parliamentary power for either Party A or C. Powell and Vanberg report that SMD electoral systems produce relatively low congruence between the median voter and the parliamentary median (Powell and

Vanberg 2000; see also Powell 2000: 192–6). As Wessels (1999) has shown, some part of this incongruence results from the sparse party offerings in those systems. A void in the party offerings could exist under PR, too, if the parties are substantially polarized. For instance, Iversen (1994) has shown as a theoretical matter that a combination of affectively infused directional voting and rationally infused spatial voting encourages parties in a multi-party system to locate themselves in a rather dispersed alignment (see also Rabinowitz et al. 1991). As a case in point, Powell and Vanberg (2000: 410) identify Sweden as a PR system where parties leave a large gap in the space around the median voter. We have investigated these possibilities in Chapter 5 with our own data, concluding that some gaps are there. We expect distortions to be more pronounced in systems with large versus small gaps, all else being equal.

Electoral systems are often investigated for their proportionality properties. This is usually treated as an issue of fairness. However, disproportionate vote-seat relations should also be recognized as an issue of how sincerely the system translates the position of the median voter into the position of the parliamentary median (Powell and Vanberg 2000). Such possibilities are likely to crop up particularly in SMD systems. For instance, after 1970, the Liberal party in Britain was more often than not the party preferred by the British median voter, yet the electoral system manufactured Labour or Conservative majorities and thereby made one of them the median party in parliament (Budge et al. 1998: 664–5).

The notoriety of SMD in this respect has made interested observers keenly aware of its potential to distort, leaving the subject of disproportionality under PR systems a specialist concern (Balinski and Young 1978; Taagepera and Shugart 1989; Lijphart 1994). From what these close observers have reported, one has to suspect more mistranslation under PR rules than meets the casual eye—due to thresholds, formulae that give mild benefits to large parties, or both. Indeed, Wessels (1999) reports that the congruence between parliaments and median voters is lower in PR systems than in SMD systems (but see Powell and Vanberg 2000).

A worry often expressed about multiparty systems is that they turn democracy into negotiations among elites.[1] After an electorate has had its say, party leaders decide who governs. Lijphart's theorizing and careful analysis (Lijphart 1977; 1984; 1999) has done a great deal to reveal the positive side of

---

[1] This argument assumes that there is a special policy role for governments over and above what might be said to be desirable policy from the standpoint of parliaments. If we do not assume that holding government office has particular importance for policy control, then the parliament to government step in the process is not of great moment. However, no one has yet marshalled strong evidence as to which institution is in control of policy, parliament, or government. Therefore, we proceed under the conventional understanding that governments as such are important policy actors in their own right.

elite negotiations. The consensus politics associated with non-majoritarian elections, Lijphart (1999: 243–301) shows, are also associated with a long list of rather positive outcomes. Even so, Lijphart (1999: 306) laments the potentially bad news that 'consensus democracy may not be able to take root and thrive unless it is supported by a consensus political culture'.[2] SMD systems, on the other hand, usually produce a parliamentary majority for one party. By definition, a member of the majority party is located at the parliamentary median. In that sense, SMD arrangements use the rules to produce correspondence between parliamentary medians and governments, rather than rely on elite goodwill.

Distortions in the representational process, as we have suggested, address only half the issue. It matters a great deal whether they cumulate or compensate from one step in the process to the next and whether they persist or compensate from one election to the next. It is cumulation and persistence that lead political systems to institutionalize representational biases.

7.1.2 Biases

Research on collective representation has usually been able to evaluate only distortions (Sullivan and O'Connor 1972; Weissberg 1978; Huber and Powell 1994; Powell and Vanberg 2000; Powell 2000), since they do not have genuinely overtime data. One exception is the pathbreaking work on the American macro polity by Erikson et al. (2002; see also Stimson et al. 1995). Other works have been unable to look at collective representation through all of its steps or along enough of a time horizon.

Compensation from one step to the next might prove important under PR as parties negotiate over which ones will enter government. Negotiation involves not just the potential for party leaders to distort the process by selecting parties distant from the parliamentary median. They can also paradoxically produce governments that are closer to the position of the median voter than the median voter is to the parliamentary median itself. An SPÖ and ÖVP coalition in Austria, for instance, might well have a position closer to the median voter compared to the position of the FPÖ (when the FPÖ was the median party).

Compensation through mutual cancellation of distortions over time could prove especially important when evaluating representation under SMD systems, which put their emphasis on the representational benefits of party alternation in government. John Ferejohn (1999: 45) said as much when he remarked, 'To me, the principal defect of PR is the weakness of electoral

---

[2] With respect to the consociational form of consensus democracy, Lijphart had earlier observed that 'Elite cooperation is the primary distinguishing feature of consociational democracy' (Lijphart 1977: 1).

responsiveness.... Electoral shifts in popular support...typically do not much alter the logic of coalition formation....' Electoral shifts under SMD rules, in contrast, often produce a wholesale change in the governing position, which is able to compensate a distortion at an earlier time with a distortion in the opposite direction today. Therefore, when voter-parliament (or voter-government) distortions are considered individually for their magnitude alone, an important element in the representational process under SMD is lost.

When it comes to biases, a useful way to think about representation through PR versus SMD rules is to entertain the possibility that both systems produce representational correspondence through averaging, with PR systems averaging across parties and with SMD systems averaging through time. In the analyses that follow we first investigate representational distortions for their magnitude and sources. Thereafter, we proceed to ask whether distortions cumulate or compensate so as to create large or small biases. Before that, however, we need to describe the data and forms of analysis we will be using.

7.2 DATA AND DESIGN

7.2.1 Data

The data we use here are familiar from earlier chapters. We omit the USA because its separation of powers renders many of the questions we ask about parliamentary democracy irrelevant. Thus the analyses are based on twenty parliamentary democracies over the period from the early 1950s to governments forming by the end of 1995. We have already described our measurement of actors' policy positions in Chapters 5 and 6 so this need not be repeated here, except for the parliamentary median. We identify a parliamentary median by the position of the weighted median party. That is, a parliamentary median is at the Left-Right position of the party with which the middle parliamentarian affiliates, given the Left-Right alignment of parties according to their CMP scores.

Among our twenty countries during the specified time period, there were 473 governments and 255 elections. However, thirty governments were caretaker, transition, or nonpartisan[3]. We exclude those thirty, and therefore our

---

[3] Nineteen caretakers are identified as such in Waldendorp, Keman, and Budge (2000). They are, by country and government number: Finland 9, 23, 30; Belgium 26, 34; France 45; Germany 8, 12, 20, 21; Italy 9, 19, 34, 37; Netherlands 6, 10, 13, 17; and Portugal 5. Non-caretaker, nonpartisan governments include the six designated as such in Waldendorp et al. (2000) plus two Finnish governments that had parties pledged to support the governments but no parties officially in government. The eight nonpartisan governments are Finland 16, 17, 27, 32, 33; Italy 55; and Portugal 3, 4. Finland 23 and Portugal 5 were both caretaker and nonpartisan. Transition governments are our designation. They include governments that served for less than two months before a parliamentary election: there are three, namely France 35, 50, and Australia 19.

TABLE 7.1. *Means and standard deviations of median voter, parliament, and government Left-Right positions, by country over the period from the early 1950s to 1995*

Country	Ns		Left-Right position [a]		
	# Govts	# Elections	Median voter	Parliamentary median	Government weighted mean
Norway	21	11	−24.3	−25.7	−23.9
			7.0	8.0	12.3
Sweden	21	15	−18.3	−21.2	−21.9
			14.7	15.3	22.4
Luxembourg	14	10	−15.6	−12.5	−14.9
			8.6	8.6	11.6
Finland	32	13	−12.7	−11.0	−8.7
			14.2	14.6	17.9
Spain	7	6	−11.9	−11.9	−12.0
			7.9	9.9	9.8
United Kingdom	18	13	−9.1	−0.1	−0.4
			12.6	25.4	25.6
Portugal	10	8	−8.7	−7.1	−7.1
			7.0	9.3	9.9
New Zealand	22	15	−8.1	−5.5	−5.5
			8.2	16.2	16.0
Netherlands	14	13	−6.8	−4.6	−5.0
			12.6	12.0	12.4
Italy	43	11	−5.6	−4.2	−4.7
			7.5	6.7	8.4
France	25	10	−5.4	4.0	5.5
			7.6	18.0	17.7
Iceland	18	13	−4.9	−2.3	2.6
			11.8	13.2	15.1
Denmark	27	19	−4.8	−7.7	−1.7
			8.4	8.7	21.9
Austria	18	13	−4.1	−3.0	−3.3
			11.7	13.2	14.7
Belgium	27	15	−4.0	−2.9	−5.1
			7.6	7.1	10.1
Canada	17	14	−2.8	0.6	1.1
			5.4	9.4	9.5
Germany	21	12	1.3	2.4	4.7
			11.3	16.6	20.2
Switzerland	45	12	4.4	4.6	5.0
			8.4	10.0	9.8
Ireland	19	14	4.9	2.8	5.7
			16.8	21.2	17.7
Australia	24	18	5.1	10.7	10.8
			10.7	20.3	20.1

[a] Cell entries under Left-Right Position are means and standard deviations over the period from the early 1950s to 1995. All calculations are weighted by either the time between elections (*Median Voter* and *Parliament*) or the time a government was in office (*Government Weighted Mean*).

total number of governments is 443. Table 7.1 reports the average Left-Right positions for each nation's median voter, parliamentary median, and government. Averages are calculated using time weights proportionalized to the number of elections or the number of governments. Weights are applied in order to give the proper emphasis to long- versus short-lived parliaments and governments (details of the weights are described below). Negative scores are left positions; zero marks the centre; and positive scores are positions on the right. The countries are arranged, top to bottom, according to the Left-Right positions of their median voters. There is a good deal of face validity in the ordering. Norway and Sweden are farthest left. Luxembourg, Finland, and Spain are also on the left, that is below -10. To the right of centre we find Germany, Switzerland, Ireland, and Australia.

Close inspection of the mean values shows that the average Left-Right positions of parliaments and governments correspond fairly well to the average Left-Right position of the median voters. To be sure, there are exceptions. The mismatches in France certainly stand out, and so, too, do the mismatches in the UK, Iceland, Australia, and Finland.

7.2.2 Design

The important principle for our design is the standard we use to evaluate differences. That standard is based on asking this question. How accurately do transitions between one stage of the representational process and another perform, compared to how accurately a transition mechanism could perform if it worked as accurately as it could under the conditions present? More or less accuracy takes two general forms, distortions and biases. Distortions record the magnitudes of mistranslation between one step in the representational process and another. Biases record the extent to which distortions cumulate or compensate. The three transition mechanisms we are concentrating on are the party system, electoral system, and elite negotiation. Party systems can distort and bias representation by the ways political parties structure choices for voters. Electoral systems can distort and bias representation by mistranslating the party position closest to the median voter into a different parliamentary median. Elite negotiations can distort and bias the process by empowering a government that is incongruent with the parliamentary median.[4]

---

[4] It would be fascinating to separate the negotiation stage into pre-election and post-election agreements. We have an indication from Powell's analyses that pre-election agreements constrain the politics of government-formation in ways that exclude the parliamentary median more often than do post-election negotiations that are unconstrained by pre-election agreements (Powell 2000: 188–92 and 206–14). Unfortunately, we do not have solid information on pre-election agreements for all of our 255 elections.

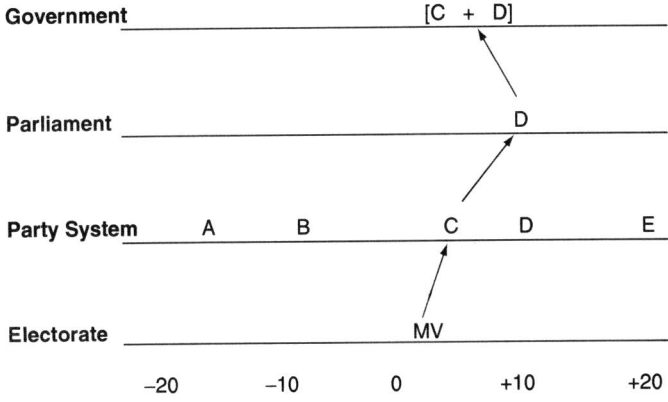

FIGURE 7.1. Hypothetical conditions at four stages in the representational process, used here to illustrate how distortions and biases are evaluated

Conditions:
- The median voter, MV, is located at +3.
- Party C is located at +5 and is the party closest to the median voter.
- Party D, at +10, becomes the parliamentary median through mistranslation from the electoral system.
- Party C and Party D form the government, and their weighted mean position is +8.

Distortion and Bias:
Distortion is the magnitude of the difference between one stage in the process and another.
Bias is the simple difference, taking into account magnitude and direction, between one stage in the process and another.

Types and sources of distortion & bias:
Overall—mismatch between the median voter Left-Right position and the government Left-Right position. This can arise from two sources, negotiation and electoral.
A. *Negotiation*—mismatch between parliamentary median Left-Right and government Left-Right positions.
B. *Electoral*—mismatch between the median voter and parliamentary median positions. It has two sources, party system and electoral system.
1. *Party system*—mismatch between median voter position and the position of the party closest to the median voter.
2. *Electoral system*—mismatch between the party closest to the median voter and the parliamentary median.

As a visual aid to help explain our approach, we use the hypothetical depiction in Figure 7.1. We have a median voter just slightly right of centre, at +3. The five available party positions are Party A = −15; Party B = −8; Party C = +5; Party D = +10; and Party E = +20. Given the party positions, the most accurate representation of the median voter would come from Party C; although even that most accurate possibility distorts the median voter's position by two points. Imagine, however, that the electoral system translates votes in such a way that Party D is the party of the median parliamentarian. That tells us that the electoral system translation distorts representation by five points, relative to what could have been. Taken together, the median voter's position compared to the parliamentary median creates an *electoral* distortion of seven points. Two of those seven points of distortion are attributable to the *party system*, and five of the seven are attributable to the *electoral system* translation. Imagine, further, that at the next step, for some reason, elite *negotiation* installs a coalition of Party D and Party C in government, with a weighted position of +8. This is a two-point distortion from what would have occurred had the parliamentary median been directly translated into a government position. The *overall* distortion, from median voter to government, ends up being just five points.

Biases are different from distortions because they take into account both the magnitude and direction of the mismatches. While there are nine total units of distortion, seven run in one direction and two run in the other. In the end, therefore, the *overall* correspondence of the government position to that of the median voter has been biased by +5 points, meaning the bias is 5 points to the political right of the median voter. By our accounting, seven points of bias come from the *electoral* process, two points of which are attributable to *party system* and five points are attributable to the *electoral system* translation. Finally, two points of compensation are given back due to government *negotiation*.

We are also interested in the representational process through time. To ignore the possibility that a distortion in the outcome of one election could be compensated by a distortion in the opposite direction at the next election, we expect, would stack the deck against SMD systems. There is good reason to believe that use of the SMD system anticipates that the system's dynamic qualities will balance distortions at one time with distortions at another time. Therefore, we evaluate biases with an eye towards how much they persist through time.

Given our attention to time, we weight calculations of government positions by the amount of time a government lasted. Calculations of median voter and parliamentary positions are weighted by the time between elections (days from the time a government took office after an election until a new government was installed following the next election). After weighting by time, the time-based weights were proportionalized so that the N for a country equals its number of governments or its number of elections. Time in government is recorded in Waldendrop et al. (2000).

7.3. COMPARATIVE FINDINGS

7.3.1. Distortions

The most important fact about distortions in the representational process is that across the end stages, comparing a median voter's Left-Right position to a government's Left-Right position, they exist in every country. It is as if there is no avoiding some misrepresentation: the question is how much?

In Table 7.2, the first column under the distortion heading reports the magnitude of the voter-to-government distortion by country and electoral system type. Within system types, countries are arranged, top to bottom, from the smallest to largest magnitude of distortion. The overall distortion in each country is statistically significant, and more than half the countries show overall distortions greater than eight units.[5] Among the countries showing especially large distortions, four of the five largest are SMD systems. Indeed, considered as groupings, countries using SMD record almost twice as much distortion as those using PR systems, 14.4 versus 7.9. Among the SMD systems, only for Canada is the distortion below the PR system average, and only for Denmark among PR systems is the distortion above the SMD system average. All of the observed countries distort; those using SMD systems do so to over one and three-quarters the extent recorded for PR systems.

What are the sources of the distortions? As expected, PR systems distort the translation principally in the step between the parliamentary median and the government. Twelve of the fifteen PR countries, Spain, Portugal, and Ireland being the exceptions, install governments with a Left-Right position that is statistically significantly different from the parliamentary median Left-Right position. Among the SMD systems, only France fails in the step from parliament to government.

Column 3 reports the mistranslation in the step from median voter to parliamentary median. No country does an accurate job, but it is at this juncture that SMD systems do an especially poor job. From voter to parliament, SMD systems, on average, create almost three times the distortion as PR systems (13.4 versus 4.7). What is more important, the poor performance of SMD systems at the electoral step creates nearly twice as much distortion as the PR tendency to mistranslate the parliamentary median into a government position—13.4 for SMD electoral mistranslation versus 7.1 for PR

---

[5] Tests of significance are paired t-tests (e.g. Snedecor and Cochran 1967: 91–109), where a pair is any two stages in the process within a nation. These tests, like nearly any parametric test, assume that each pair of observations is independent of others. Such independence is certainly not strictly true in our data, for example, elections in a country are not independent events.

We have checked to see whether time dependencies might be adversely affecting our reported standard errors—the mean values themselves are, of course, unbiased—and thereby require a qualification to our inferences. We estimated country-specific autoregressive equations and asked whether the intercepts are statistically significantly different from zero. If they are not, it is reasonable to infer that, but for a run of distortions over a few elections, the estimated through-time equilibrium—a sort of mean value estimated dynamically—may not be much different from zero. The results indicate that the statistical significance of Spain's overall distortion is in doubt, and perhaps Canada's too. The underlying details of these possible qualifications do not much affect our discussion in material ways, however; so we keep those details in the background.

TABLE 7.2. *Distortions in representing a median voter's Left-Right position, by country and electoral system type, overall and across steps in the process, from the early 1950s to 1995*

System	Country	Ns Govts	Ns Elections	Distortion[a] Overall MV to govt	Negotiation parl to govt	Electoral MV to parl	Electoral system	Party system
PR	Italy	43	11	2.2**	2.2**	2.2**	0.4	1.9*
				0.3	0.5	0.7	0.3	0.7
	Spain	7	6	3.1*	0.1	3.1*	3.0	2.9*
				0.9	0.1	1.0	2.1	0.9
	Portugal	10	8	4.1**	0.6	3.6**	0.4	3.6**
				0.8	0.4	0.8	0.8	0.8
	Switzerland	45	12	4.5**	4.4**	2.0**	0.0	2.0**
				0.5	0.6	0.6	~~	0.6
	Luxembourg	14	10	5.0**	6.6**	4.0**	1.2	3.5**
				1.1	1.0	0.7	1.2	0.6
	Austria	18	13	6.6**	9.6**	7.3**	1.2	7.3**
				1.0	2.0	1.1	0.8	1.1
	Belgium	27	15	6.7**	6.9**	2.0**	0.7	1.8**
				1.1	1.0	0.6	0.5	0.5
	Netherlands	14	13	7.5**	8.7**	2.6*	0.0	2.6*
				1.1	1.6	1.0	~~	1.0
	Iceland	18	13	8.8**	8.3**	7.7*	4.5	3.7**
				2.5	1.7	2.8	3.2	0.9
	Sweden	21	15	9.4**	6.6**	4.0*	3.3	5.2*
				2.0	2.1	1.5	2.8	1.7
	Norway	21	11	10.1**	7.7**	4.0**	1.4	3.6**
				1.5	1.8	1.0	0.8	1.0
	Ireland	19	14	11.0**	4.2	10.6**	5.9	9.9**
				2.4	2.4	2.9	3.5	2.8
	Germany	21	12	11.2**	8.7**	6.0**	0.5	5.5**
				2.1	1.8	1.6	0.5	1.6
	Finland	32	13	11.7**	10.9**	4.1*	2.6	2.8**
				1.9	1.7	1.6	1.9	0.8
	Denmark	27	19	16.3**	17.4**	4.7**	0.8	5.4**
				2.2	2.8	1.0	0.6	1.0
PR Summary		337	185	7.9**	7.1**	4.7**	1.7**	4.3**
				0.5	0.5	0.4	0.4	0.4
SMD	Canada	17	14	5.5**	0.5	5.3*	4.6	4.2*
				1.9	0.7	2.0	3.3	1.4
	New Zealand	22	15	12.3**	0.0	12.3**	1.8	11.5**
				1.5	~~	1.9	0.9	2.1
	United Kingdom	18	13	15.6**	0.3	15.3**	19.7**	7.6**
				2.9	0.7	3.4	5.6	1.6
	Australia	24	18	17.4**	0.0	17.4**	8.4*	16.0**
				1.8	~~	2.1	4.0	2.1
	France	25	10	18.5**	2.9**	16.7**	12.8*	8.5**
				1.6	0.8	3.2	4.2	2.2

TABLE 7.2. *Distortions in representing a median voter's Left-Right position, by country and electoral system type, overall and across steps in the process, from the early 1950s to 1995—cont'd*

System	Country	Ns		Distortion[a]				
		Govts	Elections	Overall MV to govt	Negotiation parl to govt	Electoral MV to parl	Electoral system	Party system
SMD Summary		106	70	14.4** 0.9	0.8** 0.3	13.4** 1.2	9.0** 1.8	10.0** 1.0

*p <0.05; ** p <0.01; two-tail critical values are used because distortion can only take a positive value. The ~ symbol indicates that the standard error is undefined because the correspondence at that step was exact at each election.

[a] Cell entries under Distortion are means and their standard errors over the period from the early 1950s to 1995. All calculations are weighted by the time a government was in office (*MV to Government* and *Parliament to Government*) or by the time between elections (*MV to Parliament, Electoral System,* and *Party System*). Weights are proportional to *Govts* or *Elections*, as appropriate, for tests of statistical significance.

Distortions are defined as follows.

- *Overall, MV to Government* is the difference between government Left-Right position and median voter Left-Right position.
- *Negotiation, Parliament to Government* is the difference between government Left-Right position and parliamentary median Left-Right position.
- *Electoral, MV to Parliament* is the difference between parliamentary median Left-Right position and median voter Left-Right position.
- *Electoral System* is the difference between parliamentary median Left-Right position and Left-Right position of the party position closest to the median voter.
- *Party System* is the difference between Left-Right position of the party closest to the median voter and Left-Right position of the median voter.

negotiation mistranslation.[6] So, while the five SMD countries install governments based accurately on the composition of their parliaments, their parliaments are at variance with their median voters.

We can go two steps further and look at the sources of distortion at the electoral step. Two features of the process are at work. One is the translation of the vote distribution into a parliamentary median, that is electoral system distortion. The other is the availability of parties in the vicinity of the median voter, that is party system distortion. Table 7.2 records the magnitudes of both sources in its last two columns.

In dealing with the party closest to the median voter, the SMD electoral system distortion is 9.0 points on average. The British SMD electoral system mistranslation is the extreme case. No step in any other country creates as much distortion as the British electoral system. Even granting that usually

---

[6] Given the small and essentially homogeneous standard errors for the PR systems' negotiation and electoral steps and the SMD systems' electoral step, both differences are statistically significant, $p < 0.01$.

TABLE 7.3. *Biases in representing a median voter's Left-Right position, by country and electoral system type, overall and across steps in the process, from the early 1950s to 1995*

System	Country	Ns Govts	Ns Elections	Bias[a] Overall MV to govt	Negotiation parl to govt	Electoral MV to parl	Electoral system	Party system
PR	Spain	7	6	0.0	−0.1	0.1	3.0	−2.9*
				1.5	0.1	1.7	2.1	0.9
	Norway	21	11	0.4	1.8	−1.4	−0.5	−0.9
				2.7	2.4	1.4	0.8	1.3
	Switzerland	45	12	0.6	0.4	0.2	0.0	0.2
				0.8	0.9	0.8	∼	0.8
	Luxembourg	14	10	0.7	−2.4	3.2*	1.1	2.1
				1.7	2.0	1.1	1.2	1.1
	Austria	18	13	0.8	−0.3	1.1	−1.2	2.3
				1.9	3.0	2.4	0.8	2.3
	Belgium	27	15	−0.8	−2.0	1.1	−0.2	1.3*
				1.7	1.7	0.7	0.5	0.6
	Ireland	19	14	0.9	2.9	−2.1	5.9	−7.9*
				3.5	2.5	4.1	3.5	3.3
	Italy	43	11	1.3**	−0.2	1.4	0.3	1.1
				0.4	0.6	0.9	0.3	0.8
	Netherlands	14	13	1.4	−0.8	2.2	0.0	2.2
				2.3	2.9	1.1	∼	1.1
	Portugal	10	8	1.5	0.1	1.6	0.4	1.2
				1.5	0.5	1.4	0.8	1.5
	Denmark	27	19	3.1	6.0	−2.9*	0.8	−3.7*
				3.8	4.3	1.3	0.6	0.8
	Germany	21	12	3.4	2.2	1.1	−0.5	1.6
				3.2	2.6	2.4	0.5	2.3
	Sweden	21	15	−3.6	−0.7	−2.9	−0.6	−2.3
				2.8	2.6	1.7	3.0	2.2
	Finland	32	13	4.9	2.5	1.6	−0.5	2.1
				2.7	2.6	1.9	2.0	1.0
	Iceland	18	13	7.4*	4.9*	2.5	4.5	−2.0
				2.7	2.3	3.5	3.2	1.3
PR Summary		337	185	1.5*	1.1	0.3	0.8	−0.5
				0.6	0.6	0.5	0.4	0.5
SMD	New Zealand	22	15	2.5	0.0	2.5	0.5	2.1
				3.0	∼	3.7	1.0	3.7
	Canada	17	14	3.9	0.5	3.4	4.2	−0.8
				2.1	0.7	2.3	3.3	1.8
	Australia	24	18	5.6	0.0	5.6	3.3	2.3
				3.9	∼	4.5	4.4	4.4
	United Kingdom	18	13	8.7*	−0.3	9.0	11.8	−2.8
				4.3	0.7	4.9	7.2	2.6
	France	25	10	10.9**	1.6	9.4	6.7	2.7
				3.4	0.9	5.6	5.6	3.4

Representing the Median Voter 129

TABLE 7.3. *Biases in representing a median voter's Left-Right position, by country and electoral system type, overall and across steps in the process, from the early 1950s to 1995—cont'd*

System	Country	Ns		Bias[a]				
		Govts	Elections	Overall MV to govt	Negotiation parl to govt	Electoral MV to parl	Electoral system	Party system
SMD Summary		106	70	6.5**	0.4	5.7**	4.9*	0.7
				1.6	0.3	1.9	2.0	1.6

*$p < 0.05$; **$p < 0.01$; two-tail test. The ~ symbol indicates that the standard error is undefined because the correspondence at that step was exact at each election.

[a] Countries are arranged by the magnitude of bias. Cell entries under bias are means and their standard errors over the period from the early 1950s to 1995. All calculations are weighted by the time a government was in office (*MV to Govt* and *Parliament to Government*) or the time between elections (*MV to Parliament, Electoral System,* and *Party System*). Weights are proportional to *Governments* or *Elections*, as appropriate, for tests of statistical significance.

Biases are defined as follows.
- *Overall, MV to Government* is the difference between government Left-Right position and median voter Left-Right position.
- *Negotiation, Parliament to Government* is the difference between government Left-Right position and parliamentary median Left-Right position.
- *Electoral, MV to Parliament* is the difference between parliamentary median Left-Right position and median voter Left-Right position.
- *Electoral System* is the difference between parliamentary median Left-Right position and Left-Right position of the party position closest to the median voter.
- *Party System* is the difference between Left-Right position of the party closest to the median voter and Left-Right position of the median voter.

the most accuracy one could expect in Britain would be having the Liberals (later Alliance and later still Liberal Democrats) as the median party in parliament, the electoral system mistranslates what could have been by more than 19 points. PR systems do a commendable job at the translation step of the electoral system. On average the distortion is only 1.7 points, and no single PR system distorts the votes-to-seats translation of medians to a statistically significant degree. PR rules are not only fair in terms of the virtually equal weight they end up assigning to each voter's vote, they are accurate in terms of creating a parliamentary median that is as close to the median voter's position as their party system allows.

Finally, the SMD system's well-known tendency to keep the number of effective parties relatively small has the associated implication of only making available parties far from the position of the median voter. Even Canada, the best performing SMD system in terms of available parties, has more distortion coming from its party system than two-thirds of the PR systems. And party offerings in SMD systems are responsible for an average of 10.0 units of distortion. PR systems fare better on average, but, even so, all PR party systems leave a gap in the vicinity of their median voters, with the result that there is a statistically significant amount of distortion created by PR multiparty systems.

The principal finding on the matter of distortions is that they exist in every one of the twenty countries analysed. It is important but not much of a surprise that the major source of distortions for PR systems occurs when going from parliament to government while for SMD systems the major source arises when going from voters to parliament. For as long as these two system types have existed, commentary has appreciated that such a tradeoff probably exists. Another important and more surprising finding is that the party system holds as much or more responsibility for electoral distortions as electoral system mistranslation. The relative contributions of electoral and party systems are expected in PR systems; the important feature of that system's rules is vote and seat proportionality. With that comes a reasonably accurate translation of the party closest to the voter median into a parliamentary median. Nevertheless, we would not have supposed PR systems everywhere would leave large enough gaps in the range of parties to distort the voter to parliament step. Also, we would not have supposed that among SMD systems the party system creates distortion to about the same extent, on average, as the electoral system.

7.3.2 Biases

What are the consequences of such widespread distortions? The answer is 'not much,' at least with respect to accurate representation of a median voter. Table 7.3 rearranges our estimates of distortion and recasts them as biases. From this perspective, the misrepresentation looks very much different. Only four of the twenty countries have a statistically significant amount of bias in the relationship between government and median voter, and just three nations—Iceland, Britain, and France—have overall biases that go beyond the difference between, say, two different centrist parties, that is beyond six points.

It is an arithmetic fact that the average magnitude of bias cannot be larger than a corresponding average magnitude of distortion. Averaging pluses and minuses necessarily results in a magnitude equal to or smaller than averaging magnitudes of absolute values. However, that arithmetic fact is itself extremely important when evaluating representation. Reporting distortions in the representational process, as do studies that focus on the relationship between seats and votes at one point in time or on the match between parliaments and governments at one time point, is a way of recording worst-case scenarios. Distortions record problems between pairs of stages in the process and have the effect of treating each single time point as independent of others. But, while each distortion is important in its own right, it ought not to be considered a summary statement of the whole issue of representation.

Within the PR and SMD system types we have been considering, the representational process unfolds to compensate one distortion with another in some ways that are similar and other ways that are different. At the beginning of the process, where we are looking at the Left-Right positions that a party system has to offer, we see a between-system similarity. In Table 7.2, the Left-Right offerings of the parties created distortions in all fifteen PR countries and in all five SMD countries, in the sense that the party closest to the median voter was at a significant distance from him or her. On average in PR systems, the party closest to the median voter was more than four units away; on average in SMD systems, it was ten units away (see Table 7.2). In Table 7.3 we see only four countries—Spain, Belgium, Ireland, and Denmark—with party system distortions that amount to statistically significant biases. By implication, everywhere else deviations between the party closest to the median voter and the position of the median voter himself or herself cancel over time. The party closest to the median voter is sometimes positioned some distance away on the right, and sometimes it is positioned some distance away on the left. Because party system distortions do not run systematically in one direction, they usually do not become biases.

Electoral system distortions under PR rules were essentially non-existent. Of course, then, they create no bias. SMD electoral system distortions are legendary, and they show themselves to be especially large in Britain and France (see Table 7.2). As biases, Table 7.3, the conclusion about SMD distortions has to be modified. In none of the five countries is the bias statistically significant. In New Zealand and Australia that is because over time electoral system distortions cancel, so much so that over more than four decades of the data the magnitude of their biases is less than one-third of their distortions. In all four nations, though most especially in Britain and France, the lack of statistical significance is a matter of biases being uncertain. In statistical terms this is reflected in their rather large standard errors. In substantive terms nearly everyone knows what it means. SMD electoral system distortions reflect the typical award of bonuses to a plurality party, whichever party wins a plurality. In some elections it is a party to the left of the median voter; in other elections it is a party to the right of the median voter. Finally, it stands to reason that the party closest to the median voter but still relatively far removed, sometimes on the right and other times on the left, creates a good deal of uncertainty. In statistical words, their standard errors are large enough to render the mean values of bias statistically insignificant.

The total electoral bias—party system effect plus electoral system effect—mostly pales in comparison to the impression one receives from distortions. Whereas all countries show statistically significant electoral distortion (see Table 7.2), only two countries, Luxembourg and Denmark, show a statistically significant electoral bias (see Table 7.3). Luxembourg becomes one of the four as a consequence of individually insignificant but reinforcing party system and electoral system biases. The party system alone is responsible for the bias in Denmark.

As with total electoral biases, negotiation biases also pale in comparison to negotiation distortions. France's bias at the negotiation stage does not amount to a statistically significant bias. And, among the thirteen PR systems with distortion at the negotiation stage, only Iceland is both distorted and biased.

All this leaves only four countries where there is overall bias to a statistically significant extent. The governments of Italy, Iceland, Britain, and France are all reliably estimated as skewed to the right relative to the position of each country's median voter.

In Italy, the bias, while reliably estimated, is so small that it has almost gone unnoticed. In today's Italy, with its new party system and electoral rules, it is too early to tell whether a similar or larger bias might creep into the representational process. Iceland arrives at its bias due principally to the negotiation step. France and Britain arrive at their biases mostly due to electoral mistranslation.

7.3.3 Compensations

In the final analysis we want to know why distortions everywhere become biases in only a small number of countries. This requires that we look at the process with a view to identifying compensations. The first column in Table 7.4 reports the proportionate reduction in overall distortions, where a proportionate reduction records the proportion of distortion that is erased due to some form of compensation. In arithmetic terms, it equals one minus the magnitude of the bias divided by the magnitude of the distortion. If all of the distortions in a country run persistently in the same direction, its bias has the same magnitude as its distortion, and thus there is zero proportionate reduction. To the extent that a country's distortions run one way and then the other, so that errors to the left cancel errors to the right, the process provides compensation.

In three of fifteen countries with PR systems, compensations reduce overall distortions by more than 90 per cent. In Spain, the magnitude of bias (see Table 7.3) relative to the magnitude of distortion (see Table 7.2) shows the reduction in distortion leaves no bias to speak of, that is $1 - (0.0 / 3.1)$, the reduction is total. The two other countries with reductions greater than 90 per cent are Norway (0.96) and Ireland (0.93). Even in PR countries with the largest biases, Iceland and Finland, distortions are reduced by 0.15 (Iceland) and 0.58 (Finland). In between countries with most and least reduction in distortions, the range in proportionate reductions is 0.41 (Italy) to 0.89 (Austria). Something about the representational processes in PR systems compensates for more than three-quarters of all the distortions.

TABLE 7.4. *Proportionate reduction in distortions, by country and electoral system type, overall and at the negotiation and electoral stages, from the early 1950s to 1995*

System	Country[a]	Overall	Proportionate reduction in distortions[b]		
			Negotiation bias cancelling electoral bias	Negotiation bias compensations	Electoral bias compensations
PR	Italy	0.41	0.11	0.93	0.38
	Spain	1.00	0.85	0.00	0.98
	Portugal	0.63	−.09	0.76	0.56
	Switzerland	0.87	−.59	0.92	0.89
	Luxembourg	0.85	0.77	0.63	0.21
	Austria	0.89	0.31	0.96	0.85
	Belgium	0.87	0.56	0.71	0.46
	Netherlands	0.81	−.38	0.91	0.18
	Iceland	0.15	−.52	0.41	0.67
	Sweden	0.62	−.22	0.90	0.26
	Norway	0.96	0.77	0.76	0.65
	Ireland	0.92	0.71	0.32	0.81
	Germany	0.69	−0.52	0.75	0.81
	Finland	0.58	−0.64	0.77	0.60
	Denmark	0.81	0.48	0.65	0.37
PR Summary		0.81	−0.26	0.75	0.94
SMD	Canada	0.29	−0.14	0.00	0.35
	New Zealand	0.79	0.00	~~~	0.79
	United Kingdom	0.45	0.04	0.00	0.41
	Australia	0.68	0.00	~~~	0.68
	France	0.41	−0.17	0.46	0.44
SMD Summary		0.55	−.07	0.52	0.58

[a] Countries are arranged, top to bottom, within system types, from smallest to largest overall distortion as reported in Table 7.2 above.

[b] Proportionate reductions are calculated from data reported in tables 7.2 and 7.3 above.

- *Overall* is one minus the magnitude of the overall bias reported in Table 7.3 divided by the overall distortion in Table 7.2.
- *Negotiation Bias Cancelling Electoral Bias* is the one minus absolute value of negotiation plus electoral biases in Table 7.3 divided by the absolute value of whichever of those two biases has the larger magnitude. It tells us the proportionate reduction brought about when the value of one bias compensates for how large the bias could have been if the larger bias operating alone had been realized. Negative values indicate negative reductions—that is, increases—because the two biases are reinforcing, not compensating.
- *Negotiation Bias Compensations* are one minus the magnitude of the negotiation bias reported in Table 7.3 divided by the negotiation distortion in Table 7.2. The ~~~ entry indicates that the proportionate reduction is undefined because there was no distortion at the negotiation stage.
- *Electoral Bias Compensations* are one minus the magnitude of the electoral bias reported in Table 7.3 divided by the electoral distortion in Table 7.2.

Our five SMD systems also show compensation, though not to the extent recorded in PR systems. In Canada, the UK, and France, the proportionate reduction in overall distortions amounts to something in the neighbourhood of 0.29 to 0.45. In New Zealand and Australia, they amount to a more substantial 0.79 and 0.68, respectively. Considered generally across all five SMD systems, the compensations in SMD systems reduce overall distortions by more than half.

Column 2 of Table 7.4 shows that not much of the greater PR compensation comes from the tendency of a negotiation bias to compensate an electoral bias. When and where this compensation does occur, it is because the median voter is often at a position between the parliamentary median and the position of the plurality party. Given that the plurality party, the party of the median legislator, or both are frequently in government under multiparty systems (Müller and Strøm 2000: 563–9), there is a tendency for the negotiation bias to run in the opposite direction of the electoral bias. SMD systems seldom involve negotiation to form governments. With a parliamentary median translating directly into a government position, little or no compensation occurs to balance one with the other. This is good news in the sense that the absence of negotiations does not bias things any more than they are already biased at the electoral stage in SMD systems. It is not good news inasmuch as there is no corrective at the negotiation stage for how much the parliamentary median misrepresents the median voter's position.

From the fact that distortions at the electoral stage are about as often reinforced at the negotiations stage as they are compensated, in both PR and SMD systems, we are led to the inference that most of the compensation comes through time. That is, most of the compensation is the consequence of party alternation in government.

The last two columns in Table 7.4 report what are mostly proportionate reductions in distortion that result from compensations across elections.[7] In both types of systems, across time compensations reduce distortions between 50 to 95 per cent, meaning that distortions do not often run in the same direction for years on end. The striking finding is that across-time compensation is larger in PR systems than in SMD systems. This conflicts with Ferejohn's notion, quoted above, that PR systems lack the admirable dynamic quality that SMD systems possess. And, at the electoral stage alone, it conflicts

---

[7] The calculation for proportionate reduction at the negotiation stage is one minus the magnitude of negotiation bias divided by negotiation distortion; likewise, the calculation for proportionate reduction at the electoral stage is one minus the magnitude of electoral bias divided by electoral distortion.

The compensations recorded by these calculations are not wholly matters of cross-time effects because the electoral biases are in some small part a consequence of countervailing tendencies between party system and electoral system biases. The country for which that form of compensation matters most is Spain. Ireland, Austria, and Iceland are other countries for which these two biases compensate one another appreciably. Otherwise, party and electoral system biases create about as much cumulation as compensation. Finally, note that at the negotiation stage two SMD systems get the parliament to government translation totally accurate (no distortion) and therefore make the concept of proportionate reduction inapplicable.

with the notion that 'plurality voting, while often defective in single elections, is probably the main force maintaining over time the simple majority decision that most people regard as desirable' (Riker 1982: 88). The irony, perhaps, is that PR systems tend to create small distortions and therefore the dynamics that they contribute to correcting distortions via alternation through time go largely unnoticed. Compensation through alternation is much more noticeable in SMD systems, because that is where it is most needed. It is as if the best thing SMD systems have going for them is alternation; when it happens it is much welcomed. When it does not happen, however, the biases under SMD systems can be substantial. In particular, the main contribution to bias in France and the UK is that parties of the left have been in power for approximately only one of every four years. In the other three SMD countries, parties of the left have been in power for one of every three years. The seemingly small difference in alternations between left and right among these five SMD systems plays a large role in creating biases, given that the magnitude of distortions under SMD systems are so large to begin with.

In summary, the tendencies of the two system types show that PR systems are less distorted and, to the extent they are, they are more nearly self-compensating. PR systems create about half as much distortion as SMD systems (see 7.9 versus 14.4, from Table 7.2), and something in the process of PR systems compensates so that their proportionate reductions in distortions are half again larger than compensation for distortions in SMD systems (0.81 versus 0.55). PR systems are likely to get it more nearly right in the first place, and to the extent they do not, there is more compensation for missteps in the process.

7.4 THE REPRESENTATIONAL PROCESS AND THE MEDIAN MANDATE

For all the distortions that arise in the representational process—and they are everywhere—an extremely important finding is that the distortions do not amount to much in terms of misrepresenting the median voter.

We now have a firm evidentiary foundation for what we observed about elections in Chapter 6. There we saw that government Left-Right positions move and line-up with movements and positions of median voters. In our concluding observations on elections, we commented that there is a dynamic fickleness to the government-voter relationship. We cannot have a high degree of confidence when predicting where along the Left-Right dimension a single government will be even with knowledge of where a median voter is located. The unpredictability of single election-government results (residual variance) was too large for high confidence. Over time, however, governments and median voters line up in something close to a one-to-one alignment. We have seen in this chapter what gives rise to both observations. At any one time and at any one step in the representational process, distortions can and frequently do disrupt an eventual government-voter alignment. Across the various stages and more especially over time, however, distortions tend to cancel one another, producing an accurate representation in general.

Among twenty parliamentary democracies during the period from the early 1950s to 1995, only Iceland, France, and Britain show heavily biased representation. Their governments, on average, have a cast similar to a liberal party whereas their median voters are in a position about halfway between a social democratic and a liberal party. Elsewhere, the misrepresentation of the median voter is no worse and often is better than the difference between two close party alternatives.

Along the way to that major conclusion, we have paid close attention to differences between PR and SMD system types. What have we learned from those details? Our empirical results on distortions are consistent with the inferences drawn by Huber and Powell (1994) and Powell and Vanberg (2000) and contrary to those reported in Wessels (1999). Distortions are generally smaller in systems using PR electoral rules than in those using SMD rules. Furthermore, when we take the next step and consider biases, PR still generally outperforms SMD. This is contrary to the thinking of scholars who have expressed support for SMD arrangements because the electoral dynamics associated with SMD systems are thought to bring SMD-based parliaments and governments more into line with a median voter than would be the case under PR (Ferejohn 1999; Riker 1982).

Perhaps the single most interesting inference to draw about the relative merits of system types is conceptual. It is time to rethink the discussion of electoral democracy that frames the system types as embodying different democratic 'visions', proportional versus majoritarian (Powell 2000; see also Lijphart 1984, 1999). The evidence here indicates that so far as representation is concerned it is more appropriate to draw a line of demarcation between institutional arrangements that operate through *consensus majorities* versus those that operate through *alternating pluralities*.

With politics set along a single dimension, the fact is that a PR system comes close to representing a median voter. Relatively judged, the facts are that SMD systems produce governments, even when averaged through time, that are more distorted and more biased than those of PR systems. Canada is a modest exception. Given that the median is the position that commands a majority along a single dimension, PR systems are the majoritarian systems. They are not majoritarian in vote and seat counting but in the deeper sense of majority rule. Furthermore, PR systems have a claim to consensus representation. This is not for cultural reasons—at least not cultural reasons alone—but because, if one were to ask the voters after the election whether they would trade the parliamentary median for the position of another party, they would likely reach a consensus that the parliamentary median is acceptable.

This is less true in SMD systems. The parliamentary median matches the available party position closest to the median voter 85 per cent of the time in PR systems but only 64 per cent of the time in the five SMD systems analysed in this chapter (see Table 2.5).

A further conclusion from this chapter therefore is that the idea of a median mandate provides us with a criterion to judge the relative performance of institutional arrangements, which its substantiation here shows is relevant to working democracies. We do not need to accept, as Powell (2000) seems to argue, that different 'visions' of democracy are incommensurable, only to be judged by the criteria that they themselves set up. We can argue against a radical deconstruction of the universal democratic ideal that there is an obligation on *all* democracies to institutionalize a necessary connection between popular preferences and public policy intentions (Saward 1998: 52). The only working form in which this can be done is, on our evidence, the median mandate. As PR operationalizes this better than SMD, it is a better election system for democracies to adopt.

This is a point to which we will return in our conclusions. Immediately, however, we need to assess how well the median mandate operates in regard to actual policymaking at the governmental level. We look at this in Parts III and IV.

PART III

The Governing Process

8

Who Controls Short-Term Policymaking?

We ended Part II by comparing electoral policy preferences with government intentions, in so far as these could be inferred from the electoral statements of the parties in government. This was appropriate in assessing the extent to which median voters are able to designate an appropriately inclined government.

We are unable to stop with party policy intentions stated at the time of elections. These are far from the end of the democratic governing process. Many factors intervene between what parties say they want at the time of an election and what they actually do once elected. In this chapter we shift our attention to what happens after parties negotiate a government. How far do they succeed in carrying out their original intentions and thereby effectuating the preferences of the median voter? This changes our focus in Part III to the processes of governing rather than the direct effect of elections, although of course we continue to consider general electoral effects by taking into account any continuing influence of the median voter.

We move in two stages towards the public policies initiated by governments. First we consider the official programme to which governments publicly commit themselves in their investiture debate, that is, government declarations. Due to bargaining, anticipated constraints, and the need to get parliamentary approval, a declaration is rather different from the preferences of the individual parties in government. This is true even of single party majority governments but applies even more to coalition governments. Programmes have to deal with immediate administrative problems and with the practicalities of policymaking, and these considerations may thwart some of the intentions analysed in Chapter 7.

Such declarations initiate rather than terminate the governing process, though they should certainly be taken as better indicators of eventual policy than simple party electoral programme intentions. They have the advantage of outlining a whole range of plans, for legislation and administration as well as spending. Legislation and administration are difficult to cover directly in a comparative study—owing to the variety of languages they are written in and great mass of documentation that embodies them. Government declarations at least provide some indication of plans for these areas, even if some later fall by the wayside.

We do have direct indicators of eventual policy outputs in the shape of the public economy, welfare, foreign aid, and defence. Most of these are spending indicators, and while spending is not all there is to policy, policies not backed up by money are unlikely to be effective, even in the regulatory field. Certainly budgeted expenditures are a central part of the government's effected policy package. We go on to analyse these actual policy outputs in Chapter 9. One interesting question of course is whether the separate analyses of declarations and expenditures lead to the same conclusions about control over public policy.

8.1 SPECIFIC POLICY AREAS

One consequence of switching from the electoral to the governmental arena is to reintroduce the question of whether policy discussion breaks out of the unified framework provided by the Left-Right shorthand that dominates elections and instead fragments into separate debates within each policy area (see Figure 3.2). There are good reasons embedded in the structure of governments and ministries as to why this might be so. Ministries issue separate discussion documents and reports on their areas of competence and sponsor legislation in their field. Cabinet business, too, is generally introduced by the appropriate minister, with discussion involving only those other ministers directly affected by the proposal.

The possibility of different policy spaces coexisting within parliament and government raises the possibility of different actors driving the policy process at different points. The most obvious of these are the ministries charged with responsibility for the area. One does not need to go as far as Laver and Shepsle (1996: 282) and regard ministries as having almost autonomous power over their areas to see them as important actors (Budge and Keman 1990: 140–56).

Another possibility already stressed is that the median parliamentary party in each area would be recognized as such and thus exercise the 'power of the median' by dominating related discussion and linked policy outcomes. Of course in many cases this might be the same as the party at the general Left-Right median, which we would regard as the one truly authorized by the median voter in the election. But sometimes the various medians might not coincide. If policy-specific medians then dominated, this would be a blow to the idea of a unified median mandate bestowed by the electorate.

Median mandate ideas would also paradoxically take a knock if the median voter him- or herself exercised a direct influence over policy. The mandate is, after all, a *mediated* process, where the median electoral preference is taken up and transmitted by the median parliamentary party. If the electoral position has a directly dominating influence this smacks more of parties and governments converging on the median position rather than following through on mandated choices made by electors.

A final possibility reasserts mandate ideas but this time in the shape of the rival, government mandate thesis. It is after all entirely plausible that when a government is constituted, however imperfectly it represents the electorate, it will have the predominant voice over all areas of policy. This is what formal constitutional theory says it should have, so it certainly gives us an alternative possibility to the overall median party.

8.2 THE IMPORTANCE OF TIME HORIZONS

Our previous analysis of congruence between median voters and government intentions emphasized the importance of the time frame we apply to the conclusions we draw. Looking at distortions in the policy correspondence based on single elections led us to the conclusion that representation runs aground everywhere, and does so most especially in SMD systems compared to PR. However, when we examined cumulative bias over a series of elections we had to tone down what we were saying. Most systems, including SMD systems, display limited bias because of party alternation over time. Across a series of elections, distortion goes in different directions if there is a different party in power, so distortion cancels out. Therefore, the final policy equilibrium is arrived at through confrontation rather than consensus. Compared across system-types, it is the way the end point is reached rather than its correspondence with popular preferences that differs between the systems.

There is a lesson here for our current analysis. Searching for influences in the context of individual elections may well lead to favouring particular actors, possibly those closest to the final decision such as governments or ministers. Viewed in a longer perspective over a series of governments their actions may cancel each other out, bringing the final outcome closer to the background median position than appears at first sight. This may also be true of the influence of overall Left-Right positions on specific issues, where effects may fluctuate in a pattern only discernable as such over time.

If we have to make a decision between an individual election perspective and a long-term one, which should we choose? In our view we have to take democracy as a process where the long-term results count more than those of any one election. After all, one point of elections is to allow voters to correct what they feel to be earlier mistakes. We have seen the way in which their decisions over time add up to 'forces restoring democratic competition'. This process can only take place in an extended period over a series of elections, however. Its policy outcomes inevitably represent an averaging of specific ones. But given that fluctuation and alternation are such characteristic properties of democracy, uniquely allowed for by democratic elections, we ought to give their end results priority in the assessment.

This is not to say, any more than in our electoral assessments, that we can afford to ignore specific elections and governments. In this and the next chapter we look at them explicitly in regard first to government declarations and then actual policies in Chapter 9. We return only in Chapter 10 to the question of time.

8.3 SPECIFYING HYPOTHESES

Previous discussion and theorizing—not only ours but also that of the general literature—have identified seven possible actors who might influence general policy, conceived in Left-Right terms, and also policy in specific areas. We have three possibilities for policy described overall, along a Left-Right continuum, and four possibilities for policymaking in a particular area.

For policy overall,

- Governments are collectively responsible for the Left-Right inclination of policy, following from the weighted mean positions of parties in government (de Swaan 1973; Huber and Powell 1994; Laver and Shepsle 1996: 280; Powell 2000).
- Parliaments are collectively responsible for the Left-Right inclination of policy, following on from the position of the median parliamentarian (Strom 1990: 38; van Roozendaal 1990; 1992)
- Voters are collectively responsible for the Left-Right inclination of policy, following on from the position of the median voter.

As for specific policies, for example, welfare,

- The minister overseeing the relevant portfolio is responsible for policy in that area (Laver and Shepsle 1996: 282).
- Governments, which have to approve putting a policy proposal before a parliament, are collectively responsible for each separate policy.
- Parliament retains the power to approve policy and, because policy considerations are separated from one another during the interelection governing period, the parliamentarian at the median position in a particular policy area (i.e. not the Left-Right median) controls policy in that area.
- Parliament retains power to approve policy and, because either the Left-Right median is congruent with a policy median in a particular policy area or because parties have agreed to logroll across issues, the median parliamentarian on the Left-Right dimension controls each particular policy.

Our purpose in this chapter and the next is to investigate all seven hypotheses. We proceed in two steps, one using government policy declarations as the outcomes of interest in this chapter and another using actual policies in Chapter 9. Of government policy declarations we ask how their general

Left-Right positions line up with the Left-Right positions of median voters, parliamentary medians, and governments. In terms of specific policies, we ask how well declarations on the role of government in economic planning, welfare, and an orientation to international affairs line up with the policy-specific positions of the party or parties in control of a ministry, policy-specific position of governments collectively, the policy position of the parliamentary policy median, and the policy-specific position of the parliamentary median on the general Left-Right dimension. In this way we cover all the possibilities mentioned in the literature and specified above, both in terms of the actors involved and of the policy areas they operate in. Of course economic planning, welfare, and foreign affairs are not the only specific policy areas in politics, but they are central and form a reasonably important subset.

8.4 GOVERNMENT POLICY DECLARATIONS

In the 1980s, the Manifesto Research Group collected data on the policy declarations of governments in eleven multiparty systems that had a strong likelihood of having coalitions (Laver and Budge 1992; see also Budge et al. 2001: 245–50). Because the declaration data reach back to the governments formed after the first constitutionally authorized elections after 1949 and go on to the early 1980s, our data match the declaration data for 137 governments. Details about governments covered by the declaration data set are provided in the appendix to this chapter. The declarations were taken from a speech by a Head of State on behalf of a recently formed government or by a prime minister of the time of investiture (see Laver and Budge 1992: 19). Quasi-sentences of a declaration were coded into the same fifty-six categories used to code party manifestoes. This enables us to construct a Left-Right score for government policy intentions comparable to those derived from manifestoes.[1] Likewise, we can construct policy-specific scores on a government planning versus market orientation to the economy, welfare support, and peace/militarist international orientation from the declarations using the same categories as those of manifestoes (see Chapter 5).

8.4.1 Left-Right Positions

Stated in its fundamental form, the question is whether the Left-Right position of median voters translates into the stated intentions of governments

---

[1] It is tempting to think that the manifesto and declaration scores are directly comparable, as they share the same interval-level metric. However, considering the amount of attention governments give to their power-sharing and other internal arrangements, which implies a strong possibility that more attention is given to matters not within the Left-Right categories in declarations compared to manifestoes (Laver and Budge 1992: 410–12), it is best not to treat the metrics as if they form a one-to-one match.

through a sequence from electorate to parliamentary median, parliamentary median to government, and government composition to government declaration, or whether the position of the median voter controls the process in such a way that it forms the common causal force creating spurious correlations between and among parliaments, governments, and policy. Diagrammatically, the two alternative situations are as follows:

Developmental sequence

Median Voter L-R ⟶ Parliament L-R ⟶ Goverment L-R ⟶ Goverment Declaration

Spurious relationships caused by median voter

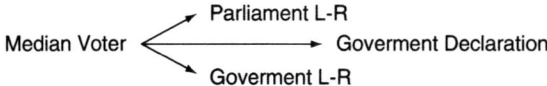

In between these polar alternatives is an intermediate causal structure, where the median voter position leads to a parliamentary position and that, in turn, creates a spurious relationship between government Left-Right positions and the governments' policy declarations. This is the causal structure that is most consistent with the median mandate thesis.

Developmental sequence and spurious relationships caused by parliamentary median

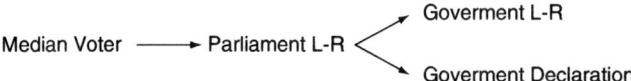

To summarize, evidence supporting the developmental sequence indicates that once one actor has been empowered by the actor immediately preceding it in the sequence, it does not look back to that preceding actor. Rather, it sets up the next step in the policymaking sequence as if its preferences are the only ones that matter. Alternatively, evidence supporting the spurious relationship indicates that one of the prime movers in the sequence, electorate or parliamentary median, holds the set of preferences that counts most. Whatever happens later in the sequence, it is one of those sets of initial preferences that exert control over what happens later.

Table 8.1 provides the results of our analyses as they relate to the general Left-Right dimension. The first column reports bivariate associations between the Left-Right emphasis of government policy declarations and the Left-Right positions of median voters, parliamentary medians, and governments. Each actor's Left-Right position relates to declarations in much the same way, but the correlation between declarations and the median voter is slightly higher than correlations from either parliamentary median or government. On this evidence, the electorate's position has as much and perhaps slightly more to do with governments' declared policy intentions than what parliaments or governments acting alone would declare as their policy intentions. Column 2 focuses on parliaments and governments, excluding consideration of median voters. These results indicate that when only these two institutional actors are considered they carry about equal weight for what governments declare they will do. When the electorate position is added, column 3, it is its position that predominates in the statistical competition. So far as we can tell from the evidence taken from government declarations, it appears that the Left-Right position marked by a country's median voter is a centripetal position towards which the stated Left-Right intentions of a government tends, at least in the multiparty systems under investigation here. Convergence by governments directly on the median preference, rather than a party-mediated relationship, seems to be what is happening.

We do not want to make too much of this. For one thing, none of the correlations, including the one between the median voter positions and government declarations is terribly high. Median voter positions standing alone account for less than 30 per cent of the Left-Right variation in governments' stated intentions. Even with the preferences of all three actors in the equation, explained variation reaches only about 31 per cent. And, what is more, much of this explained variation is cross-national, in contrast to

TABLE 8.1. *Relationships between Left-Right positions of government policy declarations and Left-Right positions of electorates, parliaments, and governments*

Left-Right position of	Bivariate correlation r	Multivariate parliament L-R median govt b (S_b)	Multivariate regression b (S_b)
Median Voter	0.53**	—	0.56**
			(0.18)
Parl. L-R Median	0.49**	0.28**	0.02
		(0.12)	(0.16)
Government	0.48**	0.28*	0.19
		(0.14)	(0.12)
Intercept	—	3.26*	6.21**
		(1.39)	(1.66)
R^2	—	0.26	0.31
s_e	—	14.0	13.6
N	137	137	137

cross-government variation within single countries.[2] Nevertheless, in a straightforward comparison between the general public policy position of what a government declares it intends to do and the Left-Right inclinations of governments themselves, the parliaments that give rise to the governments, and electorates that give rise to the parliaments, it is the position of the electorate that lines up most consistently with what is in the declarations.

8.4.2 Economic, Welfare, and Internationalist Policies

In characterizing a government's declaration as more or less left or right leaning, we may have been aggregating distinct policies that should be considered separately. That is, once a government has formed we have to recognize that policy activity is largely departmentalized. Who, we can ask, is in control of these separate policies? It is imaginable but unlikely that the electorate will be responsible for specific policies. As we view elections, their communication value comes almost totally in the form of a generalized Left-Right dimension. On specific policy questions, it makes more sense to hypothesize that parliaments, governments, or ministries are the operative actors in control.

We have scored government policy declarations with respect to a government-planned versus market-organized economy, a pro- versus anti-welfare stance, and a peaceful versus militarist orientation to international affairs. (Details of the scoring for each policy are described in the Appendix to the chapter.) Of these, only welfare policy declarations show any sizeable correlation with the Left-Right positions of median voters; in the other two areas, the correlations are meagre—planned versus market economy, $r = 0.07$ ($p = 0.21$), and peaceful versus militarist orientation, $r = 0.14$ ($p = 0.05$). Therefore, we look on these three specific policies as being controlled by one or more of the four previously identified parliamentary and government actors.

Perhaps the policy position of the party with whom the parliamentary median affiliates has control of everything, as van Roozendall (1990, 1992) hypothesized, including each separate policy. In that case, the policy position put forth in a government declaration would reflect the policy-specific position taken by that party. Perhaps, however, government formation reflects a sort of dimension-by-dimension series of negotiations from which it emerges which sort of specific policy is tenable in each area, given the alignment of parties in parliament in that area. Third, reasoning along the lines of de Swaan (1973) or Powell (2000), perhaps the government as a whole, weighted with respect to each partner's governmental presence, will characterize the policy in each

---

[2] Declaration data with more than ten cases exist for six nations. Analyses within these six nations lead to a mixed set of results: from none of the actors' preferences correlating with declarations at a statistically significant level to the parliamentary median or weighted government position showing a significant relationship.

area. Finally, following Laver and Shepsle (1996), we can hypothesize that the party in control of a ministry is the party in control of the policy under its jurisdiction.

Planned versus Market Economy. The left side of Table 8.2 reports the analysis of declarations on a planned versus market economy in relation to the planning/market position of the party of the Left-Right parliamentary median, parliamentary median on the specific planning/market policy, the weighted government position on planning/market, and the planning/market position of the party in control of the finance ministry. In a pattern similar to what we saw for the Left-Right positions of declarations (see Table 8.1), the bivariate correlations for all four actors are similar. Here, however, each correlation is noticeably weaker, and here the position of the party in control of the finance ministry has a slightly higher correlation compared to the others. In a multivariate model, only the ministry position survives statistical controls for the other actors' positions. To the extent we are receiving reliable readings from the evidence, the conclusion we reach is completely opposite to the one reached about the generalized Left-Right positions of declared government intentions. There the evidence indicated the prime mover in the process, the electorate, had control; here the end state of the process, the party holding the finance ministry, is all that matters.

Welfare. In the middle section of Table 8.2, we have the results of a similar analysis of pro-versus anti-welfare positions in government declarations. To remain consistent with the scoring we have been using, high scores indicate anti-welfare. The magnitude of the correlations with individual actor's positions are more like those we reported for Left-Right than for planned versus market economy.[3] Again, all correlations have similar magnitudes, but in regard to welfare it is the position of the parliamentary welfare median that is slightly higher than the others. When all four actors' positions are in the same equation, the positions of both the welfare median and the welfare emphasis given by the Left-Right median party in parliament carry some weight for what the government declares its welfare position to be.[4] Unlike the

---

[3] Magnitude of a correlation reflects several features of one's data, including the variation present on the variables under investigation. Low magnitudes could arise from small variation, as if, in the case at hand, all actors gave uniform levels of attention to economic matters and highly varied attention to welfare. Different degrees of variation are not the cause of the magnitude differences we are discussing. The economy and welfare dependent variables both have standard deviations between 5 and 5.5, and the standard deviations of actors' manifesto positions on both policies are in a range between 4.4 and 8.4.

[4] When just these two variables are in the equation, their coefficients look about the same. In the extended equation reported in Table 8.2, the parliamentary welfare median has a coefficient about twice as large as that of the welfare position of the Left-Right median party. Also, given that welfare is the one policy area for which the electorate's Left-Right position had a fairly sizeable correlation, we added that variable to the equation. It shows a statistically significant relationship with government welfare declarations in an equation with just the two median variables as well as in an equation with all four actors' positions.

TABLE 8.2. *Relationships, in three policy areas, between policy positions in government policy declarations and policy positions in that area of parliamentary Left-Right median, parliamentary policy median, and government, and relevant ministry*

	Market economy		Welfare		Peace/Military orientation	
Policy positions of	Bivariate correlation r	Multivariate regression (S_b)	Bivariate correlation r	Multivariate regression (S_b)	Bivariate correlation r	Multivariate regression (S_b)
Parliament L-R median	0.19**	0.08 (0.15)	0.46**	0.16* (0.08)	0.26**	0.05 (0.09)
Parliament policy median	0.21*	0.14 (0.20)	0.49**	0.31** (0.12)	0.49**	0.79** (0.29)
Government	0.18**	−0.19 (0.13)	0.39**	−0.14 (0.12)	0.44**	0.25 (0.33)
Ministry # 1[a]	0.26**	0.26** (0.11)	0.37**	0.10 (0.12)	0.44**	0.29 (0.29)
Ministry # 2[b]	—	—	—	—	0.37**	−0.20 (0.24)
Intercept	—	2.20** (0.47)	—	−2.60** (0.75)	—	0.34 (0.38)
R^2	—	0.09*	—	0.27**	—	0.27**
s_e	—	5.35	—	4.47	—	3.74

* $p < 0.05$; ** $p < .01$. One tail test for slopes and two tail tests for intercepts.
$N = 137$ for each analysis.

economic policy area, welfare policy positions of governments appear to correspond to what parliament wants, tending towards the middle—most especially of parliamentary parties in their weighted alignment on a welfare dimension.

Peaceful/Militarist Orientation. Our final policy area focuses on whether a government declares a peaceful versus militarist orientation to international affairs. Government declarations vary almost as much in their attention to this policy area as they do to the government versus market role in organizing the economy or welfare. The standard deviation for declarations on peaceful/militarist orientations is 4.3, versus standard deviations of 5.5 on the economy and 5.1 on welfare. On the other hand, party presentations to the electorate in the form of manifesto statements underplay foreign policy positions. The standard deviations of the four actors, as derived from party manifesto statements show values only about a quarter to a third as large as those addressing the economy and welfare. Government policy on foreign affairs, we surmise, is more at issue during the government formation stage than during the electoral stage of politics (see also, Laver and Shepsle 1996: 152–4).

Despite the less varied electoral position taking in this foreign area, we see on the right side of Table 8.2 that the correlations' magnitudes are similar to those on Left-Right and welfare. And, of the five actors—three that we have been using plus two different ministries, defence (#1) and foreign affairs (#2)—it is again the position of the parliamentary median in the policy area that has the strongest correlation. When variables representing all five actors are entered, only the median parliamentary policy position on peaceful/militarist orientation is statistically significant. As expected, the ministry and government positions are themselves highly correlated with one another ($r = 0.86$ with the defence ministry, and $r = 0.78$ with the foreign affairs ministry), but even when one or the other is withheld out of concern for the unreliable estimations that could result from multicollinearity, the government and ministry effects move just to the edge of statistical significance. Also, in these two alternative versions of the equation the coefficient on the parliamentary policy median remains more than twice as large as the government or either ministry coefficient.

8.5 WHO IS IN CONTROL?

Our analysis of government declarations gives mixed signals about who is in control of policy. On a general Left-Right orientation the policy position marked by a country's median voter is the most reliably consistent indicator of what a government intends to do. If this effect is causal, it would have to be due to parliaments and governments looking over their shoulders at what the election communicated about the median voter Left-Right position and anticipating policy benefits at the next election, as opposed to the median voter effectively selecting a median parliamentary position that then takes control of the general tenor of policy (cf. Stimson et al. 1995). If the parliamentary median were the major influence, it would be the variable that withstood controls for the government and electorate. It does not come close to this however. And, while the government's Left-Right position nearly withstands statistical controls, the magnitude of its effect pales in comparison to that of the electorate's position.

On the three specific policy areas, where the evidence does not support a direct role for voters and where, in any case, it would be a theoretical stretch to think voters could play much more than an indirect role, the conclusions are varied. On issues related to a government-planned versus a market-directed economy, the position of the party controlling the finance ministry provides the best indication of declared policy. However, the fit is relatively poor. On welfare and a peaceful/militarist international orientation, policies where the fit is relatively better, it is the median party position in parliament on each specific policy that best indicates government policy intentions.

None of this supports our ideas about a median mandate, couched in general Left-Right terms, being transmitted from the electorate to the Left-Right median in parliament which then controls policy. The situation appears more complicated than that. In terms of general policy orientations, parties seem to converge on the position of the median voter, a conclusion which is supported by a great deal of rational choice theorizing from Downs

(1957: 115–20) onwards. Looking more closely at the detail of specific policy areas, the proximate influence seems in one case to be the relevant ministry (but weakly) or the policy-specific median party in parliament. This is what might be expected from 'power of the median' reasoning in rational choice, where policy is handled inside separable dimensions (Shepsle and Weingast 1981), though there is still a lingering general median influence on welfare (see Table 8.2).

Such mixed conclusions might even support ideas about pluralism. In a democracy different actors have different resources and powers in different issue areas, so there are a variety of groups with influence somewhere, all jostling for position in the decision-making process (Dahl 1956: 133–4). Or it might support Kingdon's (1984) conclusions about Congress in the 1980s, that there are no clear patterns to be found and everything depends on situational factors.

All these are possibilities. One clear if negative conclusion is that we do not find evidence for median mandate or indeed government mandate effects. Perhaps, however, it is safest and wisest at this point to conclude that we cannot draw firm conclusions on the basis of declarations alone. At the very least their evidence needs to be supplemented by data on actual policy outputs, where the initial confusion may get sorted out by the constraints of practical as opposed to wishful politics. We accordingly repeat this analysis in Chapter 9 with data on actual policy indicators, both in general and in specific policy areas. This will complete our analysis of policymaking by individual governments before setting them in a broader time perspective in Chapter 10.

APPENDIX

The Government Declarations data are taken from CMP 98 (Budge et al. 2001).

Governments. The declarations data in CMP98 cover 174 governments in 12 countries. Because we have not collected electoral, parliamentary, and government data on Israel or for governments before 1950 in the other 11 countries, the declarations data used here cover 137 cases. By country, these include the following:

Country	Governments
Belgium ($n = 19$)	9, 10–14, 16–23, 26, 27, 29–31
Denmark ($n = 14$)	4, 6, 7, 8, 10, 12–14, 17–20, 23, 24
France ($n = 14$)	29, 30, 32–34, 36, 38, 39, 41–44, 46, 47
Germany ($n = 16$)	2, 5, 7, 10, 11, 13, 14, 16–19, 21–23, 25, 26
Ireland ($n = 2$)	13, 15
Italy ($n = 35$)	8–27, 29–42, 44

Country	Governments
Luxembourg ($n = 6$)	4, 6, 9–11, 13
Netherlands ($n = 5$)	12, 14, 18–20
Norway ($n = 8$)	4, 5, 7, 10, 13–15, 21
Sweden ($n = 18$)	4–21

The government numbers are those assigned by Woldendorp et al. (2000). Identification of parties in governments and ministries are also from Woldendorp et al. (2000).

Variables. The policy preference measurements of Left-Right, planning-market, welfare, and peace-military are the same as those reported in the Appendix to Chapter 5.

Actors. The actors whose positions we have measured included the following:

Parliamentary L-R median	Measured as the position, Left-Right or specific policy, of the party with whom the Left-Right median member of parliament affiliates; this is also referred to as the weighted median position of parties in parliament
Parliamentary policy median	Measured as the specific policy position of the party with whom the median parliamentarian on the policy dimensions affiliates
Government	Positions (Left-Right or specific policy) of parties in government, weighted by each one's seat percentage
Ministries	Position of party or parties holding the portfolio for a particular ministry: government planned versus market controlled economic policy = finance ministry, welfare policy = social affairs ministry; peaceful-militarist orientation to international affairs = foreign affairs and, separately, defence.

9

From Declared to Actual Policy: Short-Term Influences on Government Policies

Manifestoes and declarations state priorities for policy rather than getting down to the nitty-gritty. Actual decision-making involves the allocation of scarce resources, and it is this that we examine in the current chapter.

We have selected policies that square with those we have been investigating in government declarations. One involves two sets of indicators of the size of a country's public economy, one for 1982 and another for 1992, measured by central government spending as a percentage of gross domestic product (GDP). We analyse these in relationship both to the Left-Right positions of electorates, parliaments, and governments as well as to the planning versus market orientation of parliaments, governments, and finance ministries. A second set comes from two indicators of support for welfare. One is Esping-Anderson's (1990) scoring of welfare provision from the early 1980s; the other is the level of social spending as a percentage of GDP from the early 1990s. Our third policy is covered by another two indicators, of a peaceful versus militarist orientation to international affairs. One is the level of foreign economic aid as a percentage of GDP from the early 1980s, and the other the ratio of foreign economic aid to defence spending from the early 1990s. Detailed descriptions of these data are in the appendix to this chapter.

9.1 PUBLIC ECONOMY

A good indicator of the Left-Right ideological policy orientation of a government is the scope of its definition of public goods. A left-leaning ideology has among its core ideas a broad definition of government activities (Dahl and Lindblom 1954: 3–4; Cameron 1978). With wide scope comes an economy more directed and dominated by public activity relative to activity in the private sector. We want to investigate how the Left-Right positions of electorates and their governing institutions are related, if at all, to the size of a nation's political economy.

Figure 9.1 shows the level of political economies created by central governments in all twenty-one nations in the early 1980s and early 1990s, for 1982 and 1992 except in Italy.[1] The first obvious feature is a compression of the cross-national differences between 1982 and 1992. The range of levels in 1982 runs from below 20 to above 50 per cent but only from above 20 to below 50 per cent in 1992. The four top nations of 1982 reduced the size of their public economies over the next decade, most especially Ireland and Luxembourg. Adding to the compression, five below-average nations in the 1980s were the ones whose government spending grew most sharply (Switzerland, Iceland, Finland, Spain, and Norway). On average, excluding Ireland and Luxembourg, the size of public economies increased by two percentage points. All this makes it desirable to investigate size at more than one time point.

A second obvious feature of Figure 9.1 is that government centralization is clearly important in creating differences among these nations. Public activity can be organized by the central government itself or by devolving the funding, organization, and delivery of public activities onto regional and local governments. Given our interest in the way the size of the public sector is affected by the ideological orientations of the national actors—electorates, parliaments, governments, and ministries—we cannot mingle national and subnational governmental spending. This would inhibit any inferences about how the ideological leaning of central government actors affected public activity, over much of which it would have only partial and indirect control. We therefore have to take account of the degree of centralization in a nation by using it as an independent (control) variable. For this purpose we use revenue centralization as reported by the Internal Monetary Fund at three levels (scored −1 for low centralization, 0 for medium centralization, and +1 for high centralization; for details, see the Appendix to this chapter).

A third, less obvious, feature of cross-national differences is that the four nations with economies most open to international trade—the Netherlands, Belgium, Ireland, and Luxembourg—stand at or near the top of the ranking for government size. This is clearly true in 1982 but less so in early 1992, after a decade during which the GDPs of Ireland and Luxembourg grew at a rate one-and-a-half to two times faster than other economies. The more a country's economic activity comes in the form of international trade, the greater is the likelihood that a national government will intervene to protect its people and industry from the vicissitudes of international economic fluctuations (Cameron 1978; Boix 2000, 2001). This generalization is consistent with the data displayed in the figure, especially for 1982. The rearrangement by 1992 is also consistent with doubts that have been expressed about whether the open economy effect is robust. To attain the inferential safety that comes with thoroughness, our analysis takes account of openness as a second

---

[1] Italy's central government spending data for 1992 is missing. We have substituted the 1991 data.

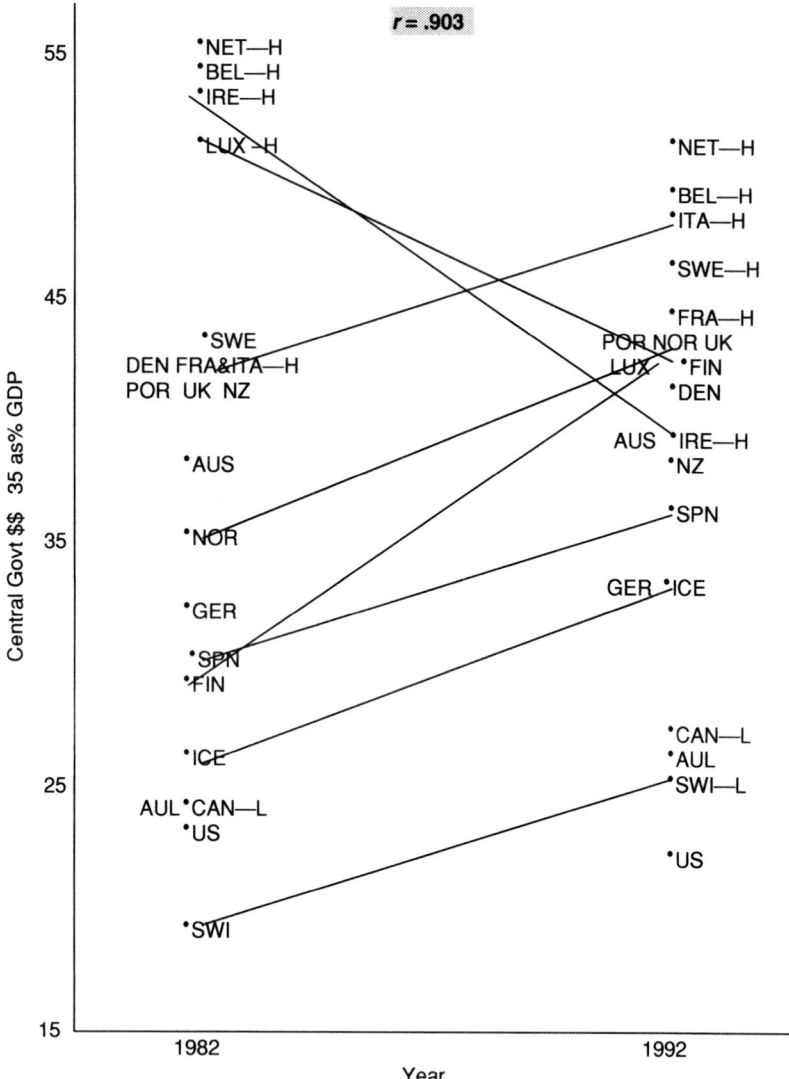

FIGURE 9.1. Central government spending as a per cent of GDP, by nation in 1982 and 1992

Legend: (a) L = low revenue centraliztion; H = high revenue centralization
(b) Lines connecting a country's 1982 and 1992 spending levels appear for those countries with public economies that changed by more than five percentage points.

Source: See appendix to chapter.

independent variable but keeps an eye open for the possibility that its effect, if a true effect, does not hold consistently.

Our main interest lies with which political actors, if any, are responsible for the varying size of public economies among our twenty-one countries while controlling for the effects of governmental centralization and economic openness. For efficient reporting of our results, we first estimate the core equations, one for 1982 and one for 1992, and then add, alternatively and in sequence, each variable representing the Left-Right position of median voters, parliamentary medians, and governments. The core equations are:

1982 Central Government (\$)
as % of GDP = 27.5 + 10.9 Centralization + 0.11 Openness
$\qquad\qquad$ (2.9) (2.4) $\qquad\qquad\qquad$ (0.04)
$\qquad\qquad R^2 = 0.76 \quad$ and $\qquad S_e = 5.6$

1992 Central Government (\$)
as % of GDP = 36.0 + 9.0 Centralization + 0.01 Openness
$\qquad\qquad$ (2.9) (2.6) $\qquad\qquad\qquad$ (0.04)
$\qquad\qquad R^2 = 0.48 \quad$ and $\qquad S_e = 6.2$

where the meaning of each variable is as described previously.

The equations repeat much of what we have already seen visually in Figure 9.1. Centralization of public activity matters a great deal, though more so in the 1980s than in the 1990s. Openness has a large, positive, and statistically significant effect in 1982, but its effect in 1992 is only a quarter to a third as large and is not statistically significant.[2]

Of course these are only control variables. The theoretical matter of concern to us is the answer to this question: What role, if any, does politics play in the cross-national differences in size? Table 9.1 reports analyses that address this point. The left-hand column of the table of coefficients reports the estimated political effects in 1982 and the right-hand column does the same for 1992. Each ideological or policy position of an actor was added as a third variable to the equations reported above, that is, with centralization

---

[2] When Ireland and Luxembourg are dropped from the 1992 analysis, the estimates look much more like those in 1982. We find
1992 Central Govt \$
As % of GDP = 31.0 + 9.7 Centralization + 0.10 Oppenness
$\qquad\qquad$ (3.5) (2.4) $\qquad\qquad\qquad$ (0.06)
with $\qquad R^2 = 0.63 \quad$ and $\quad S_e = 5.5$

We originally controlled for Lijphart's consensus democracy measure in all estimates, on the reasoning that a drive towards consensus might require logrolling that gives the government a role in various issues. Consensus democracy showed no statistically significant effect in either 1982 or 1992, regardless of whether Ireland and Luxembourg were included or excluded. We therefore decided to withhold it from our reported analyses.

158   *The Governing Process*

and openness controlled. Because the Left-Right policy positions are scored so that left positions take low values and right positions take high values, we expect the estimated effects to be negative.

What we find in 1982 is that none are statistically significant, and each has a magnitude very near zero or on the positive side. In brief, we find essentially no effect from political actors on the size of political economies in 1982. In 1992, the message is nearly the same but for one major exception. The position of the median voter is strongly marked, negative, and statistically significant. The difference between a median voter having a position similar to a social democratic party versus having a position close to a conservative party will make about a five percentage point difference in the level of a nation's political economy. This is not a consistent (robust) effect, inasmuch as it does not appear in 1982. However, it does signal the reasonable possibility that electoral politics may be playing some role in defining the scope of public activity.

9.2 WELFARE

Every Western democracy has more or less bought into the proposition that one role of government is to operate a welfare state. Figure 9.2 displays two indicators of welfare. One is Gøsta Epsing-Andersen's measurements of the early 1980s of how much a government through its welfare state provisions

TABLE 9.1. *Relationships between 1982 and 1992 central government spending as a percentage of GDP and Left-Right and economic policy positions of political and governmental actors, controlling for centralization and openness of economy*

Left-Right position of	1982 Partial slope b (S_b)	1992 Partial slope b (S_b)
Median voter	−0.02	−0.26*
	(0.15)	(0.14)
Parliament L-R median	0.00	−0.07
	(0.10)	(0.09)
Government	0.01	−0.02
	(0.09)	(0.09)
Government planning vs market position of		
Parliament L-R median	0.13	−0.06**
	(0.18)	(0.31)
Parliament policy median	0.23	−0.09
	(0.17)	(0.34)
Government	0.11	0.02
	(0.17)	(0.26)
Finance ministry	0.20	0.08
	(0.15)	(0.24)

*statistically significant at $p < 0.05$
** statistically significant at $p < 0.01$

protects persons in vulnerable circumstances—unemployed, disabled, aged—from the vicissitudes of the market. The second is the central government's spending on social welfare (pensions, unemployment, and health services) as a percentage of GDP. For ease of comparison, both measurements are displayed in Figure 9.2 in a z-score scale. The two indicators measure different phenomena, but they are closely associated ($r = 0.813$).

The age distribution in a country is an important feature that separates nations high on the welfare state index and welfare spending from those low on these indicators. The five nations with the lowest percentage of their populations aged 65 and older have low index and spending values while the five nations with the highest percentages of their populations aged 65 and older tend to cluster at the high end. We need to take that into account before attributing cross-national differences to the political preferences of parliaments and governments. It is also apparent that Lijphart's hypothesis, that consensus democracies have more generous welfare state provisions than majoritarian systems, has some empirical force. The six SMD nations—Australia, Canada, France, New Zealand, the UK, and the USA—stand near or below the mean on welfare statism and spending. Scandinavian nations tend to be among the nations with high scores on consensus democracy and stand high on the welfare indicators. As a result, we want to take the consensus versus majoritarian systemic distinction into account before interpreting welfare policy differences. We must not confuse the effects of actor preferences with the systemic effects of the political contexts in which the actors operate.

As we did in the case of central government spending, we will first estimate a set of core equations, one for the early 1980s and another for the early 1990s, and then we add to each, individually and in sequence, the welfare preferences of our four institutional actors. The four are (*a*) the welfare position of the party identified as having the member who is at the Left-Right parliamentary median, (*b*) the party of the member identified as being at the median on the welfare dimension as such, (*c*) the weighted mean welfare position of the party or parties in government, and (*d*) the welfare position of the party or parties controlling the social affairs ministry. The core equations, before the preferences of any actors are taken into account, are as follows:

Early 1980s
$$\text{Welfare Index} = 0.89 + 1.91 \text{ \% Age 65} + 3.45 \text{ ConsensusDemoc}$$
$$(7.10) \quad (0.54) \quad\quad\quad (1.11)$$
$$R^2 = 0.73 \quad \text{and} \quad S_e = 4.4$$

Early 1990s
$$\text{Welfare \$\$\$} = 3.33 + 1.54 \text{ \% Age 65} + 1.48 \text{ ConsensusDemoc}$$
$$(7.79) \quad (0.56) \quad\quad\quad (1.13)$$
$$R^2 = 0.55 \quad \text{and} \quad S_e = 4.3$$

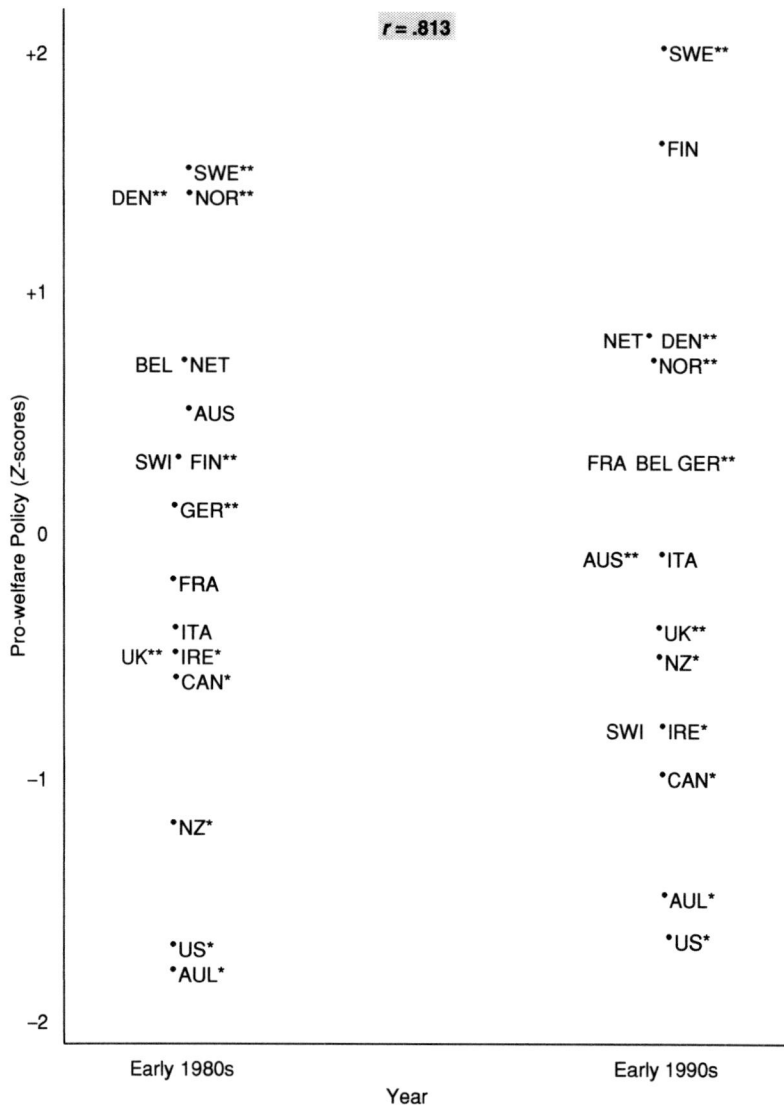

FIGURE 9.2. Central government support for welfare statism, by nation in the early 1980s and early 1990s

Legend:

* Ranks among the five countries with the lowest per cent of population age 65 and older

** Ranks among the five countries with the highest per cent of population age 65 and older

Source: See appendix to chapter (scores in both years reported on standardized z-scale)

where

- *Welfare Index* is the Epsing-Andersen decommodification variable, which in its original metric has scores for Australia = 13.0, the USA = 13.8, ..., Sweden 39.1.
- *Welfare $$$* is welfare spending as a percentage of GDP, which in its original metric has scores for the USA = 15.6, Australia = 16.4, ..., Sweden = 37.1.
- *% Age 65* is the percentage of a country's population age 65 or older.
- *ConsensusDemoc* is Lijphart's consensus democracy means on his first (executives-parties) dimension for years 1971–96 with scores among our 17 nations ranging from the UK = −1.39 to Switzerland = 1.87.

The age distribution variable has a large and statistically significant effect on both dependent variables. A percentage point difference in the population age 65 and over makes almost a two-unit change in the welfare state index and pushes up spending by a point and three-quarters. Liphart's consensus democracy measure withstands the control for the age distribution in relation to the welfare index but falls to statistical insignificance on the early 1990s spending measure[3].

The results of adding the preferences of our four institutional actors to the core equations are reported in the top portion of Table 9.2. Of the eight possibilities, only one is statistically significant. In the early 1980s, the welfare position of the party of the Left-Right parliamentary median shows a large, negative, and statistically significant effect. A ten-point difference in the welfare location of the parliamentary Left-Right median is expected to move welfare efforts about three and a half points, that is, about the difference between Italy's and Germany's scores. Even then, however, the effect is not robust in the sense that for the 1990s welfare spending measure, the parliamentary Left-Right median's welfare position shows an estimated effect of essentially zero. It would be a mistake either to make much of this transient effect or to ignore it as a one-time phenomenon. Something is going on in regard to preferences but nothing much that is consistent.

9.3 INTERNATIONAL ORIENTATION

Our third and final set of policy indicators refers to international affairs. For the early 1980s we have data on each country's foreign economic aid as a percentage of GDP and for the early 1990s aid as a percentage of its military

---

[3] The consensus democracy measure is related to welfare spending for the seventeen nations under investigation here in a manner similar to what Lijphart reports for his eighteen countries, our seventeen plus Japan (Lijphart 1999: 296). Its bivariate slope with welfare spending is 3.02 (standard error = 1.61). Thus we know it is the control for the age distribution that makes consensus democracy fall to statistical insignificance.

TABLE 9.2. *Relationships between 1980s and 1990s welfare and international policies and policy positions of governmental actors, controlling for consensus democracy on both policies and for aged population in the case of welfare*

Welfare policy position of	1980s Partial slope b (S_b)	1990s Partial slope b (S_b)
Parliament L-R median	−0.40*	0.03
	(0.20)	(0.19)
Parliament policy median	−0.29	−0.01
	(0.20)	(0.21)
Government	−0.25	0.05
	(0.20)	(0.22)
Social Affairs Ministry	−0.19	−0.16
	(0.19)	(0.18)
Peace vs militarist policy position of		
Parliament L-R median	−0.04*	−3.04**
	(0.02)	(0.89)
Parliament policy median	−0.03	−1.86
	(0.02)	(1.21)
Government	−0.02	−0.01
	(0.02)	(0.97)
Defence Ministry	−0.02	0.26
	(0.02)	(0.71)
Foreign Affairs Ministry	−0.02	0.82
	(0.02)	(0.64)

* statistically significant at $p < 0.05$
** statistically significant at $p < 0.01$

spending (missing data on Iceland, which has no military). The values on both variables for all twenty countries are displayed in Figure 9.3. The two are related but refer to different policy phenomena ($r = 0.557$). One has to do with foreign generosity relative to a country's wealth whereas the other has to do with foreign generosity relative to a country's military posture in international affairs. One example of the distinction is Denmark, which is merely above average on its generosity relative to its wealth, but is very generous relative to its investment in its military. On the other side, the USA is below average in its generosity relative to wealth and much below average in its generosity relative to its military investment.

The core equations for these two dependent variables estimate a country's international orientation as a function of Lijphart's consensus democracy indicator. The equations are:

Early 1980s

Foreign Econ Aid = 0.41 + 0.09 ConsensusDemoc, with
(0.07) (0.06)
with $R^2 = 0.10$ and $S_e = 0.29$

and

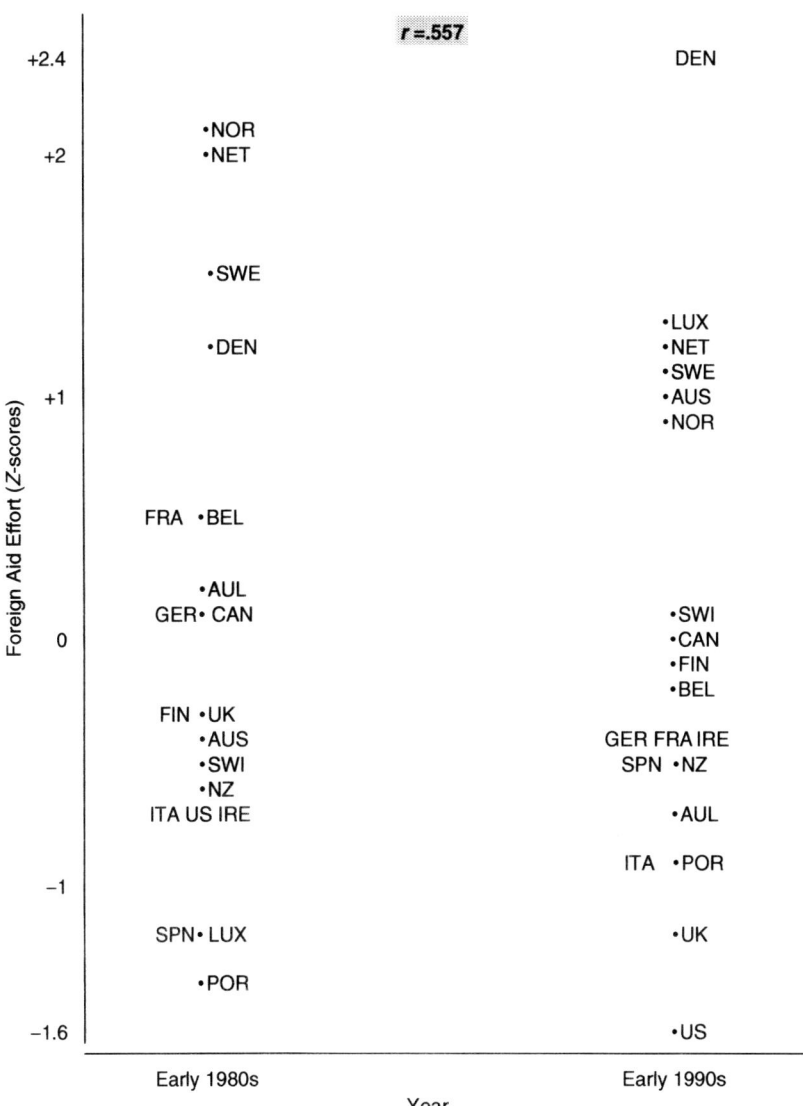

FIGURE 9.3. Foreign aid support (1980s) and foreign aid relative to defence spending (1990s), by nation

Source: See appendix to chapter (scores in both years reported on standardized *z*-scale)

Early 1990s
$$\text{Aid/Defence \$\$\$} = 21.60 + 5.85 \text{ ConsensusDemoc, with}$$
$$(2.47) \quad (2.37)$$
with $R^2 = 0.25$ and $S_e = 10.6$

where

- *Foreign Econ Aid* is foreign economic aid as a percentage of gross national product averaged over the period 1982–5, which in their original metric have scores for Portugal $= 0.04$, the USA $= 0.24, \ldots$, Denmark $= 0.79, \ldots$, Sweden $= 0.94$.
- *Aid/Defence \$\$\$* is foreign economic aid as a ratio of military spending averaged over the period 1992–5, which in their original metric have scores for the USA $= 4$, Portugal $= 12, \ldots$, Sweden $= 36, \ldots$, Denmark $= 52$.
- *ConsensusDemoc* is Lijphart's consensus democracy measure on his first (executives-parties) dimension for years 1971–96 with scores among the 20 nations ranging from the UK $= -1.39$ to Switzerland $= 1.87$.

The effect of consensus democracy is just short of statistical significance ($p = 0.086$, one tail test) on foreign economic aid as such, but it has a significant effect on aid in relation to military spending.

The bottom half of Table 9.2 reports the estimated effects of the preferences of the five actors hypothesized as potentially being in control of policy. Only the party of the Left-Right median parliamentarian appears to have a significantly estimated effect on the aid and aid/defence policies. The estimated effects of the preferences of other actors are usually in the proper (negative) direction, but none is statistically significant. If any actor's specific policy preferences are important for the policies in these countries, it appears to be those of the party with which the parliamentary Left-Right median affiliates, as was the case for welfare policy.

9.4 CAN WE GET OUT FROM HERE?

Far from taking us to the firm ground of democratic control, the analyses of actual policy carry us further into the quaking morass where we were left by government declarations. There is some very modest evidence of transient representational processes going on, with the median voters' preferences linked to government activity and size in the 1990s but not the 1980s. In specific policy areas the overall median party in parliament seems to get its preferences through, except for welfare in the 1990s—strange because welfare is so integral to Left-Right positions. At least this influence of the parliamentary median supports the corresponding mandate ideas while the influence of the median voter in Table 9.1 is at least interpretable as democratic control being exercised. All the positive results demonstrate the power of the median.

Yet, when we think that only four of our thirty-two potential coefficients are statistically significant this is decidedly underwhelming. Four are slightly more than one might expect by chance but not by much. Moreover, in two cases, overall spending and welfare, the statistically significant relationship appears at one time but not another. Such transient relationships hardly provide the 'necessary connection' between popular preferences and policy demanded by democratic theory (Saward 1998: 51).

A first question in light of these discouraging results is methodological—whether the policy data are so crude and unrefined that they are simply incapable of revealing the relationships that do exist. It is hard to imagine that our elaborate representative procedures simply do not produce consistent democratic control—though some authors have argued this (King and Laver 1993). On the other hand our policy measures are well attested ones, used by authors of the stature of Lijphart (1999) and Esping-Anderson (1990), with positive results. It seems unlikely that they have simply pegged out on us. Certainly spending data are slow moving and hard to prove causal connections on (Hofferbert et al. 1993) but it can be done (McDonald et al. 1999). The nature of spending data may give us clues to what is going on (see later) but is not in itself an explanation for the relative absence of relationships.

Furthermore, spending patterns confirm some of what we have already got from the Government Declarations. Certainly there are criticisms to be made of these as policy measures, the main one being of course that they are an intent rather than a fulfilment in regard to policy. Still, they do include proposals for legislation and administration not covered by expenditures. What mostly came out from Table 8.1 was the direct control of the median voter over general matters of policy (Left-Right orientation of governments) as with overall Government expenditure in Table 9.1. On specific policy the individual median party was influential over declarations whereas the overall median party took the lead in expenditures. At least there is convergence between the analyses on the median being important in some shape or form, even if it is not the same one.

Inconsistent and partial validation of weak relationships does not sum to very much however. At best it seems to indicate that authorized democratic agents exert a patchy influence over policy but seemingly struggle against other influences which crowd them out.

What could these influences be? Possibly they are the ones we have recognized as control variables: cultural predispositions linked to negotiations which give everybody a little but nobody everything (consensus democracy), economic forces operating in a certain direction without regard to political actors (open economy), and demographic developments which leave no room for manoeuvre (aged population). Or a bureaucracy or power elite might be controlling things behind the scenes. Alternatively there may be overall confusion, with decisions determined by situational conjunctures which vary largely by chance (Kingdon 1984).

Or so at least it may look from the short-term perspective of individual elections and governments, where the only way of explaining the outcome is to retell the story—the typical focus of the historian rather than the scientist. An alternative, however, which is facilitated by the overtime nature of our data, is to examine the long-term processes which underlie individual outcomes. Our strong suspicion is that what obscures the real decision-makers is none of the factors listed above but the actual operation of democracy itself over time—the very alternating forces restoring democratic competition of Chapter 6. It is the transient nature of power holding in democracy, constantly threatened by and changed by elections, that prevents clear-cut short-term control from emerging. If any one party or ideological persuasion were fixed in power over a long period they could well take policy in the direction they prefer. But of course that is precisely what representative democracy as a system guards against. Either it produces coalitions where policy has to be negotiated and compromised between partners. Or it creates an 'elective dictatorship' where everything a government does in its limited term of office is subverted by the next one.

Seen from close hand, elections create the somewhat chaotic policy processes we have been examining. Standing further back one may well see regression to the mean or median just as with representational biases versus distortions in Chapter 7. Long-term processes are at least worth examining from this point of view. We start by re-analysing the nature of our dependent variable—policy expenditures—in Chapter 10, before seeing how it can be related in a long-term perspective to democratic actors in Chapter 12.

APPENDIX

Data used in this chapter come from various sources. Government spending figures are taken from the International Monetary Fund's *International Financial Statistics Yearbook* (2001) and *Government Financial Statistics Yearbooks* (1984 and 2001). Data on the two welfare variables have been supplied by Arend Lijphart, as have the figures on foreign economic aid and defence spending.

All data are available in electronic form on a website at Binghamton University. The address is http://binghamton.edu/polsci/research/facdata For the convenience of readers and for the written record, we describe the details of the data and the coding choices we made to construct these data.

Policies: Policy and related data cover government activities during the early 1980s and early 1990s. As independent variables referring to policy preferences of electorates, parliaments, and governments we used one government from the early part of each decade. Below, we identify those governments and thereafter provide the definitions of our variables, their sources, and special considerations.

Governments: The governments of the twenty-one countries according to which we identified the election, parliament, governments, and ministers are listed below. Government numbers, one for the 1980s and a second for the 1990s, refer to those assigned by Woldendorp et al. (2000).

Country & Governments	Country & Governments	Country & Governments
Australia: #s 22, 27	Germany: #s 19, 25	Norway: #s 18, 24
Austria: #s 15, 19	Iceland: #s 16, 21	Portugal: #s 8, 12
Belgium: #s 32, 35	Ireland: #s 13, 17	Spain: #s 3, 6
Canada: #s 15, 18	Italy: #s 41, 50	Sweden: #s 17, 23
Denmark: #s 22, 27	Luxembourg: #s 13, 15	Switzerland: #s 38, 48
Finland: #s 38, 44	Netherlands: #s 16, 20	United Kingdom: #s 15, 18
France: #s 46, 52	New Zealand: #s 16, 22	United States: #s 10, 12

Variables: We use five policy indicators as dependent variables in this chapter. We also used indicators of political preferences for five actors. And we controlled for four different systemic features. The policy variables include the following:

1. *Consolidated central government spending as a percentage of GDP*—this refers to expenditures within the territorial jurisdiction of the central authority and includes items that are sometimes off-budget, such as pensions. The government spending data come from the IMF's *Government Finance Statistics Yearbook*. The 1992 data are from the 1999 yearbook Table B, line I; the 1982 data come from the 1992 yearbook, Table B, line I. GDP are from the IMF's *International Financial Statistics Yearbook 2002*, on line 99b.c. Data cover all twenty-one countries in 1982, but Italy's central government spending is missing for 1992. We used Italy's 1991 spending data.
2. *Welfare state support (early 1980s)*—Esping-Anderson's scoring of welfare state efforts (see Epsing-Anderson 1990). Arend Lijphart kindly supplied these data to us. They exist for seventeen of our twenty-one nations. Data for Iceland, Luxembourg, Portugal, and Spain are missing.
3. *Social spending (early 1990s)*—the level of social spending as a percentage of GDP from the early 1990s. Social spending includes expenditures on pensions, unemployment, aid to the disabled and health. Arend Lijphart supplied these data to us. They exist for seventeen of our twenty-one nations. Data for Iceland, Luxembourg, Portugal, and Spain are missing.
4. *Foreign economic aid (early 1980s)*—foreign economic aid as a percentage of GDP, averaged over the years 1982–85. Arend Lijphart supplied these

data to us. They exist for twenty of our twenty-one nations; data for Iceland are missing.

5. *Economic aid as percentage of Defence spending (early 1990s)*—foreign economic aid as a percentage of defence expenditures, averaged over the years 1992–95. Arend Lijphart supplied these data to us. They exist for twenty of our twenty-one nations; data for Iceland, which has no military, are missing.

6. *Government centralization*—the extent to which government tax revenue collection is concentrated in a country's central government. This comes from the IMF's *Government Finance Statistics Yearbook 1984* (p. 46), the last year the IMF reports these figure. Experimentation with the variable indicated that a threefold classification—scored low = -1, medium = 0, and high = $+1$ —distinguished among the countries in a linear manner. The cutpoints in the classification are at central government percentages of less than 70 (low), 70 to 90 (medium), and 90 and above (high).

7. *Open economy*—the degree of openness of international trade. This is calculated as imports plus exports as a percentage of GDP. Data on imports and exports are from the IMF's *International Financial Statistics Yearbook 2002*, on line 98c.c. (imports) and line 90c.c (exports). GDP data are from the IMF's *International Financial Statistics Yearbook, 2002,* line 99b.c. Data exist for all twenty-one countries, but for Italy we use the 1991 data to match its government spending data.

8. *Percentage of population age 65 and older*—this is self-explanatory. Data come from OECD. Data exist for all seventeen countries for which we have welfare data.

PART IV

The Democratic Process

10

Long-Term Policy Regimes: Incrementalism Put in Context

One way to resolve the dilemma of no one seeming to control short-term decision-making is to shift our focus to long-term outcomes. We already know from earlier studies of public policy in advanced industrial democracies (cf. Lindblom 1959, 1965) that policy has a dynamic, but also that most policy decisions are rather sticky. Policies change from one government to the next but not much and not rapidly.

This point has been most cogently and powerfully made in theories of incrementalism, particularly in regard to expenditures which are the most easily available and comparable indicator of policy outcomes (Davis et al. 1966). But it also seems to apply to a range of other policies. Among most of the twenty-one democracies we are investigating, policies related to issues as diverse as voting rights and railways look much the way they did a generation ago. The same can be said of abortion, capital punishment, euthanasia, health services, unemployment compensation, highways, and taxes on income. Of course, all of these look very different over the long term, from the middle of the nineteenth century for example. Then, women were disenfranchised nearly everywhere and the property-less almost everywhere; rail systems were being laid; abortion was self-induced or performed in some back alley; a death sentence was a commonplace punishment for capital crimes, euthanasia was murder, treatment for health concerns existed only for the well to do; unemployment was a hard fact of life; and taxes were on property and through indirect levies.

The long-versus short-term contrasts are facts on the historical record. However, we will arrive at the same conclusion of short-term stability if we engage in plausible hypothesizing about what is likely to happen during the tenure of any one government. Which hypothesis is more plausible?

> *H1:* A bourgeois coalition of parties with a majority in parliament and control of government in Norway will adopt welfare and defence policies like those of Australia or the USA.
> *H2:* A bourgeois coalition of parties with a majority in parliament and control of government in Norway will adopt welfare and defence policies like those in Norway in the year before the coalition took control.

Our money is on continuity in Norwegian policies over time. Policies change, but not in a way that has them veering sharply left and right every few years.

Of course these arguments can be, and have been, employed against the influence of democratic actors like parties and in favour of permanent bureaucrats or impersonal, unchanging forces influencing decisions. Wildavsky and his associates (Davis et al. 1966) maintain that slow incremental change in expenditures points more to the impossibility of changing departmental budgets and to bureaucratic bargaining involving only minor adjustments and tradeoffs, than to the influence of elected legislatures or presidents over budgetary decisions. King and Laver (1999) strongly endorse this position, remarking that government expenditure can as well be related to national baseball scores as to the priorities of political parties.

These conclusions rest simultaneously on a position of statistical strength and statistical weakness. Their strength lies in the fact that expenditures in one year correlate very highly with expenditures in the next. It is difficult to argue over the existence of a relationship when r^2 values are 0.9 and higher. The statistical weakness of the evidence is that autocorrelation in the dependent variable is not by itself a satisfactory basis on which to erect a theory of politics, particularly when it excludes the very elections and parties which substantive theory points to as the democratic movers in the process. Indeed, if the incrementalists are right, there is no democratic control over decision-making. This conclusion however rests more on the absence of satisfactory indicators with which to measure potential democratic influences, and on the restrictions on single country cases, than on any rigorous statistical analysis of the possibilities (McDonald et al. 1999).

This is not of course to decry the insight that one year's policy will be mostly like last year's, with only minor (perhaps technical and bureaucratic) adjustments. Limited variation, and slow change in the short-run, have the capability of making it seem as if no one in particular, or very different actors in different situations, control policy making (just as we ourselves found in Chapters 8 and 9).

However, other studies hint at the possibility of long-term political influences being at work. (Stimson et al. 1995; Erikson et al. 2001; McDonald et al. 1999). If in the USA we relate presidential policy intentions to long-term (mean party position) and short-term (current election position) policy positions of presidential parties, we find the former exert most influence, though short-term responses are not lacking.

One point that incrementalist theories seem to miss is who sets and maintains the base-point around which short-term changes oscillate? To continue the example used above, policy one year in Norway looks much like policy next year in Norway. But it is substantially different from American policy in all sorts of areas. Is this simply because both operate within the context of (different) crucial decisions taken far back in time? Or is it a continuing response to set preferences on the part of some political actor, possibly the median voter, as mandate theory would indicate?

10.1 THE PACE OF POLICY CHANGE

That is the point we intend to investigate in this part of our book. To do so we need first to look more closely at the nature of the dependent variable (actual policy outputs). In Chapter 11 we shall look at the independent (political) variables and, in particular, look to see how their fluctuation and rate of change compare with that of policy. In Chapter 12 we put the two together in a long-term context showing how they can be related in a way consistent with median mandate ideas about the working of democracy. Chapter 13 relates these findings explicitly to our earlier theoretical concerns and to the electoral process.

Figure 10.1 provides an illustrative picture of six public economies annually from 1973 to 1995. (Figures are taken from the IMF sources described in the Appendix to Chapter 9.) The six countries include two highly centralized states (Belgium and the Netherlands), two moderately centralized states (the UK and Germany), and two relatively decentralized states (Canada and Switzerland). The dynamics are apparent. There are upward trends, and there are similar cyclical/seasonal movements where government size increases noticeably in the late 1970s to early 1980s and levels off thereafter. Even more apparent, however, are the persistent similarities and differences between and among nations. The two countries starting the period with large public economies stay persistently larger than the others. The two that start in the middle stay in the middle. And, the two that start low stay low. Even more revealing are the facts that, of all the variation in the political economy among these six countries, 93.2 per cent is associated with cross-national differences and only 5.8 per cent is associated with time.[1] If we were trying to understand policymaking in these six democracies, our best hope would rest with differences across nations rather than differences across time.[2]

---

[1] These percentages come from estimating two naïve models of public economy size differences. One model uses five dummy variables for the six countries. The other uses twenty-two dummy variables for the twenty-three years. The naïve nation model for the six nations in Figure 10.1 has an R^2 of 0.932; the naïve time model for the six nations has a R^2 of 0.058.

[2] Observed constants make it impossible to test one's explanation, because no degrees of freedom exist. Any explanation will do, and therefore no alternative explanations can be ruled out. For the same reasons, near constants make testing an explanation difficult. In the case at hand, the difficulty is even more severe than the R^2 value of 0.058 for the years suggests. Of the 5.8 per cent variation associated with time, nearly 60 per cent is attributable to a simple trend. If we take the usual step of writing off common trends (to say nothing of common cycles and seasons) as consequences, so far as we can tell, of unspecified maturation processes, our efforts to explain time differences would focus on explaining 2.4 per cent of the overall variation we are observing. In short, while explaining variation is far different from explaining a phenomenon, having variation to explain is a vital prerequisite for testing a proposed explanation.

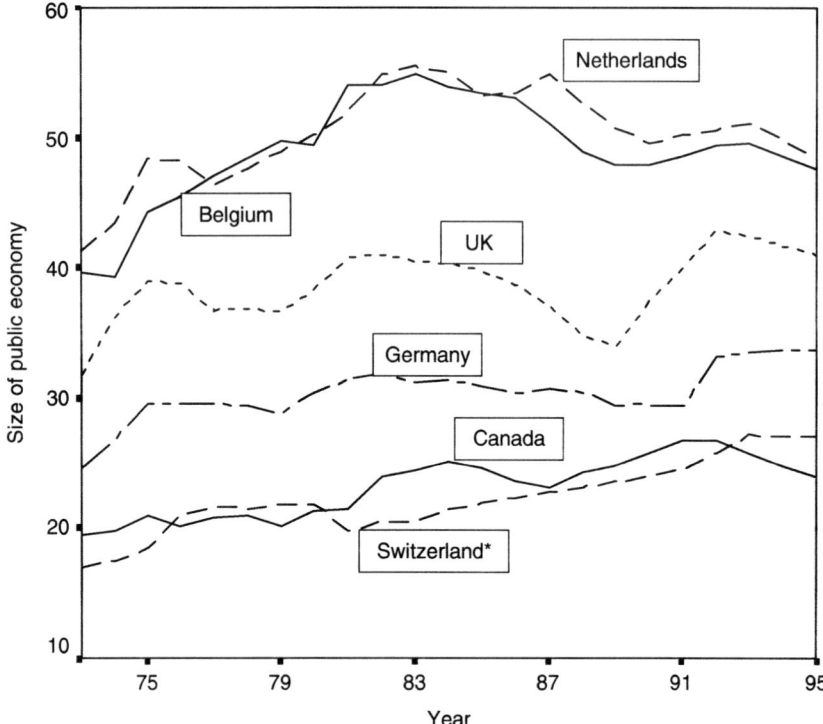

FIGURE 10.1. Long-run cross-national differences in six countries' public economies
*Swiss data are missing from 1985 to 1990

Does this pattern generalize to all twenty-one countries under investigation here, or is it the mere consequence of having selected six nations that differ fundamentally on how centralized their public sectors are (or on some other characteristic relevant to the size of a public economy)? Table 10.1 reports the means and standard deviations for public economies, welfare spending, and defence spending over twenty-one nations in the period 1973–95. So far as the political economy is concerned, the six nations stack the deck, though only modestly, in favour of cross-national versus cross-temporal differences. Nevertheless, as reported in the summary statistics at the bottom of the table, a nation-based statistical model accounts for 77 per cent of the variation among the twenty-one countries across twenty-three years. The year-based statistical model accounts for just 11.7 per cent of the variation, of which two-thirds is attributable to a common trend (0.78/0.117 = 0.667). When we turn to welfare spending as a percentage of GDP, the cross-national versus cross-temporal contrast is even more apparent. For welfare spending, the nation-based model has a R^2 of 0.837 compared to the

TABLE 10.1. *Policy regime estimated by mean spending on public economy, welfare, and international relations in twenty-one democracies, 1973–1995*

	Public economy			Welfare			Defence		
	Mean	s	N	Mean	s	N	Mean	s	N
Australia	24.4	2.6	23	7.0	1.3	23	2.2	0.2	23
Austria	37.6	2.9	23	17.2	1.2	23	1.1	0.1	23
Belgium	48.9	4.1	23	20.4	1.8	16	2.7	0.2	16
Canada	23.1	2.3	23	8.6	1.7	22	1.7	0.1	22
Denmark	37.8	4.0	23	15.4	1.5	23	2.1	0.2	23
Finland	31.2	5.9	23	10.7	4.4	23	1.5	0.2	23
France	40.8	4.1	23	17.6	1.5	19	2.7	0.2	19
Germany	30.4	2.1	23	14.8	1.3	23	2.5	0.6	23
Iceland	29.6	3.0	23	5.2	1.4	23	0.0	0.0	23
Ireland	44.4	5.8	23	11.7	1.1	14	1.4	0.2	14
Italy	41.4	6.8	19	13.6	2.2	14	1.6	0.2	14
Luxembourg	42.4	5.4	23	20.9	2.9	23	0.9	0.2	23
Netherlands	50.3	3.6	23	18.7	1.2	22	2.7	0.3	22
New Zealand	37.5	4.5	22	11.4	2.2	21	1.7	0.3	21
Norway	36.5	4.0	23	12.7	2.0	21	2.9	0.2	21
Portugal	37.3	7.7	23	9.3	1.0	13	2.9	1.1	13
Spain	30.0	6.2	23	13.8	2.6	22	1.4	0.3	22
Sweden	40.4	6.1	23	19.1	3.3	23	2.9	0.3	23
Switzerland	22.0	3.3	17	10.5	1.6	17	2.0	0.2	17
UK	38.5	2.8	23	11.6	2.3	23	4.8	0.8	23
USA	21.7	1.5	23	6.7	0.7	23	4.9	0.6	23
% Variance explained by									
Nation		77.0			83.2			90.9	
Year		11.7			6.9			2.9	
Trend		7.8			5.0			1.6	

year-based 0.069 (of which three quarters is attributable to a common trend). And, on defence spending as a percentage of GDP, cross-national variation scores even higher against time. The nation-based model has an R^2 of 0.909, and the year-based model has an R^2 of just 0.029 (of which half is attributable to a common trend).

What do all these statistics tell us? First, the policies we are observing differ a great deal between countries. Second, the cross-national differences in one year persist to the next. Countries are marked as being on different policy tracks, which persist. We term these tracks their 'policy regime', to emphasize their long-term nature and to underline their stability.

We can take the analysis of policy dynamics a step further and estimate just how much of a policy adjustment there is from one year to the next. The core feature of our dynamic analysis is an equation linking current to previous spending. This is constructed by adding an autoregressive term (spending in the previous year) to the equation with the nation dummy variables. That is,

$$\text{Govt Spending}_t = \alpha + \beta \text{Govt Spending}_{t-1} + \Sigma\lambda(N) + \varepsilon_t$$

where *Govt Spending* at t and $t-1$ are the size of the public economy in the current (t) and the previous ($t-1$) years; and N is a matrix of dummy variables for the nations. This equation estimates two substantively important features of the policy process: (*a*) the speed per annum by which spending moves, and (*b*) the equilibrium level of spending within a country. The speed is estimated by the value of one minus the slope, that is $1 - \beta$. A country's equilibrium spending is estimated by dividing the speed of adjustment into the intercept plus the slope of the country's dummy variable, that is, $(\alpha + \lambda_i)/(1 - \beta)$.

An example will help to clarify the substantive implications of this calculation. Given a slope equal to 0.8, the per annum speed of adjustment to spending is 0.2; we can expect spending in a country to move from where it is to where it is going (the equilibrium value) by increments of 20 per cent. Imagine a country is at a 30 per cent level of spending in year $t-1$ and is headed for 35 per cent. The next year spending in that country moves to 31 per cent, a 20 per cent closing of the five-unit gap between 30 per cent and 35 per cent. From year t to $t+1$ the country closes the four-unit gap by another 20 per cent, going from 31 to 31.8. Slope values with lower magnitudes indicate a more rapid yearly adjustment. Given a slope of 0.5, then to whatever extent spending is removed from its equilibrium it will move halfway towards that equilibrium in one year. If the slope is 0.7, so that the speed of adjustment is 0.3 ($1 - 0.7$), then it will take about two years to move halfway. Generally, the time it will take to move halfway is given by $b^k = 0.5$, where b is the slope and k is the number of years it will take to move halfway (i.e. 0.5). For $b = 0.8$, it will take a little over three years; for $b = 0.9$, it will take between six and seven years. We expect policy outputs in our twenty-one developed democracies to be slow moving and therefore the speed of adjustment to be perhaps 0.9, meaning a 10 per cent adjustment towards equilibrium each year.

Finally, imagine that the country whose dummy variable has been withheld from the equation (so as to stand as the baseline against which equilibriums of other countries are estimated) has an equilibrium of 35. Then the intercept of the equation will be 7, since then the intercept divided by one minus the slope is 35, that is, $[7/(1 - 0.8)] = 35$. A country whose equilibrium is 40, 5 units higher than the baseline country, will have a dummy variable coefficient of 1, since the intercept plus the dummy coefficient divided by one minus the slope is 40, that is $[(7 + 1)/(1 - 0.8)] = 40$.

In the present context we are most interested in the speed with which policies change. For each of three policy variables—size of public economies, welfare spending, and defence spending—we have estimated those speeds. We find the following.

Size of the public economy

$$\text{Government Spending}_{it} = \alpha + 0.846 \text{ Govt Spending}_{it-1} + \Sigma \lambda_{it-1}(N=it) + \varepsilon_{it}$$
$$(0.019)$$

Welfare

$$\text{Welf Spending}_{it} = \alpha + 0.869 \text{ Welf Spending}_{it-1} + \Sigma \lambda_{it}(N_{it}) + \varepsilon_{it}$$
$$(0.021)$$

Defence

$$\text{Defence Spending}_{it} = \alpha + 0.852 \text{ Defn Spending}_{it-1} + \Sigma \lambda_{it}(N_{it}) + \varepsilon_{ie}$$
$$(0.021)$$

In all three cases, the slope is close to 0.85 and thus the speed of adjustment in spending overall as well as welfare and defence is only about 15 per cent per year. For a parliament or government 5 points away from its equilibrium, movement towards that equilibrium in the first year is only three-quarters of a percentage point. In the second year the movement is just over five-eighths of a percentage point. Indeed, to move half way towards its equilibrium is estimated to take more than four years, which is about double the average duration of a government and about the length of an average parliament. Policies do not change rapidly.

What are the consequences of slow moving policies? Take a situation where a social democratic party takes full control of a country's governing apparatus after four years of conservative rule. We can expect the social democrats to expand the size of the public economy relative to the conservatives. Let us assume that the difference is to have a public economy set at 30 per cent by the conservatives and 35 per cent by the social democrats. Also, assume that when the conservatives took office four years earlier the public economy was 32 per cent. By the end of the conservative tenure, its size is expected to have moved halfway between 32 and 30, to 31 per cent. After four years of social democratic control, the expected movement is halfway between 31 per cent, where they found it when they took control, and 35 per cent, where they want to be. Given four years of social democratic government, the size of the public economy will move to 33 per cent, halfway from 31 to 35. Thus across eight years of watching this tug of war over spending play out, the expected time series of spending will have been 32 per cent to start with. Then, by year, it unfolds as follows.

Conservatives have control

$$Y_0 = 32\% \rightarrow y_t = 31.7 \quad y_2 = 31.4 \quad y_3 = 31.2 \quad y_4 = 31.0.$$

Social democrats take control

$$Y_5 = 31.6 \; y_6 = 32.0 \; y_7 = 32.5 \; y_8 = 32.9.$$

Over an eight-year governing period, involving two governments with quite different ideological colorations, the size of the public economy centres around thirty-two, moving around that position within a range of 32 ± 1. The political ideological inclinations make a difference, for we have imposed that on our hypothetical set up. But the fact of the political situation, that no one party is in control continually, in combination with the slow movement of policies, have the effect of centring the system near a 32 per cent level over the course of the eight year period. An electorate that moves back and forth from conservative to social democrat most likely has a median voter somewhere in the middle, between these two parties, This implies that the alternations inherent in democratic politics have led to a long-term outcome somewhere near to what the median voter prefers.

10.2 COMPARATIVE EVIDENCE

In the foregoing example we have identified both a policy regime—measured through the stable point or equilibrium around which actual outcomes oscillate—and possible influences on it, in the shape of the median voter. The dynamics of median voter position taking we investigate in Chapter 11. Here, however, we can examine the points around which actual policies have fluctuated in each of our twenty-one democracies. The numbers in Table 10.2 flesh out the idea of stable, national, policy tendencies that endure over time. Actually we have three examples of this in the areas of the public economy, welfare, and international relations.

The dynamic equilibrium estimates in Table 10.2 come fairly close in numeric terms to the means reported as alternative measures of policy regimes in Table 10.1. This in itself is an important substantive finding which we can make clear through a simple analogy with estimates of body weight.

Suppose we had a sample of twelve- to twenty-two-year-olds and measured their weight each year. If we took the overall mean as an estimate of typical weight it would be quite misleading as a statement of what each would be expected to weigh as adults, or children. It would probably come out to what they weighed when they were about eighteen but differ considerably from their average weight at twelve or twenty-two. Much better to use the dynamic equilibrium point which gives an indication of where they are heading as adults (or where they have come from as children). As dynamics dominate these differences, the equilibrium point will differ substantially from the mean.

Contrast this with the same group from twenty-two to thirty-two. Assuming these are normal healthy young adults, their body weight should remain

TABLE 10.2. *Policy Regimes estimated by spending equilibria on public economy, welfare, and international relations in twenty-one democracies, 1973–1995*

	Public economy			Welfare			Defence		
	Estimated Equilib	*Observed*		*Estimated Equilib*	*Observed*		*Estimated Equilib*	*Observed*	
		Min	Max		Min	Max		Min	Max
Australia	26.3	18.1	27.8	8.5	4.2	9.2	2.0	1.9	2.6
Austria	40.6	31.1	41.4	18.6	14.4	19.0	1.0	0.9	1.3
Belgium	51.0	39.2	54.8	22.5	16.1	22.7	2.6	2.3	3.0
Canada	24.2	19.4	26.8	9.8	6.5	11.6	1.7	1.5	2.0
Denmark	40.3	29.1	42.8	16.9	12.2	18.4	2.0	1.7	2.5
Finland	35.4	22.8	44.4	13.5	6.2	20.2	1.5	1.2	1.9
France	44.1	31.6	46.2	18.8	14.9	19.8	2.6	2.5	3.2
Germany	32.7	24.7	33.7	16.4	11.0	16.9	2.1	1.4	3.2
Iceland	31.0	25.5	34.4	6.0	3.8	7.7	0.0	0.0	0.0
Ireland	45.1	34.1	53.1	10.6	10.2	13.0	1.0	1.1	1.8
Italy	48.0	29.6	50.8	17.4	10.5	17.8	1.7	1.2	1.9
Luxembourg	44.7	31.5	46.2	22.8	14.1	26.0	0.9	0.4	1.2
Netherlands	52.6	41.3	55.5	19.5	15.7	21.0	2.4	1.9	3.1
New Zealand	38.0	28.4	44.4	13.1	6.9	14.7	1.7	1.1	2.2
Norway	38.6	30.1	43.3	14.0	9.9	15.8	2.9	2.5	3.3
Portugal	44.0	14.7	46.2	10.8	6.6	10.4	1.4	2.1	6.2
Spain	34.2	19.4	39.4	15.8	9.6	19.7	1.2	1.0	2.2
Sweden	45.2	28.0	51.7	22.4	11.9	24.5	2.7	2.5	3.4
Switzerland	24.8	17.0	27.1	12.9	7.9	13.2	1.9	1.6	2.3
UK	40.8	31.8	42.8	13.5	7.5	15.5	4.2	2.0	5.6
USA	22.4	18.7	23.9	6.8	5.8	8.1	4.3	3.6	6.0

fairly constant. The main differences will now be between individuals rather than ages. Hence the mean, reflecting weight around twenty-seven, will provide a good overall estimate. Moreover it will coincide closely with the dynamic equilibrium point, reflecting the fact that there is little dynamic growth going on, so the end state of the group resembles closely that at the starting point and the middle.

The coincidence of mean spending (see Table 10.1) and spending equilibria (see Table 10.2) thus powerfully reinforces our earlier findings on the main differences—at any rate within the time period we cover—being cross-national rather than temporal. There is little dynamic; policy regimes are stable; and we should look to relate them to long-term factors distinguishing countries rather than short-term fluctuations in the political forces within each country.

10.3 ANALYTIC IMPLICATIONS

The major conclusion of this chapter is that we must take a long-term approach to studying policy and build into this a recognition of its underlying stability. Looking at policy regimes rather than individual policy decisions further implies that we focus on the major, cross-national differences that create enduring policy regimes rather than the minor over time ones which create oscillation rather than enduring change. Dramatic announcements about radical change often mask underlying steadiness and stability.

This finding explains a commonly observed phenomenon of democratic party politics—the unbounded enthusiasm of activists after an election followed by disillusion with 'their' government a year or two on. Change never goes far enough or fast enough as radicals either of left or right want. The reason is not that changes are not made but that they are slow, because of pre-existing budgets, contracts, commitments, and entitlements in the field of expenditure; time constraints, due process, legislative and social opposition, and administrative bottlenecks in the field of legislation. Effective change takes the whole of a government's term of office and then some. So the very existence of 'forces restoring competition' and putting in a government or parliamentary median of a different ideological complexion reverses the direction of policy change and leaves it near a long-term equilibrium point.

It is not that short-term policy change does not occur but that its effects are limited. Only when a party establishes an hegemony over government—like the New Deal Democrats in the USA, or the Thatcher-Major conservatives in Britain, or the Scandinavian Social Democrats from 1930 to 1980—will policy regimes change and new ones be set up. But this is a rare occurrence. Bush and Blair may aim at it in the USA and UK, but it remains to be seen whether they will succeed. Even so, many old policies will remain unchanged, as it is too difficult to deal with everything even over twenty years.

The varying success of would-be hegemonic parties in different countries perhaps explains the differences in policy regimes. For the moment, however, this remains an untested hypothesis. What we have to do in Chapter 11 is to examine the political forces at work over time within the different countries and see whether they have the necessary stability to affect long-lasting policy regimes. If they simply fluctuate rapidly between one election and another they will not have the ability to produce major change. Policy outputs will simply oscillate marginally around an underlying equilibrium somewhere in the middle, close to the long-term preference of the median voter.

This may well be normal politics in a democracy and no bad thing in itself. Policy will reflect majority opinion that may not change so very much. We now turn to an examination of this very point in Chapter 11.

11

Fluctuating Political Forces

Having examined the dependent variable—policy outputs, the end results of the democratic process—in Chapter 10, we turn to the hypothesized political forces at work on them. In terms both of theoretical perspectives and previous findings these are median voters', median parliamentary party's, and government's preferences. We want to see, as with policy, what their dynamics are and how important these are compared with cross-national differences. Is there a 'political regime' we can match with the 'policy regimes' identified in Chapter 10?

We need to do more than replicate the policy analysis of speed of change and cross-country variation. We also want to examine relationships between the political forces themselves, especially how far median voter preferences affect those of the parliamentary median and how these in turn affect the government position. This is particularly relevant in light of the median mandate argument (see Table 2.4) that there is a sequence at work, one in which the median voter chooses the median party and the median party influences the government.

We already examined relationships between these political forces in Chapter 7. However, that analysis averaged the dynamics rather than accounting for them. Here we need to look at relationships in terms of how they carry over time and, in particular, how responsive the median party preference is to that of the median voter and how responsive the government is to the median party. If one does not shift in response to the other in the way indicated by a median mandate, an essential link in our argument will be missing.

The chapter proceeds from the 'political rate of change'—which after the evidence reported in Chapters 6 and 9 we must clearly expect to be greater than that of actual policy—to the analysis of election by election responsiveness within countries. On the way we consider the extent to which elections coordinate the forces at work and the way in which both parties and voters shape election outcomes.

11.1 POLITICAL DYNAMICS

We now come at the policy situation from the other side; that is, we consider what we know and can estimate about political dynamics. We have already seen in Chapter 6 that electoral dynamics move quite rapidly. In particular, the evidence showed that electorates whose party-vote percentages deviate from their average (a form of equilibrium value) can be expected to return very quickly to their typical levels.[1] We also saw in Chapter 7 that our twenty-one nations have different sets of ideological equilibria.

In light of the previous analyses we can take these median voter, parliamentary median, and government mean values as pointing to the approximate political equilibrium in the countries concerned and ask what the political dynamics of these three actors look like. To do this we once again estimate the speed of adjustment, now with respect to political ideological change, with our autoregressive term included in an equation with a set of national dummy variables. We find the following:

Median Voter
($N = 245$ elections)

$$MV_{ie} = \alpha + 0.276 MV_{ie-1} + \Sigma \lambda_{ie}(N_{ie}) + \varepsilon_{ie}$$
$$(0.067)$$
$$R^2 = 0.395 \quad \text{and} \quad S_e = 10.5$$

Parliamentary Median
($N = 245$ parliaments)

$$\text{Parl Median}_{ie} = \alpha + 0.294 \text{ Parl Median}_{ie-1} + \Sigma \lambda_{ie}(N_{ie}) + \varepsilon_{ie}$$
$$(0.064)$$
$$R^2 = 0.316 \quad \text{and} \quad S_e = 14.2$$

Government
($N = 411$ governments—excluding caretaker, nonpartisan, and transition governments)

$$\text{Government}_{ig} = \alpha + 0.481 \text{Government}_{ig-1} + \Sigma \lambda_{it}(N_{it}) + \varepsilon_{ie}$$
$$(0.044)$$
$$R^2 = 0.394 \quad \text{and} \quad S_e = 14.0$$

where

- MV_{ie} and MV_{ie-1} are the Left-Right positions of median voters for nation i in the current (e) and preceding ($e-1$) elections.

---

[1] Means are one way to characterize equilibriums, positions towards which a system tends to move when it is not at its equilibrium position and from which it tends not to stray too far when it is at its equilibrium position. What our analysis showed in Chapter 6 is that the mean is the appropriate dynamic equilibrium point for government vote percentages, as parties in government tend over time to revert to it.

- *Parl Median$_{ie}$* and *Parl Median$_{ie-1}$* are the Left-Right positions of parliamentary medians for nation I at the time of the parliament sitting after the current (e) and preceding ($e - 1$) elections.
- *Government$_{ig}$* and *Government$_{ig-1}$* are the aggregate Left-Right positions of government parties weighted by the parliamentary seats held by them, in nation i at the time of the current (g) and preceding ($g - 1$) governments.
- $\Sigma\lambda_{i,e \text{ or } g}(N_{i,e \text{ or } g})$ is a matrix of nation dummy variables and respective coefficients for nation i at a given election or government.
- $\varepsilon_{ie \text{ or } g}$ is (assumed to be) a well behaved error term.

Clearly the speed of adjustment towards a country's electoral, parliamentary, or governmental equilibrium is much faster than the speed of adjustment of policy. Indeed, with coefficients between 0.25 and 0.5 on the autoregressive term (i.e. the Y at t-1 variables), our estimates tell us that political movements are between three and five times more rapid than policy movements.

11.2 TAKING STOCK OF POLICY AND POLITICAL DYNAMICS

It is now time to bring our bits of scattered evidence into direct association with one another so as to form a unified picture of what might be going on. In Chapter 7 we saw that the average ideological positions of various countries on these measures are more or less left-leaning versus centre-leaning versus right-leaning and that representational distortions around each country's national ideology tend to cancel out through time. In Chapters 8 and 9 we saw that the connections between policy and the political ideological positions of voters, parliaments, governments, and ministries at each individual time-point are weak and fleeting. In Chapter 10 we have seen that policy is slow moving and we have just shown that politics are highly dynamic. The overall picture of politics that emerges is one where political influences oscillate around country-specific ideological equilibria. These in turn mark a rather steady central tendency within a single country despite dramatic temporary upsets. However, these steady ideological inclinations differ quite considerably across countries. They thus have the potential to mark out a divergent track for policy in each country.

Contrary to hypotheses that point to governments and ministers as the operative policymakers (e.g. Laver and Shepsle 1996) we suspect that governments are relatively less important than parliaments and individual ministers are even less important than governments. More than that, we suspect that no single parliament can be assigned responsibility for the policy it makes. A parliament necessarily has to work within the policy regime it inherits. One half of our contrary thesis is this: if a party or coalition takes control of government's policymaking apparatus without the people being with them, and the people never do come to see things in the way the party or coalition would like, it is difficult to imagine that government having a lasting policy impact in the sense of changing the policy regime. The other half of our thesis is this: if a party or coalition takes control of the apparatus of policymaking, and the people come along initially, but popular support evaporates, it is difficult to imagine *that* government having a lasting policy impact.

11.3 ELECTIONS AS COORDINATING INSTRUMENTS

At this juncture we have varying but interlocking pieces of evidence that give rise to the interpretation above. Interpretations are not final answers, however; they are hypotheses we arrive at after viewing the evidence. We therefore need to ask what independent evidence would make this hypothesis untenable. At the centre of our median mandate thesis is the proposition that elections have the power to animate the policymaking process. If this proposition fails, then so does the whole thesis.

Chapter 7 found that ideological positions held by median voters over a series of post-war elections in twenty democracies match the parliamentary and government positions well enough for us to conclude there is not much representational bias, except in France and Britain. This is a necessary piece of evidence for thinking there is coordination of median and government positions by elections. But it is hardly sufficient. At the very least, for elections to coordinate the politics and policies of a country, we have to show direct responsiveness of parliamentary and government positions to electoral ones. We know from Chapter 7 that the ideological positions of parliaments are usually not much biased with respect to the ideological positions of their electorates. But, then, two random series can have the same mean; two trends running in different directions can have the same mean; two series zigzagging in antithetical response to one another can have the same mean. If similar means arise for reasons other than parliamentary medians being directly responsive to election medians, we do not have evidence of elections having the potential to coordinate politics and policy.

11.4 ELECTORAL RESPONSIVENESS: THEORETICAL POSSIBILITIES

We begin with a disclaimer. It is unnecessary to ask in some general sense whether electoral responsiveness exists. It undoubtedly does. A vast and important literature constructed around the concepts of representational responsiveness, with a concern for bias as well, has repeatedly shown that party seat percentages respond to shifting vote percentages (Tufte 1973; see also Edgeworth 1898; Kendall and Stuart 1950; March 1957–8; Taagepera and Shugart 1989; King and Gelman 1991). No one doubts that particular generalization. However, those investigations have not been much concerned with another generalization—about whether there is policy responsiveness. Their concern has been the precise magnitude and absolute reliability of responsiveness of seat shares to party vote shares under different rules (Taagepera and Shugart 1989), under the same rules in different places (March 1957–8; Tufte 1973; Taagepera and Shugart 1989), or under the same rules in the same place at different times (Tufte 1973; King and Gelman 1991).

The issue of responsiveness looks much different when infused with a concern for policy. It changes the question from who wins how much of the valued currency, namely seats, to how accurately the policy position of an electorate empowers a similar policy position in parliament and government. The distinction is readily apparent when one contrasts the consequences of different electoral systems, most especially SMD versus PR systems.

From a seat-vote perspective, SMD systems are said to be overly responsive compared to the near definitional requirement of proportional responsiveness under PR. When policy is allowed into the consideration, this simple distinction needs to be qualified. Varying seat percentages in response to shifting vote percentages is essentially a rule-based, mechanical operation. Whether such shifts have consequences for policy preferences and, if so, to what extent, depends on whether the vote shifts are relevant to changing the parliamentary median and whether the change in the parliamentary median is large or small. Furthermore, as we have said, the answer to these questions depends on more than the behaviour of voters. The changing policy positions of the parties can shift the parliamentary median even when the voters stand still, and changing party positions can make the parliamentary median stand still even when the party choice of voters changes.

A few examples help us explore these possibilities and think through the possible consequences. A three-party system operating under PR rules (as in Germany) might record an electoral shift to the left. But as long as the middle party, fixed in its policy position, remains the party with which the parliamentary median affiliates there is no effect on policy preferences at the decision-making level. A two-party system (as in the USA) might record an electoral shift from 52 to 60 per cent of the vote. But as long as the electoral rules properly identify the majority party, one with a fixed policy position in both elections, there is no recorded policy consequence. In both cases, seat shifts in response to vote shifts are not relevant to changing the parliamentary median and thus are unlikely to have any direct policy consequences.

As regards policy responsiveness when the parliamentary median does change as a consequence of vote-percentage shifts, the magnitude of the response is likely to depend as much or more on the distribution of party positions as on the redistribution of party vote percentages. Seat-percentage changes in response to a percentage point shift in votes are two to three times as large under Canada's SMD rules as under Sweden's PR rules.

Nevertheless, when the vote change produces a change in the parliamentary median in both countries, the effect on policy preferences is about a six unit movement along the Left-Right dimension in Canada—where the Liberals and Progressive Conservatives stand about six units apart, on average—versus a twenty-five unit Left-Right movement for Sweden—where Social Democrats and Liberals stand about twenty-five units apart, on average. The proximity of parties to one another, especially of the two parties normally adjacent to the median voter, matters a great deal for policy responsiveness.

Consider also that voters alone are not the only electoral force that can move the policy position of the parliamentary median. Parties hold that power too. In the three-party case (here Austria might be the operative example), if the middle party abandons its middle position by moving to the right of the one-time right-wing party, this will put the heretofore party on the right in the position of the parliamentary median even if the party movement had no effect on the vote distribution.

These are hypothetical possibilities, of course. It is very hard to imagine that marked programmatic shifts by parties have no effect on their vote (Adams 2001). In the case of Austria, the Freedom Party's move rightwards undoubtedly lost it some voters while it gained others. The electors who stuck with it expressed, through their revealed preferences (votes), a willingness to record a change in their own opinions.

What these examples illustrate is that election outcomes generally reflect both the party alternatives on offer and the electoral reactions to them. There is no way of entirely distinguishing the two.[2] Over time, indeed, electors might support new parties or movements that provide different alternatives for them. In any one election, however, the only way they can reveal their preference is by selecting one of the parties competing, or by abstaining. These are points we take up again in methodological comments on the results from our analysis of responsiveness.

11.5 ELECTORAL RESPONSIVENESS: COMPARATIVE EVIDENCE

A failure to find shifts in parliamentary and government preferences in response to electoral ones would be enough to dismiss our median mandate

---

[2] However, in the Appendix to this Chapter, we do try to separate them out, partially, by 'fixing' party positions. Certainly in the estimation of median vote preference one might attempt to go beyond the aggregate vote to ascertain preferences. Within the context of an individual country one might use surveys to get at electors' 'real' preferences. However, this would take us into a general debate as to whether spontaneous survey responses are any more 'real' than a considered vote for a party programme. There is the additional question of which survey question is more 'real'—general Left-Right positioning or, for example, attitudes to immigrants. As pointed out in Chapter 3, survey responses are not entirely comparable between countries, rendering the survey option inoperative for a comparative investigation like ours.

thesis, even if their discovery is not enough to substantiate it finally. So the first thing we need to know is whether the electoral process can be viewed as moving the centre of the policymaking process. Our answer starts with the most general form of the relationship—across all elections in our data set—and moves down through levels of aggregations through system types to individual countries.

Figure 11.1 shows the relationship for all 265 elections. The graph is distinctly linear with a slope very near to one-to-one direct responsiveness and with a reasonably good fit. The associated linear equation is

$$Parl\ Median_{ie} = 1.47 + 1.01 MV_{ie} + \varepsilon_{ie}$$
$$(0.70)\ (0.05)$$
$$R^2 = 0.598 \quad S_e = 10.5 \quad N = 266$$

where *Parl Median*$_{ie}$ is the Left-Right position of the parliamentary median in nation i following election e, and MV_{ie} is the position of the Left-Right position of the median voter in election e, and ε_{ie} is assumed to be a well behaved error term. Policy responsiveness is estimated with respect to the slope. There is a remarkably consistent degree of responsiveness. The solid line represents hypothetical one-to-one policy responsiveness; the dotted line is the estimated relationship. We find each shift of a median voter's position by one unit along the Left-Right dimension associated with a one-unit shift of the parliamentary median position. Representational bias is estimated by the intercept. Given its statistically significant value of +1.47, there is about a one and a half unit rightward bias in the parliamentary median relative to the position of the median voter. This is not much; it amounts to the difference between a Christian party or progressive Liberal party being at the ideological centre of parliament following an election. The difference is, however, statistically significant and thus indicates a reliably consistent bias in election outcomes.

We saw earlier, in Chapter 7, that SMD systems tend to have a rightward-tilting representational bias. We have added a dummy variable for SMD systems to the above equation to check on how that bias might affect the estimated responsiveness and how this analysis records the bias by system. The statistical results show

$$Parl\ Median_{ie} = 0.02 + 0.98 MV_{ie} + 4.35 SMD_{ie} + \varepsilon_{ie}$$
$$(0.84)\ (0.05) \quad\quad (1.39)$$
$$R^2 = 0.612 \quad S_e = 10.3 \quad N = 266$$

where SMD_{ie} is a dummy variable scored 0 for elections held under PR rules and scored 1 for elections held under SMD rules, and where other variables

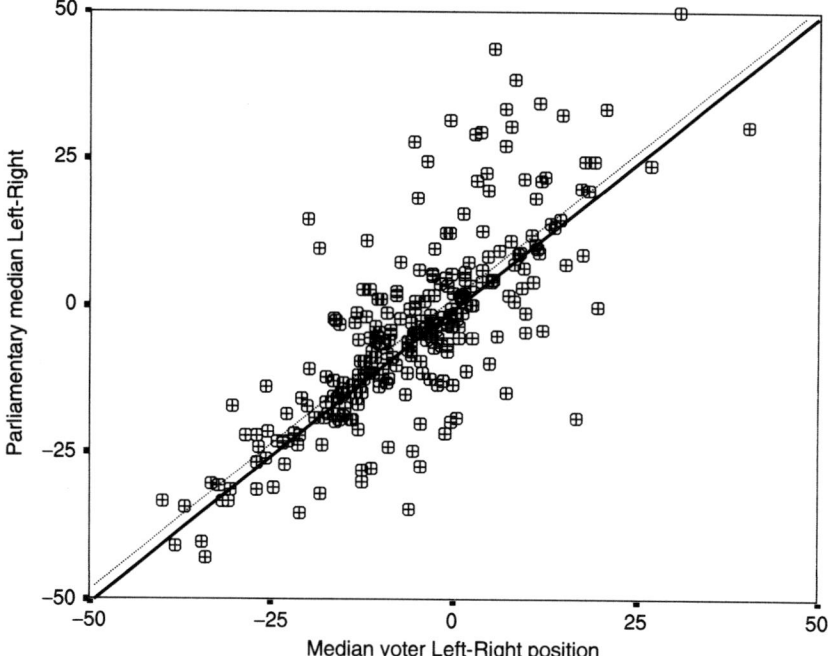

FIGURE 11.1. Responsiveness of median parliamentary Left-Right policy position to median voter Left-Right position over 266 elections in twenty-one democracies, 1950–95

are as previously defined. Controlling for system type does virtually nothing to the estimated magnitude of responsiveness—it is still nearly one-to-one—but the re-estimation tells us that representational bias is entirely within the ambit of SMD elections. There is essentially no bias under PR rules. The intercept, which records PR system bias, is a negligible 0.02, but the bias under SMD rules amounts to a rightward tilt of outcomes over four units to the right of a median voter's position.

This second equation, as did the first, imposes the assumption on the analysis that the responsiveness in PR systems and SMD systems has the same magnitude. From what we know about translating vote percentages to seat percentages, that might seem a dubious assumption. We therefore separate the analyses by system.

PR Systems

$$Parl\ Median_{ie} = -0.14 + 0.96\ MV_{ie} + \varepsilon_{ie}$$
$$(0.57)\ \ (0.04)$$
$$R^2 = 0.779 \quad s_e = 6.9 \quad N = 185$$

SMD Systems

$$Parl\ Median_{ie} = 4.63 + 1.08\ MV_{ie} + \varepsilon_{ie}$$
$$(1.80)\ \ (0.17)$$
$$R^2 = 0.341 \quad s_e = 15.7 \quad N = 81$$

where all variables are as previously defined. The responsiveness in both systems is similar; in statistical terms they can be considered to be the same.[3] And, as we have already seen, representational bias exists only under the SMD system. Another point of distinction is the more reliable responsiveness under PR rules than under SMD rules. Mispredictions for SMD compared to PR systems are much larger; standard errors of estimate show PR = 6.9 and SMD = 15.7. A consequence is that direct reliability estimates for responsiveness (i.e. standard errors of the slopes) are about four times better under PR than under SMD systems (0.04 versus 0.17).[4]

The responsiveness equations just presented run the risk of drawing on essentially cross-national differences to gain leverage for the responsiveness estimates. That is not wholly legitimate from all theoretical perspectives, because responsiveness is most often a theoretically important system-specific phenomenon. Table 11.1 breaks the responsiveness analyses down by country. The results are nothing less than stunning. In twenty of twenty-one countries under investigation, responsiveness exists to a statistically significant extent. France is the lone exception. That the existence of responsiveness is so widespread is an important electoral fact. Electoral rules are supposed to ensure that responsiveness exists. What we learn here is that they fulfill their purpose not just in terms of votes and seats but of policy as well. What makes the results especially impressive is that in every country policy responsiveness can be said to be one-to-one. There is no country for which we can reject the hypothesis that the policy responsiveness slope equals 1.0. That means we are justified in saying for all countries that a one unit shift in the Left-Right position of the median voter produces something like a one unit shift in the Left-Right position of the parliamentary median. France in particular, but also Germany, Iceland, Canada, the UK, and the USA, permit the one-to-one inference because their estimated responsiveness is

---

[3] This set of equations could be estimated with an algebraic equivalent single equation, which has a less obvious interpretation than the set presented but which does provide a more straightforward view of whether the difference in slopes (0.96 versus 1.08) is statistically significant. As stated, it is not. The difference, 0.12, has a standard error of 0.13, thus $t < 1$ ($p = 0.181$, one tail test).

[4] This corroborates what we reported in Chapter 7. Viewed in a regression format, so as to take account of responsiveness, the standard error of estimate is the regression analogue to distortion, which is greater under SMD rules than under PR rules. The intercept is the regression analogue to bias, which is tilted to the right among SMD systems compared to PR systems.

TABLE 11.1. *Responsiveness of the median parliamentary party's Left-Right position to the median voter Left-Right position, by country*

	Intercept	(s_a)	Slope	(s_b)	r^2	s_e
Austria	0.57	(2.56)	0.89**	(0.17)	0.706	8.8
Belgium	0.57	(0.82)	0.88**	(0.09)	0.875	2.8
Denmark	−3.07	(1.51)	0.83**	(0.15)	0.658	5.9
Finland	−0.56	(1.70)	0.92**	(0.09)	0.903	4.5
Germany	0.52	(2.21)	1.31**	(0.21)	0.798	7.6
Iceland	−0.35	(3.44)	0.65*	(0.28)	0.326	11.1
Ireland	−1.12	(3.96)	0.92**	(0.26)	0.510	14.3
Italy	0.67	(0.89)	0.86**	(0.10)	0.889	2.6
Luxembourg	1.37	(2.30)	0.89**	(0.13)	0.849	3.6
Netherlands	1.30	(1.18)	0.95**	(0.08)	0.926	3.6
Norway	−4.85	(6.45)	0.86**	(0.26)	0.556	5.7
Portugal	2.91	(1.91)	1.15**	(0.19)	0.862	4.0
Spain	2.49	(3.36)	1.18**	(0.24)	0.854	4.3
Sweden	−3.75	(2.54)	0.95**	(0.11)	0.851	6.8
Switzerland	−0.76	(1.07)	1.12**	(0.12)	0.902	3.2
Australia	3.40	(5.33)	1.09*	(0.45)	0.264	20.0
Canada	0.46	(2.38)	0.73*	(0.37)	0.250	8.0
France	7.52	(6.46)	0.53	(0.74)	0.061	16.9
New Zealand	4.97	(5.21)	1.08*	(0.45)	0.313	13.7
UK	12.30	(6.14)	1.57**	(0.39)	0.593	16.5
US	−2.26	(6.47)	2.81*	(1.44)	0.297	17.5

* $p < 0.05$; ** $p < 0.01$; one-tail test for slopes and two-tail test for intercept.

not especially reliable; elsewhere it is because the slope itself is in the interval between 0.8 and 1.2.

How can it be, given the ways in which we usually think about electoral responsiveness, that electoral policy responsiveness is one-to-one? Does not a shift from Conservative to Labour (or vice versa) in Britain or from the SDA to FP (or vice versa) in Sweden create large differences in policy positions? There are two points to be made in answer to these questions. First, some shifts in median voter positions create no difference in the parliamentary median. Those non-responsive elections compensate the highly responsive elections. Over a series of elections, average responsiveness is somewhere between 0 and some large value, the magnitude of which depends on the difference between parties adjacent to a median voter in the Left-Right space. Second, being close to the median voter is usually what it takes for a party to be the one with which the median parliamentarian affiliates. Were parties to stand at fixed policy positions, so that only movements by voters towards one or another party policy position were the source of redirecting the parliamentary median, there would likely be larger degrees of responsiveness in Britain and Sweden. That is to say, importantly, that shifting voter positions are not the only force that redirects the parliamentary centre. Party positions move too. Policy position movements by parties contribute their own policy dynamics to elections, and those dynamics contribute to the policy responsiveness we have been observing.

This explicitly reminds us that sometimes parties lead and voters follow, while at other times voters lead and parties follow. Taking notice of this two-way street makes it best not to consider the pervasiveness of the one-to-one policy responsiveness an unconditional fact. Instead, one-to-one responsiveness exists under two conditions, (*a*) a country's voters know which Left-Right positions the parties are proposing at the time of an election; (*b*) parties mean what they say about policy at the time of each election. Of course these are major assumptions, stressed classically (e.g. in Downs 1957: 96–114), on which mandate theory also has to base itself (see Tables 2.1 and 2.4), and there is no reason to doubt them. Doing so would undermine the foundation of democracy itself, certainly as embodied in the countries we are examining here, not just the idea of the mandate.

11.6 RESPONSIVENESS: METHODOLOGICAL CONCERNS

Our responsiveness analysis raises in acute form methodological concerns already discussed elsewhere in the book, particularly in Chapters 3 and 7. We return to them here because they very much affect what we report and infer about responsiveness. Two sets of questions come up, both concerned with interdependency between electoral and parliamentary positions. To what extent can we regard them as truly independent when parties at one and the same time fix the policy alternatives voted on in elections and the policy positions taken up in parliament? Is not any correspondence purely tautological or even manipulated, certainly not a spontaneous reflection of voter preferences?

The other, related, set of questions are more narrowly technical, but relevant nonetheless. If party positioning along the Left-Right continuum enters centrally into defining what electors are voting for, through the estimation of the median voter position, and is then used to define the median party in parliament, is responsiveness not ensured definitionally by this measurement overlap? If so, what are our findings worth for actually testing the existence of a median mandate in the democracies under study?

These questions can be answered in terms of substantive theories of modern democracy, which put political parties at the centre of the representative process. Parties are in fact often likened rhetorically to a transmission belt between electors and governments. Mandate theories (see Tables 2.1 and 2.4) explicitly see them as defining policy alternatives for electors to choose between and then effecting them at the level of government and parliament.

Parties' dual electoral and governance role is not merely an artefact of our measurement procedures but exist as a central feature of theories of democracy, clearly echoed in contemporary practice. Parties are *supposed* to define the policy alternatives for electors and then to advance these in government or parliament. If they did not, decision-makers would act outside the frame of reference used by voters, and, therefore, popular preferences would not have a 'necessary connection' with policy outputs. It is precisely the dual party role in defining the electoral alternatives and then effecting them that ensures democracy works effectively to transmit popular preferences to decision-makers.

Seen from this point of view the parties' part in defining the electoral alternatives and ordering them so as to produce median positions, both in electorates and parliaments, appears not as tautological and manipulative but as essential in democratic terms. Without party definition and ordering, democracy would not have a common frame of reference for debate, nor would there be any clear-cut indication as to what an election outcome implies for decision-making. From this perspective, the parties' ability to change the meaning of election outcomes by moving their own position appears not just acceptable but essential in substantive terms.

Clearly democracies work on this assumption. Party votes constitute the recorded preferences on which the whole process is based. We cannot try to second guess this normative principle of democracy (Downs 1957: 18) by using some other measure of preference. We have research techniques to use the currency—votes and published party programmes—that democracies themselves use, and we analyse these within the framework of democratic theory to test and evaluate that theory.

These substantive democratic considerations also underpin our measurements. These measure median voter preference on the basis of the party Left-Right ordering and their share of votes, and relate it to party Left-Right ordering and their share of legislative seats. To the extent this is tautological it is a tautology embedded in the structure of elections and legislatures, both of which are ordered and organized by parties. The only way electors can express their preferences is by choosing between parties. The only way legislative voting can be ordered and coordinated is through parties. The overlap between the two is substantive and entailed by the very set-up of party democracy.

What this implies is that responsiveness is not so much a causal function as a translation function, in much the same way that the vote-seat relationship is not so much causal as translational. Voters record their preferences for parties so that we know the distribution of voter preferences. The voter preference distribution is translated into a distribution of preferences in parliament according to rules. Entry and exit of parties affect the preference distributions we observe on both sides of the translation. Nevertheless, *given* the parties on offer, it is important to descriptive, empirical, and normative democratic theory to investigate whether shifts in the parliamentary distribution respond to shifts in the voter distribution. That importance is attenuated not in the least by knowledge that the parties on offer affect the shape of both distributions.

In the Appendix to this chapter we modify the effects of current party position on estimates of the median voter by varying our measure to take in average party positions over three elections rather than just one. We still relate this to the parliamentary median as reflected in the results from the one election in question. The overall results of this 'distancing analysis' of the two electoral and parliamentary measures are much the same as reported in Table 11.1, indicating that legislature responsiveness to median voter preference is not just a measurement artefact based on using the same party ordering in both measures.

From the evidence mustered in this methodological review, as well as from our substantive analyses, we can draw two important conclusions. First, elections do a remarkably accurate job in creating responsiveness between the Left-Right medians of voter and parliamentary distributions. Where voters are well informed about party positions, the centres of the two distributions move in tandem over a series of elections and track each other in one-to-one movements. The tandem movements are more reliable in countries using PR electoral systems, but the same (but less reliable) pattern exists in and among SMD systems. Second, and equally remarkable, party movements along the Left-Right dimension have a large hand in creating the accurate responsiveness. Were party positions fixed, so that shifts in the vote distributions were the only source of election change, responsiveness would exist in many countries but it would be less reliable and less accurate. This finding makes clear that voters have a responsibility to themselves to know what the parties are offering beyond general, long-term differences. Electorates that do not accept that responsibility will get in the way of the coordinating potential of elections. The centre of the vote distribution will mean one thing but the parties, who know what they themselves have proposed, will take it to mean something different. This is not an onerous burden on voters; accurate responsiveness will exist in most countries even if voters have an imprecise sense of party positions (see Appendix to this chapter). All-in-all, the principal message is that elections are good, accurate coordinating instruments for marking the Left-Right preferences of electorates and re-presenting their Left-Right positions in parliaments over the course of several elections, even though they are not especially reliable for any single election.

11.7 COORDINATION FROM PARLIAMENTS TO GOVERNMENTS

Thus far we have taken for granted that parties mean what they say. Can we really expect that what parliaments produce will reflect the ideological disposition we infer they have, given the distribution of party seats? We learned from the analysis of government declarations that parliaments, perhaps looking over their shoulders at the position of the median voter, expressly declare policy intentions in line with the centre of their ideological distribution. However, that relationship was not especially tight; the correlation was only in the neighbourhood of 0.5. One has to wonder whether the slippage during the step from parliament to government arises as a consequence of the nature of the government installed or the policy objectives those governments say they will pursue? To investigate this we can look directly at ideological responsiveness in the step from the parliamentary median to the weighted Left-Right position of parties in government. As we did for our analysis of the voter to parliament step previously, we start at the most general level, looking across nations and time simultaneously, and proceed to disaggregate the analysis by system type first and then by nation.

We know from Chapter 7 that Left-Right positions of parliaments and governments match each other with a high degree of accuracy. We also know from other analyses (Laver and Budge 1992; Müller and Strøm 2000) that the party of the parliamentary median is in government under multiparty PR systems about 80 per cent of the time. And, we know from simple logic that the party of the parliamentary median is almost always the single-government party in dominant two-party systems. The results of the following equation tell us further that all this is in large part a matter of government policy intentions reflecting parliamentary median positions on a nearly one-to-one basis. The translation in the step from parliamentary median to the weighted position of government, as given by the associated linear equation, is:

$$Govt_{ig} = 0.40 + 0.93 \; Parl \; Median_{ig} + \varepsilon_{ig}$$

$$(0.48) \quad (0.03)$$

$$R^2 = 0.687 \quad s_e = 9.9 \quad N = 456$$

where $Govt_{ig}$ is the weight mean Left-Right position of parties in government for nation i in government g, $ParlMedian_{ig}$ is the Left-Right position of the parliamentary median in nation i in government g, and ε_{ie} is assumed to be a well behaved error term.

The modestly surprising aspect of the results is the slight but statistically significant tendency for the government positions to tend towards the centre, the zero point on the Left-Right dimension. There is essentially no bias in this translation, as can be seen in the small and statistically insignificant magnitude of the intercept, but the slope is lower than 1.0. This we suspect is due to governments created through legislative negotiation tending slightly more towards the centre than the parliamentary median itself. Separate analyses of PR and SMD systems show a one-unit movement in the parliamentary median produces slightly less than a 0.9-unit movement in the position of government under PR, whereas the foregone conclusion of normally single-majority parliaments under SMD is a one-to-one relationship.

PR Systems

$$Govt_{ig} = 0.13 + 0.88 \; Parl \; Median_{ig} + e_{ig}$$
$$(0.67) \; (0.04)$$
$$R^2 = 0.555 \; s_e = 11.3 \; N = 337$$

SMD Systems

$$Govt_{ig} = 0.32 + 1.01 \; Parl \; Median_{ig} + \varepsilon_{ig}$$
$$(0.34) \; (0.02)$$
$$R^2 = 0.963 \; s_e = 3.7 \; N = 119$$

where all variables are as previously defined.

The nation-by-nation results of government to parliament responsiveness in Table 11.2 reveal where and therefore how PR systems as a group have a slight tendency to install a more centrist government relative to the position of the parliamentary median. The parliament to government translation in Denmark is so unreliably responsive as to be indistinguishable from zero. It is anyone's bet as to what the ideological disposition of a Danish government will be, regardless of knowing the ideological disposition of a Danish parliament. This may be due to the frequent minority governments there having to carry out legislative wishes regardless of their own ideological predilections. Whatever, the essentially zero slope for Denmark helps to drag the responsiveness of PR systems as a group below 1.0.

That is not all, however. Austrian, Irish, Dutch and Swiss governments are less responsive, more centrist, than the parliaments that produce them. On reflection, these tendencies come from widely recognised facts about these countries, which may reflect their tendencies to 'consensus democracy' (Lijphart 1984). Austria and Switzerland often install grand coalition governments. Given that a weighted mean of positive and negative scores is more likely than a weighted median to sum to a value of zero, that is, the median is based on the position of a single party that is involved in the calculation of the positive and negative scores that make up the weighted mean—Austrian and Swiss governments tend towards a centrist position relative to their parliamentary median.

Similarly, Irish governments throughout much of the post-war period stood as binary alternatives of Fianna Fail in government alone or Fine Gail and Labour in a coalition. That coalition often involved Fine Gail splitting the weighted difference between itself on the right, where it marked the centre of parliament, and Labour to the left, which created a government closer to the centre than the parliamentary median.

TABLE 11.2. *Responsiveness of the government's Left-Right positions to the median parliamentary party's Left-Right position, by country*[a]

	Intercept	(s_a)	Slope	(s_b)	r^2	s_e
Austria	−3.33	(3.15)	0.59**	(0.20)	0.346	13.3
Belgium	−2.01	(1.52)	0.80**	(0.20)	0.399	7.1
Denmark	−1.68	(5.30)	0.29**	(0.46)	0.016	22.0
Finland	3.24	(4.30)	0.94**	(0.23)	0.357	17.1
Germany	1.31	(2.40)	1.00**	(0.15)	0.711	10.9
Iceland	1.66	(2.74)	0.83**	(0.19)	0.540	10.6
Ireland	2.30	(1.83)	0.78**	(0.10)	0.774	7.8
Italy	0.86	(1.15)	1.15**	(0.07)	0.866	3.1
Luxembourg	−2.03	(3.16)	1.09**	(0.22)	0.674	7.0
Netherlands	−2.56	(2.87)	0.65**	(0.21)	0.442	9.4
Norway	2.96	(9.30)	0.97**	(0.35)	0.291	11.7
Portugal	0.61	(0.66)	1.02**	(0.07)	0.965	1.9
Spain	0.00	(~~)	1.00**	(~~)	1.00	0.0
Sweden	2.99	(4.30)	1.19**	(0.17)	0.716	11.7
Switzerland	1.24	(0.99)	0.81**	(0.09)	0.634	6.0
Australia	0.00	(~~)	1.00**	(~~)	1.00	0.0
Canada	1.37	(1.38)	0.92**	(0.14)	0.736	5.6
France	1.63	(0.88)	0.98**	(0.05)	0.942	4.3
New Zealand	0.00	(~~)	1.00**	(~~)	1.00	0.0
UK	−1.14	(1.46)	1.04**	(0.06)	0.950	6.0
US	0.00	(~~)	1.00**	(~~)	1.00	0.0

* $p < 0.05$; ** $p < 0.01$; one-tail test for slopes and two-tail test for intercept.
[a] Caretaker, nonpartisan, and transition governments excluded.

The Dutch case is more complicated. Until Kok's 1994 coalition government involving PvdA, D 66, and VVD, Dutch Christians were the core around which all governments formed. During the 1950s through to the late 1960s, when the Christians were slightly to the right of centre, they had a slightly greater tendency to coalesce with the left-of-centre PvdA than the right-of-centre VVD. Since 1967, after which time the Christians themselves moved slightly left of centre, they had a slightly greater tendency to coalesce with the right-of-centre VVD than with the left-of-centre PvdA.

A fact not to be missed in this discussion of the centrist tendencies of governments in five countries, is the important flip side. The ten remaining PR systems show something close to a one-to-one responsiveness in the ideological positions of governments to the ideological centres of parliaments.

SMD systems make this translation one-to-one almost by definition. Their statistical results are only needed at the bottom of the table as numerical reminders that on a few occasions after elections in Canada, France, and the UK there was no single-majority party in parliament and thus a once-in-a-while slip took place between the parliamentary median and the government positions.

Finally, the unreliability in moving from the ideological centre of parliaments to governments under PR systems deserves mention. In all but four PR countries (Iceland, Italy, Portugal, and Spain), the errors from our predictions of government Left-Right positions from parliamentary Left-Right positions—using the standard errors of estimate as the measure of mispredictions—are about twice as large as the errors in predicting parliamentary positions from median voter positions (see Table 11.1). Even with substantial difficulty predicting any particular government's Left-Right position, an important fact stands out. The general tendency is for government positions to hover around a one-to-one relationship with the centres of their parliaments. Politics swirl in seemingly chaotic ways one day to the next, one year to the next, one government to the next, one parliament to the next, and one election to the next. Nevertheless, in the long run, the swirling politics centre themselves around the middle political ground in each country, marked by the positions of the countries' median voters.

APPENDIX

Distancing Median Voter Estimates from the Measure of Median Party in Parliament

We have argued that using party Left-Right orderings as an element in the measures both of Median Voter Positions (MV_{LR}) and Median Parliamentary Party (MPP_{LR}) reflects the actual practices of democracy rather than a tautology in our measures. Nevertheless it is always useful methodologically to validate measures by varying their procedures and seeing if one gets similar results.

We 'distance' the measures here first by using the moving average of party positions over the last, current and next elections to estimate Left-Right orderings for the median voter calculation. Substantively this implies that voters may be a bit hazy about current party policy but have a good general idea about where they have come from and where they are moving to, over a nine to twelve year period. In contrast the MPP_{LR} position is still estimated in terms of where it is after the current election. This realistically assumes greater knowledge of the actual party position on the part of its leadership, and approximations (but not unrealistic ones) by electors. Methodologically it implies that there is less overlap between the two measures so the results of the responsiveness analysis can be taken more at face value.[1] Of course, the great

---

[1] One could of course take the mean-party position over 20–30 years or the whole post-war period. This seems unrealistic however in terms of the current electorate's information horizons. In the 1990s they are unlikely to take much account of what politics were like in the 1950s or 1960s. Even if party positions do not change greatly (see Chapter 5) this information will be transmitted through the current decade's positions.

interest in the analysis is whether it corroborates the substantial responsiveness already observed.

Statistical results are reported in Table 11.A.1. Responsiveness is evident in sixteen out of twenty-one countries. Along with France, for which there is no evidence of responsiveness even were voters to be aware of the precise party positions at each election (see Table 11.1), responsiveness is absent in Germany, Iceland, Portugal, and New Zealand. That is the negative news. Elsewhere, which is to say in over three-quarters of our twenty-one countries, responsiveness not only exists but is often statistically indistinguishable from one-to-one. In a large majority of PR systems and 50 per cent of SMD systems, even if voters have only an imprecise sense of what party positions are, elections will create accurate responsiveness between the position of median voters and parliamentary medians.

The coincidence in general results between Tables 11.1 and 11.A.1 increases confidence in the validity of our median voter measure for all our analyses.

A further investigation of validity was offered by an anonymous reviewer of our book MS for OUP, who allowed us to make public the following comments and analysis which we report here verbatim:

TABLE 11.A.1. *Alternative estimation of responsiveness of the median parliamentary party's Left-Right position to the median voter Left-Right position, by country: median voter position measured with a three-election moving average of party positions*

	Intercept	(s_a)	Slope	(s_b)	r^2	s_e
Austria	−0.08	(3.37)	0.89**	(0.27)	0.448	11.6
Belgium	0.90	(1.86)	0.81**	(0.23)	0.489	5.7
Denmark	−1.74	(1.64)	1.03**	(0.18)	0.654	5.9
Finland	11.26	(5.42)	1.74**	(0.26)	0.675	8.2
Germany	0.43	(5.00)	0.76	(0.94)	0.062	16.4
Iceland	−3.68	(3.83)	0.21	(0.93)	0.005	13.5
Ireland	−4.04	(4.32)	1.21**	(0.35)	0.494	14.6
Italy	−1.32	(1.25)	0.76**	(0.15)	0.742	4.0
Luxembourg	1.37	(4.06)	0.97**	(0.26)	0.628	5.6
Netherlands	7.50	(4.52)	1.56**	(0.43)	0.540	9.0
Norway	−0.45	(5.93)	1.04**	(0.24)	0.682	4.8
Portugal	3.83	(6.23)	1.04	(0.62)	0.309	8.9
Spain	9.73	(3.73)	1.60**	(0.26)	0.904	3.5
Sweden	0.03	(7.24)	1.02**	(0.33)	0.420	13.4
Switzerland	−1.86	(1.85)	1.07**	(0.19)	0.754	5.0
Australia	3.46	(5.88)	1.08*	(0.58)	0.179	21.1
Canada	1.19	(2.45)	0.90*	(0.42)	0.282	7.9
France	8.04	(7.75)	0.46	(0.81)	0.38	17.1
New Zealand	0.88	(7.95)	0.53	(0.70)	0.043	16.2
UK	16.86	(6.61)	2.15**	(0.51)	0.622	15.9
US	3.46	(5.88)	1.08*	(0.58)	0.179	21.1

* $p < 0.05$; ** $p < 0.01$; one-tail test for slopes and two-tail test for intercept.

In considering the likely critical reception of this book, the most radical aspect of the authors' methodology involves their reliance on election results to infer the location of the median voter. Briefly, the authors use the distribution of votes across parties, combined with the parties' Left-Right positions as coded by the Comparative Manifesto Project (CMP), to locate the median voter in each election (this is an adaptation of a method originally developed by Kim and Fording, 1998). Now, I believe that this is a reasonable procedure, and indeed I think this is the *only* feasible procedure given that the obvious alternative approach—namely, to employ survey data to estimate the voter medians—is unworkable, since reliable, cross-nationally comparable survey data on voter ideologies is not available over the range of countries and time periods the authors analyse.

The authors point out that even if such survey data were available, its use in cross-national analyses is problematic because respondents' Left-Right self-placements are not necessarily comparable across different countries (i.e. the fact that the median respondent self-placement in Norway is similar to the median respondent self-placement in Britain does not prove that the distributions of Norwegian and British citizens' ideologies are actually similar). This is a good point, and to this I would add that even if this problem could somehow be overcome—which it cannot—an additional problem with relying on survey data to measure citizens' ideologies is that strong evidence exists that citizens' Left-Right self-placements are subject to *assimilation* effects, that is, that citizens tend to place themselves unduly close to parties they like for non-policy-related reasons. Huber, for instance, reports that this is the case with Eurobarometer respondents' ideological self-placements in Ireland, Germany and Belgium (see Huber, 'Values and Partisanship in Left-Right Orientation: Measuring Ideology', *European Journal of Political Research* 17 (1989: 599–621). These effects render the use of public opinion survey data problematic, if the goal is to understand how shifts in voters' ideologies affect their voting behaviour.

The above observations notwithstanding, I expect that some readers will nevertheless find the Budge-McDonald methodology for locating voter medians to be problematic. The authors have anticipated this, and they present several reasons why their approach is reasonable (for instance they demonstrate that election results are not substantially influenced by economic conditions—thereby eliminating one possible outside influence that might bias their ideological estimates—and they have also just demonstrated that their ideological estimates are similar if they use party positions over three elections rather than just using the current election). While these arguments are reassuring, a natural question that arises is: 'Would the authors' substantive conclusions have been different, had they been able to rely on cross-national survey data to estimate the ideological medians'?

Since the authors do not explicitly report their estimates of the median voter positions I cannot answer this question directly. However I *do* have access to the Kim–Fording median voter estimates—which are presumably quite similar to the Budge–McDonald estimates, since the latter were constructed using a variation of the Kim–Fording coding procedure—and I also have survey-based measures of voters' ideological positions, as reported in Eurobarometer surveys. I therefore decided to compare the Kim–Fording estimates of the median voter positions against mean voter positions as computed from Eurobarometer respondents' Left-Right self-placements.

I based my comparisons on the Eurobarometer data from eight countries—Britain, France, The Netherlands, Greece, Spain, Denmark, Luxembourg and Italy—since Huber's (1989) analyses of the Eurobarometer surveys suggest that the ideological self-placements from the remaining countries included in the Eurobarometer surveys are unreliable. This data are presented in Table 11.A.2, which reports the Kim–Fording estimates of the voters' median Left-Right positions, compared with voters' mean positions as computed from the Eurobarometer data. (Ideally these tables should report *median* Eurobarometer respondents' self-placements, not means, so

TABLE 11.A.2. *Voters' median Left-Right positions as coded by Kim and Fording using the CMP data, versus voters' mean Left-Right positions as computed from Eurobarometer data*

Country	Election year	Left-Right median Kim-Fording coding	Left-Right mean Eurobarometer
Denmark	77	−6.38	5.33
Denmark	79	1.37	5.59
Denmark	81	−0.71	5.63
Denmark	84	−10.22	5.67
Denmark	87	−23.17	5.56
Denmark	88	−1.52	5.87
Denmark	90	−6.69	5.57
Denmark	94	−2.67	5.62
Denmark	98	−3.20	5.54
Netherlands	77	−10.87	5.72
Netherlands	81	−19.06	5.31
Netherlands	82	−11.39	5.44
Netherlands	86	−3.34	5.3
Netherlands	89	−10.74	5.28
Netherlands	94	1.34	5.3
Netherlands	98	−10.95	5.01
Luxembourg	79	−15.03	5.63
Luxembourg	84	−16.32	5.65
Luxembourg	89	−2.36	5.61
Luxembourg	94	−17.10	5.46
France	78	9.22	5.09
France	81	−11.34	4.78
France	86	5.40	5.22
France	88	−0.52	5
France	93	−5.15	4.92
France	97	2.10	4.6
Italy	76	−1.00	4.13
Italy	79	−8.17	4.3
Italy	83	−4.50	4.63
Italy	87	4.91	4.73
Italy	92	9.00	4.85
Spain	86	−7.01	4.8
Spain	89	−21.40	4.55
Spain	93	−22.32	4.55
Spain	96	−18.10	4.71

TABLE 11.A.2.—Cont'd

Country	Election year	Left-Right median Kim-Fording coding	Left-Right mean Eurobarometer
Greece	81	16.39	6.12
Greece	85	−8.56	5.04
Greece	89	5.30	5.38
Greece	89	14.48	5.38
Greece	90	2.41	5.66
Greece	93	−7.92	5.59
Greece	96	−12.37	5.61
Great Britain	79	−3.60	5.89
Great Britain	83	2.38	5.87
Great Britain	87	3.28	5.92
Great Britain	92	−5.52	5.41
Great Britain	97	11.55	5.02

Notes: The Left-Right medians as coded by Kim and Fording are taken from the CD-ROM included with Budge et al., *Mapping Policy Preferences* (2001).

that they would be more directly comparable to the Kim–Fording median voter estimates. However I happened to have the mean data at hand and so relied on that; my assumption is that the median Eurobarometer self-placements are virtually identical to the means).

The time period covered is from 1976, the first year for the Eurobarometer surveys to 1998, the most recent year for which the CMP data is available. Note that the Kim–Fording codings of the voter medians are on a scale running from −100 to +100, while the Eurobarometer scale runs from 1–10.

Using these data, I computed the correlation between these two measures of voters' positions. The correlation is only 0.14, which is not statistically significant. To me this strongly suggests that use of the Eurobarometer surveys might have supported quite different conclusions than the ones the authors report, in cross-national analyses based on data from a single time period. (This assumes, of course, that the Budge–McDonald codings of voter medians are similar to the Kim–Fording codings.) However I then computed the correlation between the *changes* in voters' Left-Right positions between elections, as computed from the Eurobarometer data and from the Kim–Fording method. To clarify, the variable I constructed was the difference between the median voter's Left-Right position in the current election and the median voter's position at the previous election, using both the Budge–McDonald measure and the Eurobarometer data. So for Denmark 1977–79, for instance, the change in the Budge-McDonald coding of the median voter's position is given as [1.37−(−6.38)]=7.75, while use of the Eurobarometer data gives a value of (5.59−5.33)=−0.26.)

The dynamic correlation was 0.55, which is statistically significant at the 0.01 level. What this result states is that in situations where the Kim–Fording method registers that the median Left-Right voter position in a country has shifted, there is a strong tendency for the Eurobarometer surveys to register an ideological shift in the same direction. To me this suggests that the authors' central conclusion, that *over time*

Western democracies tend to faithfully translate the preferences of the median voter into government policy, would likely have been unchanged, had the authors employed survey data to measure shifts in voters' ideologies, rather than relying on their own method for estimating these shifts.

We thank this conscientious reviewer for his comment and analysis. We are naturally pleased that it strengthens confidence in our main findings, even though we do feel for the reasons that we have stated that the survey-based measure of median (mean) position is less valid than our own estimate.

12

Politics and Policy Regimes: Setting a Long-Term Equilibrium

Out of the chaos of democratic politics comes the order of democratic policymaking. Such was the message from Chapters 10 and 11, potentially. Policies in our twenty-one democracies give the appearance of different regimes, situated at persistently different levels in different countries. Politics, too, in our twenty-one democracies, give the appearance of different regimes, swirling dynamically, left and right, from one election, one parliament, and one government to the next, but with centripetal tendencies drawing politics back to its ideological core in each country, over the long run. The remaining question is whether the policy and political regimes have much to do with one another. Are the politics in each separate country, drawn as they are towards an ideological core, among the forces that bring about distinguishable policy regimes in each separate country? Such is the issue we pursue in the current chapter. We do so by using the national means for each country, for both policy and political variables, as our input to the analyses. This enables us to get at the enduring relationships behind the short-term fluctuations analysed above.

12.1 FRAMEWORKS FOR ANALYSIS

The principal differences in both politics and policies exist cross-nationally. We therefore concentrate on using the median mandate thesis to explain cross-national policy differences. If the thesis fails to provide that explanation, it fails a most important test in terms of its practical applications. The theoretical structure of our explanation starts with the same reasoning as spelled out previously for short-term relationships, in Chapter 8. We ask whether policy is (*a*) an end stage of a developmental sequence, (*b*) a direct consequence of an early stage in the sequence, (*c*) both, or (*d*) neither. Here, however, instead of investigating whether and how the policy preferences adduced from elections, parliaments, governments, and ministries at one particular time produce policies more or less in line with preferences, we ask how policy preferences at the core of each country's politics through time set and keep policies in line with core preferences. To remind everyone of the possible forms that political-policy sequences may take, we represent them in the following schema.

Developmental Sequence

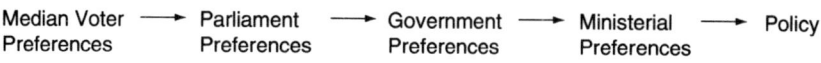

Spurious Relationships Caused by Median Voter

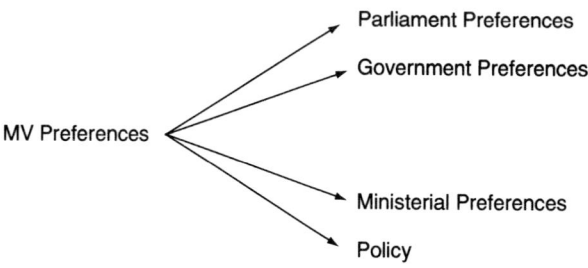

Developmental Sequence and Spurious Relationships Caused Through Either (a) or (b)

(a) Parliamentary Median [the median mandate]

(b) Government

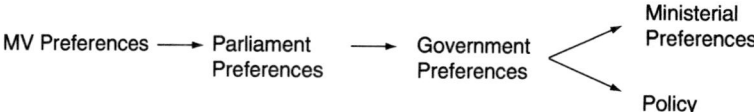

To recap:

1. The developmental sequence holds that democratic politics unfolds in a sequence from initial mover, the electorate, to end-game control, a ministry, such that any slippage along the way effectively turns policy control over to the subsequent stage of the sequence, with the effect that it is the ministry that has the final say, and therefore, policy control.
2. The spurious relationships caused by the median voter hold that democratic politics is set in motion by the electorate and that any slippage along

the way is largely noise compensated by a subsequent stage of the sequence or by subsequent elections, with the effect that policy tends to revert to a position consistent with the preferences of median voters.
3. The spurious relationships caused by the parliamentary median hold that democratic politics, though set in motion by an electorate, empowers the median party in parliament and any slippage between electorate and parliament that goes largely uncompensated, as in France and Britain, has the effect that policy tends to be held by or revert to a position consistent with the preferences of parliamentary medians. If no slippage occurs this is the median mandate process outlined in Table 2.4.
4. The spurious relationships caused by government hold that democratic politics, though set in motion by an electorate and translated through a parliament, empowers a government and any slippage between parliament and government goes largely uncompensated while any slippage between government and ministries is largely noise, with the effect that policy tends to be held by or revert to a position consistent with the preferences of governments.

One qualification is needed. The frameworks just discussed refer to policies that have a plausible connection to preferences along the Left-Right dimension, such as the size of a public economy. On specific policy issues, such as welfare and defence, it may be the preferences with respect to each policy that will be important. Thus, on particular policies, we will be especially interested in the policy preferences of parliaments, governments, and ministries. In those cases, the theoretical framework is similar but either the specific policy position of the Left-Right parliamentary median, or the parliamentary specific policy median as such, is hypothesized to be the prime moving force. We shall examine these alternative possibilities below, after our general Left-Right analysis.

12.2 POLITICAL RELATIONSHIPS VIEWED FROM A GENERAL LEFT-RIGHT PERSPECTIVE

The political relationships observed in Chapter 11 indicate substantial coordination through the electoral process. All countries under investigation showed a degree of responsiveness between parliamentary and electoral Left-Right positions reasonably close to one-to-one. Moreover, seldom did we see persistent biases in Left-Right positions of parliaments in relation to their respective electorates. It follows, necessarily, that long-run positions of national electorates over time are coordinated with highly similar long-run national positions of parliaments.[1] Figure 12.1 illustrates this

---

[1] This is necessarily so since Y-mean $= a + b\,X$-mean. Given a small bias, a is near zero. Given a near one-to-one correspondence, b is close to one. In that case, the equation can be written as Y-mean $= X$-mean.

consequence.[2] Differences between Left-Right positions of national parliamentary medians are aligned in near one-to-one correspondence with differences between the Left-Right positions of national electorates. If one country's electorate is 10 units to the right of another, then that country's parliament, as marked by its Left-Right median, is about 10 units to the right of the other.

The cross-national relationship between the Left-Right positions of parliaments and governments is similarly coordinated. Figure 12.2 illustrates

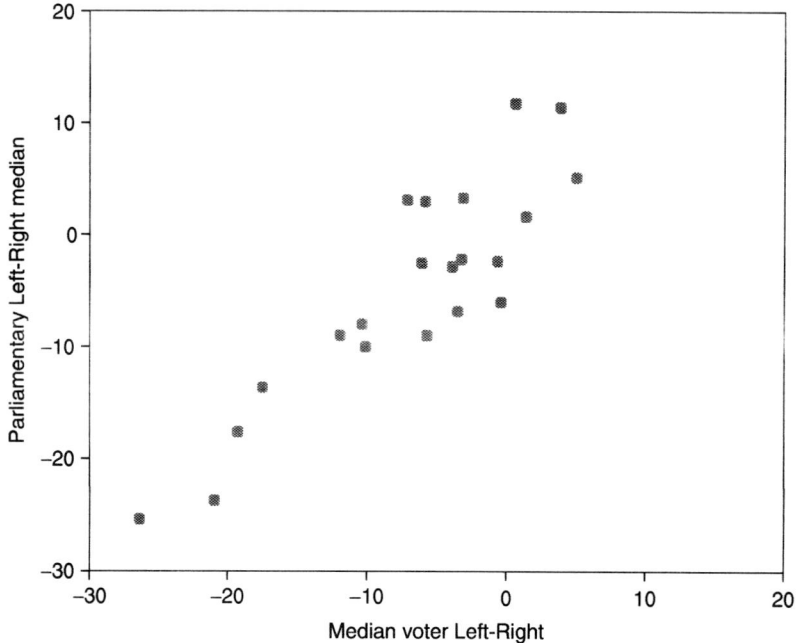

FIGURE 12.1. Correspondence between mean Left-Right positions of median voters and median parliamentary party over twenty-one countries

---

[2] Data used in Figure 12.1 and for other relationships under discussion immediately below, are based on average positions for each actor weighted by time from 1968 to 1990. The time frame is used so that the analyses we report here inform the policy analyses we report later in the chapter, where we focus on policies in the period of the mid-1970s to the mid-1990s. The relationship between parliaments and median voters over the period from the early-1950s to 1995 looks similar to that for the shorter period. Over the longer period, we find

$$Parl\ Median_{ie} = 2.27 + 1.07MV_{ie} + \varepsilon_{ie}$$

$$(0.92)\ (0.10)$$

$$R^2 = 0.869 \quad S_e = 3.25 \quad N = 21$$

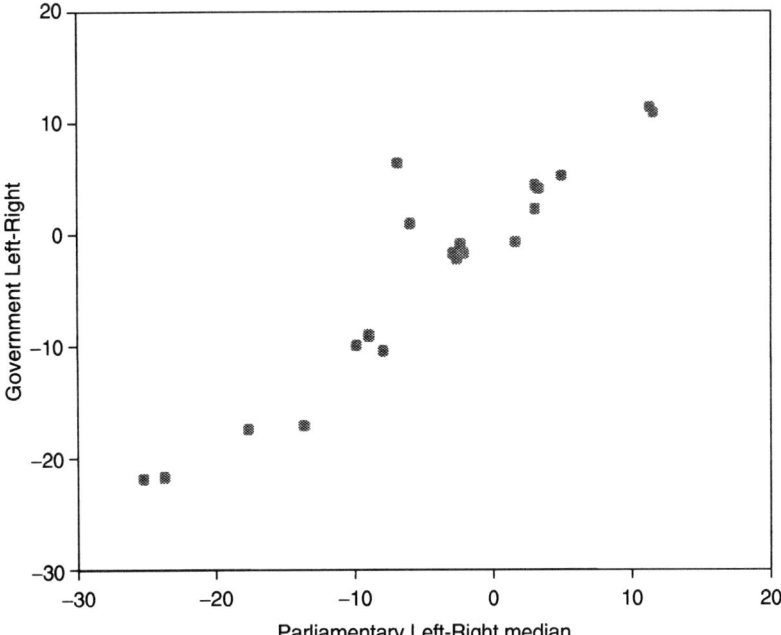

FIGURE 12.2. Correspondence between mean Left-Right positions of median parliamentary parties and of governments over twenty countries

this relationship. Again we see a distinctly linear relationship with little or no bias and a correspondence close to one-to-one. Thus, once again, each country's long-term core Left-Right government position is very nearly the same as its long-term core Left-Right parliamentary position.

Our schematic set-up contrasts the possibility of a political-policy sequence with the possibility that an actor early in the sequence controls or coordinates all subsequent steps. Across the stages involving political preferences, if coordination takes place in sequence, the process is supposed to go from median voter to parliamentary median to government—the two steps we have just observed and discussed. For the sequence-hypothesis to stand, a simultaneous consideration of the effects of the median voter and the parliamentary median on the Left-Right position of the government should reveal that governments are affected by their parliaments but not by their median voter. For the sequence hypothesis to fail, completely, the same analysis should reveal that the position of the median voters is the sole prime mover, creating a spurious relationship between Left-Right positions of parliamentary medians and governments, as indicated by the estimated parliamentary effect falling to zero.

The results of our estimation of the effect of both the median voter and parliamentary positions on government Left-Right positions show that we can distinguish between the two. The equation is

$$Govt\ L\text{-}R_i = 2.13 + 0.64\ Parl\ Mdn_i + 0.41\ MV_i + \varepsilon_i$$
$$(1.03)\quad (0.16)\qquad\qquad (0.19)$$
$$R^2 = 0.903\quad S_e = 3.3\quad N = 21$$

where *Govt L-R* is the average government Left-Right position for nation i, *Parl Mdn* is the parliamentary median position in nation i, *MV* is the median voter position in nation i, and ε is the error term.

Both estimated effects are positive and statistically significant. The parliamentary median carries one and a half times the weight of the median voter position, so we can say that the process operates more like a sequence than a single prime mover, the median voter, creating a spurious parliament–government relationship. Still, the effect of the median voter is significant. For a country with a closely matched median voter and parliamentary median, say, with both at ten, we can expect the government's position to be about 12.6, that is, receiving 6.4 units of impetus from the parliament, 4.1 units of impetus from the median voter, and 2 units of impetus from a rightward bias (recorded by the intercept). For a poorly matched parliament and median voter, say, with parliament at 10 and median voter at 0, we can expect the government's position to be more responsive to the parliament than the median voter, but the different median voter position draws the result towards it, that is, $2.13 + 0.64(10) + 0.41(0) = 8.53$.[3]

12.3 POLITICAL RELATIONSHIPS IN SPECIFIC POLICY AREAS

What can we say about political coordination in specific policy areas like welfare and international affairs? Which actor at a prior stage in the hypothesized sequence has a policy position leading directly to the policy

---

[3] One possibility is that parliaments give consideration on any mismatch between their position and that of the median voter when installing a government. Perhaps they have their eye on the next election and want to pre-satisfy the median voter with whom they are not rightly matched (Austen-Smith and Banks 1988). That is not the only possibility, of course. It is probably not even the most plausible, and it is one that is especially difficult to test. A plausible alternative explanation is that the median voter effect reflects tendencies in one or more of the coalition systems to install governments that tend towards the political centre. Were we to remove Ireland (a country with relatively low responsiveness when going from parliament to government, with a centrist tendency in its government formation, because of the constrained nature of its coalition governments) and re-estimate the equation, the effect of the parliamentary median increases to nearly 1.0 and the effect of the median voter falls to statistical insignificance.

position of governments and, next, ministries?[4] The answers allow us to check whether there is political coordination within each policy area and, if so, whether it unfolds in sequence or is driven by one actor in an early stage. However, before producing the results of those investigations we need to take account of the possibility that the initializing stage is itself of some importance. We have not hypothesized and cannot suppose that electoral preferences translate into specific policy positions. The electoral issue dimension is Left-Right, not policy-specific. That means the policy-specific positions of parliaments with respect to economics, welfare, and international affairs, as marked by the median within each policy area, might arise as electoral by-products. Alternatively, the policy-specific positions of parliaments might align with each separate policy position of the parliamentary Left-Right median so that elections in one fell swoop of a collective voice, along one broad dimension, provide a single message across all policy areas.

The linear relationships between parliamentary policy medians, and the policy-specific positions of the parliamentary Left-Right median party take the following forms, by policy area.

$$EconMdn_i = 0.03 + 0.81 \ Econ \ Parl \ L\text{-}R \ Mdn_i + \varepsilon_I$$
$$(0.29) \ (0.07)$$
$$R^2 = 0.873; \quad S_e = 1.3; \quad N = 21$$

$$WelfMdn_i = -1.18 + 0.92 \ WelfParl \ L\text{-}R \ Mdn_i + \varepsilon_I$$
$$(0.81) \ (0.07)$$
$$R^2 = 0.896; \quad S_e = 1.5; \quad N = 20$$

$$Int'lMdn_i = 0.05 + 0.70 \ Int'l \ Parl \ L\text{-}R \ Mdn_i + \varepsilon_i$$
$$(0.16) \ (0.08)$$
$$R^2 = 0.818; \quad S_e = 0.7; \quad N = 21$$

where, for nation i, *EconMdn*, *WelfMdn*, and *Int'lMdn* are the parliamentary median policy positions in each of three policy areas: *Econ Parl L-R Mdn*, *Welf Parl L-R Mdn*, and *Int'l Parl L-R Mdn* are the policy-specific positions of the party at the parliamentary Left-Right median, and the ε's are the respective error terms in each area. The results show no sign of bias to the

---

[4] All bivariate associations are statistically significant. In all policy areas, the policy positions of the parliamentary Left-Right median and of the parliamentary policy median, considered singly, are related to government policy positions. Likewise, the policy positions of the parliamentary Left-Right median, the parliamentary policy median, and the government, considered singly, are related to ministry positions.

Left or Right between the policy position of the Left-Right median party and each separate issue-specific median position in parliament (all three intercepts are statistically indistinguishable from zero). There are, however, centrist tendencies in the economic and internationalism policy areas relative to the policy-specific positions of parties at the centre of parliament in general Left-Right terms.

When a median voter's position is translated into an essentially one-to-one reappearance of the median position in parliament, over the long run, there is a tendency for that party's economic and internationalism policy positions to be slightly more extreme than parliament is as a whole. A Left-Right parliamentary median with an economic policy position at 5 or −5 is expected to exist in a situation where the economic policy median for parliament is about 4 or −4. Also, a Left-Right parliamentary median with an internationalism policy position at 5 or −5 is expected to exist in a situation where the internationalist policy median for parliament is about 3.5 or −3.5. These are consistent tendencies, in the sense of being significantly below one-to-one relationships, though as the examples make clear the centrist tendencies are not large. It should also be noted that a centrist tendency does not exist in the welfare policy area. With respect to welfare, elections produce policy positions in parliament for the Left-Right parliamentary median party that is essentially the same as parliament would look when aligned and assessed for its specific welfare policy median.

The policy specific medians that emerge in parliament are, therefore, mostly consistent by-products of what elections produce. But they are to some modest extent by-products nonetheless. This alters our theoretical view of the developmental sequence for politics to policy described earlier. Perhaps a more faithful representation, in light of the slippage on economics and internationalism, is the following.

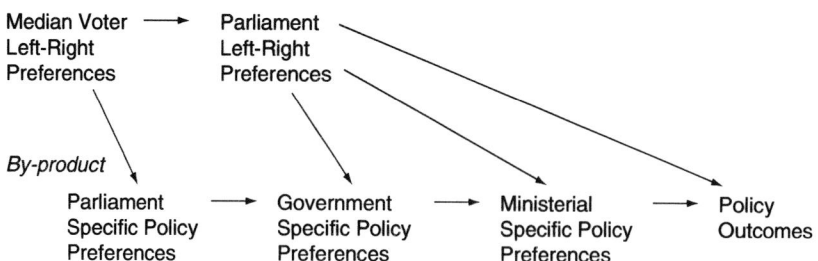

In this view, elections directly set median voter political preferences in accord with parliament so far as the centre of the Left-Right distribution in parliament is concerned. As a by-product this creates parliamentary policy preferences in separate policy areas. Given that the two sets of parliamentary policy positions are close (if we base the comparison on the separate policy preferences of the Left-Right parliamentary median versus the specific parliamentary policy median as such) the by-product is not so different from the main Left-Right product. The big remaining question is whether the policy preferences flowing directly or incidentally from elections initiate the remainder of the process. We take up this issue, in relation to government and ministerial policy preferences, immediately below. In the second half of this chapter we investigate the ultimate question: Which actor, if any, sets the track for policy regimes in the various countries?

12.4 CORRESPONDENCES BETWEEN POLITICAL PREFERENCES IN THREE SPECIFIC POLICY AREAS

The results of our quest for sequences as opposed to spurious relationships within each policy area are reported in Table 12.1. The Table is organized so that the dependent variable in each multivariate regression equation heads a column, with the regression coefficients reported for each independent variable defining the rows. On the left side of Table 12.1 are regression results for the economic policy area—preferences for a government-planned economy versus preferences for an economy organized through market forces.

TABLE 12.1. *Analyses of policy transitions from parliaments to governments to ministries in three areas*

	Economic policy		Welfare policy		International affairs policy		
	Govt position	Finance ministry position	Govt position	Social affairs ministry position[a]	Govt position	Defence ministry position[b]	Foreign affairs ministry position
Parl. L-R Median	0.46 (0.31)	−0.43** (0.13)	0.25 (0.15)	−0.16 (0.17)	−0.41 (0.24)	0.05 (0.13)	−0.28 (0.21)
Parl Policy Median	0.51 (0.36)	0.17 (0.15)	0.81** (0.16)	0.15 (0.25)	1.31** (0.31)	−0.03 (0.22)	0.54 (0.36)
Govt Position	~	1.29** (0.09)	~	1.01** (0.24)	~	0.97** (0.12)	0.83* (0.19)
Intercept	0.45 (0.45)	−0.55** (0.19)	0.13 (0.59)	−0.40 (0.60)	0.17 (0.22)	0.23 (0.11)	−0.35 (0.17)
Summary Statistics							
R^2	0.783	0.971**	0.960**	0.964**	0.704**	0.936**	0.853**
s_e	2.0	0.8	1.1	1.1	1.0	0.5	0.8

* $p < 0.05$
** $p < 0.01$
[a] Switzerland has no Social Affairs Ministry; $N = 20$ for this analysis.
[b] Iceland has no Defence Ministry; $N = 20$ for this analysis.

Column 1 shows that we cannot distinguish statistically between the possibilities that the economic policy position of governments, viewed cross-nationally, are aligned more directly with the parliamentary policy median on that particular issue or with the economic policy preferences of the party at the parliamentary Left-Right median. In statistical terms, both effects estimated simultaneously are statistically insignificant. Each effect estimated on its own is statistically significant with linear translations (slope values) close to 1.0— economic policy positions of Left-Right parliamentary median $= 0.87$ ($S_b = 0.11$) and economic policy parliamentary median $= 1.01$ ($S_b = 0.13$). One, the other, or both of these forces are associated with the government economic policy positions, but on this evidence we cannot be sure which.

The next stage in the sequence, the economic policy positions of finance ministries, shows the effect of government economic policy positions to be beyond what we could reasonably consider to be one-to-one, and the effect of the economic policy position of the Left-Right parliamentary median to be negative. The combined effect, when parliamentary and government positions are on the same side, positive-positive or negative-negative, is to produce a finance ministry position that essentially matches the government policy position, as the overly large effect from government is compensated by a negative effect from the parliamentary Left-Right median. However, when parliamentary and government positions stand on opposite sides, positive-negative or negative-positive, the consequence is to push the policy position of the finance ministry to a point that is, relative to a government's position, extra-positive when the parliamentary policy median is negative and extra-negative when the parliamentary policy median is positive.

Considering the overall evidence, the economic policy area operates something like, but not entirely like, a sequence. Government economic policy positions reflect the economic policy position in parliament, though it is unclear whether the parliamentary position is that of the overall centre party or the median party on economic policy. The position of the finance ministry is primarily a reflection of a government's policy position, but there appears to be a holdover, compensatory effect from parliament that operates to distinguish the finance ministry position from the parliamentary position when parliaments and governments line up on different sides.

The middle section of Table 12.1 gives results for welfare. The situation here is very much more in line with a simple sequence than is economic policy. Welfare policy positions of governments reflect the welfare median position of parliaments, and the social affairs ministry welfare positions reflect the welfare position of governments. For both steps, the translation is essentially one-to-one. The simple association between the welfare parliamentary median and government welfare position has a value of 1.06 ($S_b = 0.05$), and the simple association between the government welfare position and the social affairs ministry welfare position has a value of 1.00

($S_b = 0.05$). Briefly stated, welfare positions of institutional actors develop in sequence, with close to one-to-one correspondence, with the parliamentary position on welfare as such giving the impetus to the welfare positions of governments and with the government welfare position giving the impetus to the welfare position of the social affairs ministry.

International affairs produce results similar to welfare. In the step from parliament to government, the parliamentary policy median translates into a government position, without discernible effect from the policy position of the overall centre party. Uncoupling the estimated policy median effect from the estimated centre party effect gives a value of 0.83 ($S_b - 0.14$). Also, it is the government's position, not the parliament's position, on international affairs that matters in relation to ministry policy positions, both for the defence and foreign affairs ministry. There is one qualification however. There appears to be a sort of trade-off. When the foreign affairs ministry position is added to the government's policy position to form a twofold set of predictors for the policy position of the defence ministry, the foreign affairs ministry effect is negative. The equation is:

$$Defn\ Min\ Int'l_I = 0.11 + 1.32\ Govt\ Int'l_i - 0.32\ FA\ Min\ Int'l_i + \varepsilon_i$$
$$(0.16)\ (0.13) \qquad\qquad (0.12)$$
$$R^2 = 0.954 \quad S_e = 0.4 \quad N = 20^5$$

where *Defn Min Int'l* is the internationalism policy position of the defence ministry in nation i, *Govt Int'l* is the government's internationalism policy in nation i, and *FA Min Int'l* is the foreign affairs ministry's internationalism position. When the foreign affairs ministry is on the same positive/negative side, the defence ministry, government, and foreign affairs ministry all line up in something close to one-to-one policy correspondence. In nations where the government and foreign affairs ministry are, on average, on opposite sides of the issue, the defence ministry operates as a sort of counterbalance.

All the translations just discussed follow in part from institutional arrangements and in part from the choices of actors. Parliaments with majority parties, which almost always occur under SMD systems, create a sequential translation by their institutional arrangements alone. One party defines the parliamentary Left-Right median, and that party's policy specific position, on welfare, say, is by virtue of its majority status also the welfare policy median in parliament. This is no minor throwaway empirical fact; it is a consequence of organizing the system so that elections identify the same party as being at the median on every policy. Later, the parliamentary majority (and therefore by definition its median) takes over governments by weight of its numbers and puts one of its members in each ministry.

[5] Iceland does not have a defence ministry and therefore is not included in the analysis.

What happens where parliaments with more freedom to choose a sequence actually do so? We have estimated all equations in the three policy sequences based on our fifteen PR systems. All the substantive results obtained in the overall analysis (see Table 12.1) hold for these countries considered as a separate subset. Moreover, this is true not just for general tendencies but also with respect to each analytical subtlety.

1. There is no bias in any step of the sequence.
2. Economic and international parliamentary policy medians, but not welfare, are by-products of elections (i.e. not directly defined by their outcome) because they relate to the specific policy positions of the parliamentary Left-Right median in less than a one-to-one relationship.
3. The parliamentary economic policy median and the centre party's economic position have statistically indistinguishable effects on government's economic policy positions.
4. The parliamentary policy median alone is related to government policy positions and the relationship is essentially one-to-one for welfare and internationalism.
5. The government policy position alone is related to ministry policy positions and the relationship is one-to-one.

12.5 CONNECTING POLICY REGIMES TO POLITICS

The final stage in the politics-to-policy sequence is a critical one. We want to know who is tracing the track for the policy regime in each of the separate countries. As in previous analyses we have three sets of policy variables. One indicates the size of the public economy, here aggregated as the 1973 to 1995 average of a country's consolidated central government spending as a percentage of GDP. Two others are the same welfare policy indicators used in Chapter 9, the Esping-Anderson welfare index and the 1992–5 social spending figures collected by Lijphart. The third set includes the two international affairs policies, also used in Chapter 9, foreign aid as a percentage of GDP in the early 1980s and 1992–5 foreign aid as a ratio of defence spending. Additional data details are provided in the Appendix to this chapter.

The independent variables of greatest interest for the median mandate thesis are those that reference the policy positions of various institutional actors, namely median voters, parliaments, governments, and ministries. As the thesis has developed in Chapters 10 and 11, normal democratic policy-making is viewed as consolidating policy regimes that change only slowly with time. The hypothesized role of politics is to mark out the track for those policy regimes. Our measurement of policy positions for each institutional actor is its average policy position during the period of governments sitting in 1968 to any government installed before 1 July 1991. This allows us to cover governments with budget authority from the late 1960s to the early 1990s.[6]

It is easier to appreciate the details that follow by sketching out our conclusions first. We therefore begin here by going directly to what the details of our evidence support with respect to the wider-scope view. This is outlined in Figure 12.3. We know already that the political-governmental process develops mostly in a sequence starting with a step from voters to parliaments in such a way that median voter Left-Right preferences are, over the long- run, accurately re- presented in parliament as a whole. We also know that parliamentary re- presentation along the Left-Right dimension is sorted out in reasonably faithful ways policy area by policy area; but the reasonable faithfulness has to allow for some slippage in this sorting. In particular, the parliamentary party at the Left-Right median—the centre party as we shall call it—holds specific policy preferences slightly less centrist than when parliament is considered by itself on the specific issues of the economy and international affairs. Thereafter, in the steps involving selection of governments and ministries, it is the policy-specific median positions that translate most directly into government policy positions as a whole and into the policy positions of individual ministries. When we arrive at the policy end-stage, however, our evidence below points to the conclusion that in all three areas of policy it is the Left-Right position of the centre party that operates to mark the tracks for policy regimes. It is never possible to reject the idea that the centre party's Left-Right position shapes both the long-run look of the political-governmental process and policy regimes in each specific area.

This is our major finding. It strongly supports the median mandate thesis. The median voter speaks at the time of an election. At any one time his or her voice is liable to be distorted. But over the long run the political process tends to work out the general tendency of what the electorate has been saying and, again in the long run, accurately represents that voice in parliament. Certainly the electoral voice never speaks in a direct, knowable sense on specific policies. This allows its parliamentary reflection to become slightly biased in a centrist direction. However, in the end, the Left-Right position of the parliamentary overall median is what provides the most

---

[6] We settled on this period a priori, for two reasons. A lag over five years is required to move policy over half way from where it was when a party took control of an institutional sector, to where its own policy position indicates the party would like to see it. Also, the time period reasonably matches the time frame that Lijphart (1999) used to investigate the relationships between consensus democracy and several policy indicators, including the four of his variables that we are using. We experimented with alternative divisions in time, going back to starting points in the early 1960s and up to starting points in the early 1970s. Each alternative made some sort of marginal difference, of course, but in the main the findings reported later hold without much concern for the detail of the time period selected.

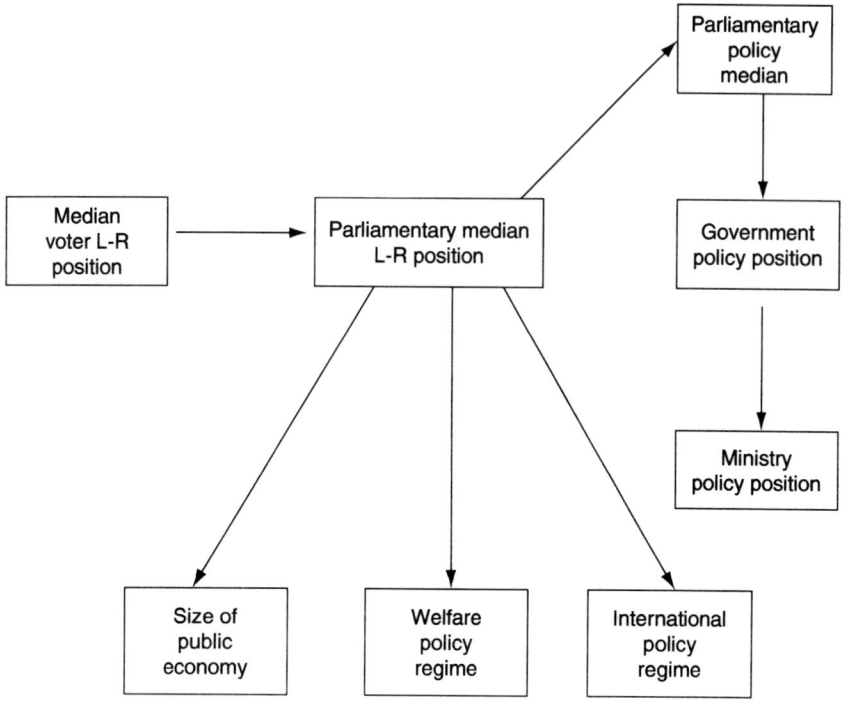

FIGURE 12.3. A validated overview of the long-term policy process under representative democracy

consistent information about the tracks followed by the specific policy regimes. It is difficult to imagine a more faithful representational process that connects electors' preferences to the actions of governments.

That is the wide-scope perspective; now we turn to the details.

12.5.1 Size of the Public Economy

The size of a country's public economy is a significant indicator of what governments do. It tells us how wide is the scope of a country's definition of public goods and how broad is the coverage of goods and services coming under public organization and control. The question is whether there is a discernible role for politics beyond the largely constitutional framework that divides control between a central government, on the one hand, and regional and local governments on the other.

Table 12.2 presents a detailed view of three possible political effects operating on the size indicator of a country's policy regime.[7] In column 1,

---

[7] In order to have comparable mean values of spending for the period, 1973–95, we had to exclude Portugal and Spain from the analysis and interpolate government spending values for a

TABLE 12.2. *Average central government spending estimated as a function of Left-Right positions of institutional actors, controlling for centralization and international economic openness*

	Y = Central government spending (1973–95) average			
	(1)	(2)	(3)	(4)
Centralization	10.80**	10.74**	10.92**	9.87**
	(1.84)	(1.77)	(1.84)	(1.99)
Median Voter	−0.25*	~	~	~
	(0.13)			
Parliamentary Median	~	−0.24*	~	−0.20
		(0.11)		(0.12)
Government	~	~	−0.20*	~
			(0.11)	
Openness	~	~	~	0.04
				(0.04)
Intercept	31.90**	32.47**	32.83**	30.30**
	(1.45)	(1.22)	(1.23)	(2.55)
Summary Statistics				
R^2	0.725**	0.744**	0.723**	0.759**
s_e	4.9	4.7	4.9	4.7

* $p < 0.05$
** $P < 0.01$

we have an equation that estimates the effect of median voters, controlling for centralization. The results indicate that for a country with middle-range centralization (e.g. Germany) and a centrist median voter, the average size of its political economy would be about 32 per cent of GDP. Move to a more centralized system (e.g. the Netherlands) with a centrist median voter and the size grows to about 43 per cent; move to a less centralized system (Switzerland) with a centrist median voter and the average size drops to about 21 per cent. The position of the median voter can make a difference, too. Its −0.25 coefficient is statistically significant. Recall that the scale of the Left-Right variable runs low to high as political preferences go from left to right, so a negative effect is to be expected. Substantively it means that a median voter near the position of a typical social democratic party (around −10 on the

---

few countries. Spending by Portuguese and Spanish central governments changed noticeably when constitutional democracy came to Portugal and Spain in the latter years of the 1970s, rising quickly between 1974 and 1980. This means the 1973–95 average political economy value is not an indicator of the policy regime set by democratic forces alone. Italy, New Zealand, and Switzerland have missing values on central government spending in at least one year (see Table 10.1). The available versus missing years can lead to an over- or understatement of a country's spending average for the period, depending on which years are missing. We compensated for this by estimating an autoregressive equation for spending in each country and using its results to assign the missing year or years a value equal to the predicted value.

Left-Right dimension) leads a country to a level of spending about two and a half points higher than a centrist median voter, while a country with a median voter near the position of a typical conservative party leads a country to a level about two and a half points lower than with a centrist median voter. Thus, moving across the Left-Right spectrum from social democrat to conservative is expected to create about a 5-unit difference in the size of a public economy. The political effect might be said to be small in comparison to the centralization effect, 10 units for a movement when going from low to medium centralization and another 10 units of movement when going from medium to high centralization. But the political effect is substantial in and of itself. A 5-unit difference is equivalent to that between the Australian and German, or between the Irish and the Dutch, political economies.

In column 2 of the table, we report the same sort of analysis but substitute the Left-Right position of the overall parliamentary median for that of the median voter. The fit in this case is better, compared to the equation with the median voter, but the improvement is modest. The degree of overtime coordination between the median voter's and the parliamentary median's Left-Right positions makes it difficult to say which set of political preferences is the principal force in setting the size of a political economy. The sizes of public economies will look much the same whether we estimate them from the median voter or the parliamentary median. When the two variables are included in the same equation, the parliamentary median effect retains its magnitude of about -0.25 while the estimated median voter effect falls to near zero. However, the collinearity between them makes both estimated effects less reliable, to the extent that both are statistically insignificant.[8] It is safe to say that one or the other exerts an effect, though we would prefer firmer evidence as to which one. Forcing a choice on the basis of our evidence gives the nod to the parliamentary median, but not with much assurance.

Column 3 of Table 12.2 reports the results of estimating the government's Left-Right position on public economy size. Since it lines up rather neatly with the parliamentary median position, it is to be expected that it will show an effect similar to those we estimated for median voters and parliaments. It, too, cannot be assuredly distinguished from the effect or effects of those other actors, and its magnitude is similar. The fit is slightly worse than the others, but our statistical

---

[8] By removing the UK from the analysis the evidence lines up more clearly in favour of the parliamentary median over the median voter. Without the UK, controlling for the median voter and estimating the effect of the parliamentary median shows that the parliamentary median effect withstands the control and that the effect of the median voter is essentially zero. This is because while the sizes of political economies elsewhere line up more squarely in accordance with the parliamentary median than with the median voter, the size of the political economy in the UK lines up more squarely with the average position of the median voter. We do not remove the UK case because doing so provides us with no potent inferential leverage. With the UK included we are left to wonder whether voters or parliaments are having a general, uniform effect. With the UK excluded we are left to wonder whether the effect is usually but not everywhere exerted by parliament.

ability to distinguish among the three is impaired by the close associations each bears to the others. We are left once again to say that political forces appear to make a difference to the scale of a public economy, even though we cannot say with assurance which political force makes it.

The fourth and final column of the table reinserts the parliamentary median as the most likely operative political force and then controls for the openness of a country's economy. We saw earlier, in Chapter 9, that the effect of an open economy comes and goes depending on how rapidly an economy is growing, but there may exist a generalized effect from openness that we do not want to confuse with an estimated political effect. The results show an unreliably estimated effect, though one that might make as much difference as 4 per cent of GDP in the public economy for a large difference in openness. Imports plus exports as a percentage of GDP that is 100 units higher in one country versus another, that is, about the difference between Belgium and the USA—would, if the coefficient of 0.04 is accepted as accurate, lead to about a 4 percentage point difference in the size of a public economy.[9] The control for openness reduces the magnitude of the political effect modestly and moves it to the edge of statistical significance ($p = 0.054$). Given that we cannot tell with much assurance whether an open economy itself carries weight in pushing up the size of a public economy and the consistent estimation that shows a parliamentary median effect of -0.2, we feel reasonably secure in concluding that the political regimes in our twenty-one countries do move the size of their public economics by approximately two to two and a half points across the range of Left-Right positions between social democrats and centrists (e.g. Liberals or Christians) and another two to two and a half points between centrists and conservatives.

Possibly the political effect is more directly a function of where the political actors stand on economic matters than on the general Left-Right dimension. Debates over whether to organize economic activity under government control as opposed to relying on market forces is fundamental to defining what is a public good and stipulating the breadth of its coverage. This is checked with the analyses reported in Table 12.3. The structure of the report is the same as we have just gone through with respect to the Left-Right dimension. The policy preferences of each actor are investigated separately, and then the one appearing to hold the best explanatory promise is investigated further with a control for openness. The summation is easy to provide: the estimated effects from all three political actors are properly signed—a preference for market forces over governmental action reduces the size of a public economy—but none has a statistically reliable impact at conventional

---

[9] As we have been reminded, it is proper to keep in mind that the openness variable gains some potential statistical force due to having GDP as a common denominator of both the dependent variable (central government spending/GDP) and itself, as an independent variable, ([imports + exports]/GDP).

TABLE 12.3. *Central government spending estimated as a function of economic policy positions of institutional actors, controlling for centralization and international economic openness*

	(1)	(2)	(3)	(4)	(4)
Centralization	10.93**	10.58**	11.32**	11.32**	9.54*
	(1.92)	(1.97)	(1.94)	(1.96)	(2.13)
Economic Policy Position of Parl. L-R Median	−0.40	~	~	~	~
	(0.29)				
Economic Policy Position of Parl. Policy Median	~	−0.47	~	~	−0.32
		(0.34)			(0.36)
Economic Policy Position of Government	~	~	−0.31	~	~
			(0.29)		
Economic Policy Position of Finance Ministry	~	~	~	−0.24	~
				(0.27)	
Openness	~	~	~	~	0.05
					(0.04)
Intercept	33.83**	33.90**	33.80**	33.60**	30.71**
	(1.26)	(1.27)	(1.30)	(1.28)	(2.95)
Summary Statistics					
R^2	0.701	0.701	0.687	0.681	0.727
s_e	5.1	5.1	5.2	5.2	5.0

* $p < 0.05$
** $p < 0.01$

levels of statistical significance. Controlling for economic openness performs as one would expect. Its estimated effect is unreliable but it tends to reduce the appearance of political effects, if such effects actually do exist in the form of these economic policy preferences.

On the size of a political economy the political forces appear to operate more clearly from general Left-Right positions than from specific policy positions taken on the sub-issue of a government-controlled versus a market-force directed economy. There is good reason for this. The Left-Right dimension provides the ideological underpinning for the economic debate and it accounts for something more—other aspects of policy that are important components of the public economy. A willingness to define, for example, health care as a publicly provided service—one aspect of general Left-Right positions—leads to expanding the public economy. Combining that willingness with an orientation that favours welfare spending—another aspect of general Left-Right positions—gives the size of the public economy an extra push, which the analysis here indicates is worth taking into account.

12.5.2 Welfare

Providing welfare support systems is a large part of what advanced industrial democracies do. The organization of social and economic life takes the activity fairly much for granted and so do the politics of all twenty-one countries we are investigating. We saw earlier that no party system offers a choice between anti-welfare versus pro-welfare stances (see Chapter 5). The political debate is mostly over how extensive the system should be. We look at two indicators, a general index of welfare effort and the extent of social spending (welfare plus health care), and ask whether the political preferences of political actors add to our understanding of the welfare commitments that the political systems of different countries provide.

To cut to the centre of our findings we can say that the politics of welfare policies operate fairly much in the same way as they do when it comes to setting the size of political economies. Simply put, the long-run Left-Right position of the parliamentary median provides the clearest estimate of an effect from political preferences, and those preferences survive controls for age distributions and the organization of politics along consensual versus majoritarian lines.

Table 12.4 presents the details that lead us to this conclusion. In the first four columns on the left of the table we have the estimated effects, presented one by one and, in turn, of the welfare policy preferences of the centre party in parliament, the parliamentary median on welfare, the government, and the social affairs ministry. In each case we have controlled for the percentage of the population aged 65 and over, as that is the segment on whom most welfare effort is expended. The political preference efforts of each political factor are properly signed, and each is just over conventional levels of statistical significance (p values slightly lower than 0.05). In column 5 we see that the effect of the Left-Right parliamentary median is properly signed and even more reliably estimated. And, from column 6, we see that even controlling for Lijphart's measure of consensus democracy, which itself has an effect at the edge of statistical significance ($p = 0.037$), leaves us with evidence showing that parliaments leaning to the political right have less extensive welfare systems compared to those with parliaments leaning to the political left.

As expected, the relative size of a country's aged population exerts a large effect, moving the values of the welfare index two points higher for each percentage point difference. That alone can account for about a 14-unit difference in the welfare index values, for those who are familiar with Esping-Anderson's welfare state difference between Sweden and Canada (Esping-Andersen 1990). The political effect is smaller, but alone it amounts to more than a 5-unit difference in the index values coming from Sweden's left leaning parliament and Canada's centrist parliament.

Analyses of social spending over the years 1992–5 leads to much the same inferences about the connection between politics and welfare policy. These analyses are shown at the right of Table 12.4. In the first four columns we see that the specific welfare policy positions of the four actors bear a strong and

TABLE 12.4. *Welfare policies estimated as a function of policy positions of institutional actors, controlling for aged population and consensus democracy*

	Welfare index 1980s						Social spending 1990s					
	(1)	(2)	(3)	(4)	(5)	(6)	(1)	(2)	(3)	(4)	(5)	(6)
% Age ≥ 65	2.50** (0.60)	2.55** (0.58)	2.46** (0.61)	2.48** (0.62)	2.20** (0.49)	1.95** (0.47)	1.23** (0.43)	1.44** (0.43)	1.32** (0.45)	1.36** (0.45)	1.09** (0.41)	1.03* (0.44)
Welfare Position of L-R Parliament Median	−0.46* (0.26)	—	—	—	—	—	−0.67** (0.18)	—	—	—	—	—
Welfare Position of Parliament Policy Median	—	−0.48* (0.25)	—	—	—	—	—	−0.66** (0.19)	—	—	—	—
Welfare Position of Government	—	—	−0.43 (0.24)	—	—	—	—	—	−0.61** (0.18)	—	—	—
Welfare Position of Social Affs[a] Ministry	—	—	—	−0.43* (0.23)	—	—	—	—	—	−0.53** (0.17)	—	—
L-R Position of Parliament Median	—	—	—	—	−0.35** (0.10)	−0.26* (0.11)	—	—	—	—	−0.35** (0.08)	−0.32** (0.09)
Consensus Democracy	—	—	—	—	—	0.02* (0.01)	—	—	—	—	—	0.004 (0.010)
Intercept	−9.87 (7.53)	−10.87 (7.48)	−9.43 (7.56)	−9.95 (7.74)	−3.05 (6.34)	0.13 (6.03)	2.51 (5.46)	1.19 (5.56)	3.15 (5.64)	1.93 (5.63)	9.58 (5.23)	10.25 (5.60)
Summary Statistics												
R^2	0.661	0.670	0.659	0.667	0.779	0.828	0.680	0.672	0.658	0.672	0.729	0.733
S_e	5.0	4.9	5.0	5.1	4.0	3.7	3.6	3.6	3.7	3.7	3.3	3.4

a. Switzerland does not have a social affairs ministry.
* $p < 0.05$
** $p < 0.01$

statistically significant relationship to social spending, controlling for the age distributions of the populations. Each actor's position looks as if it could move social spending between five and six points for a 10-unit difference in welfare support (e.g. the difference between overtime welfare support of parliaments and governments in Britain compared to Norway). Column 5 shows that parliamentary Left-Right positions are an even better predictor of social spending. The difference between a parliament persistently controlled by social democrats compared to one persistently controlled by Christian democrats leads to a six to seven percentage point difference in social spending.[10] Controlling for Lijphart's consensus democracy at this point makes no difference. Consensus democracy appears to have been standing in as indicator related to both the age distributions and Left-Right differences in political preferences.[11]

In the welfare policy area, whether viewed from the perspective of a welfare policy index or from the perspective of social spending, the Left-Right position of the parliamentary median exerts a consistent and substantively important influence on welfare policy regimes.

12.5.3 International Affairs

Our two indicators of international affairs policies are foreign economic assistance as a percentage of GDP and foreign economic assistance expressed as a ratio of defence spending. The results once again support the proposition that these policies reflect the Left-Right position of parliaments rather than specific internationalism policy positions of other institutional actors. They also tell us that the relationship is more clearly evident when we look at economic assistance relative to defence spending than when we look at economic assistance on its own.

The left of Table 12.5 focuses on economic assistance, and we see that the internationalism policy positions of none of the actors bear a statistically strong relationship with it. The coefficient on all actors takes the proper sign, but the only actor whose coefficients are statistically significant is the parliamentary policy median ($p = 0.04$). The internationalism position of the Left-Right parliamentary median party and the Left-Right position of the

---

[10] It is possible that political preferences operate as a conditional translation mechanism, rather than an additive force. More left-leaning parliaments could translate the relative size of the aged population into higher levels of social spending. That is what one could expect if left-leaning preferences were operating as a matter of generosity. We explored the possibility of this sort of interactive effect and found no strong indication of it.

[11] When consensus democracy is added to an equation with either the age-distribution variable or the Left-Right parliamentary median, its statistically significant bivariate effect is reduced to statistical insignificance. When both the age distribution and the parliamentary median are controlled, the effect of consensus democracy falls to essentially zero, as we can see in Table 12.5.

TABLE 12.5. *Internationalism policies estimated as a function of policy positions of institutional actors, controlling for consensus democracy*

	Foreign aid as % GDP 1980s							Foreign aid as ratio of defence spending 1990s						
	(1)	(2)	(3)	(4)	(5)	(6)	(7)	(1)	(2)	(3)	(4)	(5)	(6)	(7)
Int'lism Position of L-R Parl Median	−0.05 (0.03)	—	—	—	—	—	—	−3.06* (1.12)	—	—	—	—	—	—
Int'lism Position of Parl Policy Median	—	−0.07* (0.04)	—	—	—	—	−0.06 (0.04)	—	−4.05** (1.42)	—	—	—	—	—
Int'lism Position of Government	—	—	−0.04 (0.04)	—	—	—	—	—	—	−1.67 (1.61)	—	—	—	—
Int'lism Position of Defence Ministry[a]	—	—	—	−0.05 (0.04)	—	—	—	—	—	—	−1.89 (1.56)	—	—	—
Int'lism Position of Foreign Affs Ministry	—	—	—	—	−0.02 (0.04)	—	—	—	—	—	—	−1.27 (1.44)	—	—
L-R Position of Parl Median	—	—	—	—	—	−0.01 (0.006)	—	—	—	—	—	—	−0.73** (0.22)	−0.57** (0.25)
Consensus	—	—	—	—	—	—	0.0005 (0.0010)	—	—	—	—	—	—	0.03 (0.03)
Democ Intercept	0.41** (0.06)	0.41** (0.06)	0.44** (0.07)	0.44** (0.07)	0.43** (0.07)	0.38** (0.07)	0.40** (0.07)	21.40** (2.41)	22.81** (2.33)	23.16** (2.67)	23.54** (2.65)	23.76** (2.74)	19.51** (2.45)	19.43** (2.41)
Summary Statistics														
R^2	0.141	0.168	0.052	0.072	0.015	0.138	0.197	0.292	0.310	0.056	0.075	0.042	0.375	0.428
S_e	0.3	0.3	0.3	0.3	0.3	0.3	0.3	10.3	10.2	11.9	11.8	12.0	9.7	9.6

[a] Iceland does not have a defence ministry
* $p < 0.05$
** $p < 0.01$

parliamentary median as such are close to meeting statistical significance (p values = 0.051 and 0.052, respectively). On the issue of foreign economic assistance it is not at all clear that the preferences of any of those actors matter much. The levels of significance of none of the three withstand a control for Lijphart's consensus democracy indicator, which itself is not statistically significant ($p = 0.09$). Maybe one or more of these actors or the consensus condition influence economic assistance allocations, but, if they do, the effect is neither large nor as reliable as our standards would call for.

The role of the parliamentary Left-Right median is more clearly visible as we turn attention to the ratio of economic assistance to defence spending. For this indicator, the international affairs policy orientation of both the centre party and the policy-specific policy median bear reliable relationships. That is not true for government international affairs policy positions; nor is it true for the policy positions of the defence or foreign affairs ministries. In the end it is once again the Left-Right position of the centre party that bears the most reliable relationship to the economic-assistance and defence-spending ratio. Furthermore, it withstands a control for Lijphart's consensus democracy. Across the Left-Right dimension a 10-point movement (as from a social democratic party persistently at the centre to a liberal or Christian party at the centre) gives rise to the expectation of a sixfold change in the ratio of economic aid to defence spending.

As with other policies, it is the centre party's general political position that provides us with the best sense of how international affairs policy, at least in terms of economic assistance versus military orientations, will be set up in the long-term—what we have called a policy regime. Should we be surprised that for each separate policy we have considered the general Left-Right parliamentary median provides the most consistent political force? No, there is no particular surprise. Considering policies over the long run it would have been more surprising to have found no coordinating force across different areas. It is possible to have guns and butter but not in a centrist political regime that imposes a budget constraint on its size.

12.6 CONCLUSION

The democratic process looks orderly and coherent from the perspective taken here. Over the course of approximately one generation political actors in a country are well aligned with one another. That description applies to parliaments as representatives of median voters, governments as embodiments of the preferences of parliaments, and ministers as agents of government. All of this leads to a set of national policy regimes that are easy to understand in terms of politics. Clearly, important pre-existing political choices, such as how centralized the state apparatus should be, exert substantial effects, as do demographic forces that signal how much of what sort of policy a population could be said to need. Still, elections and political arrangements that are shuffled every few years create a cumulative signal about policy preferences that itself is easy to read and that on our evidence *is* read.

Let no one mistake or mischaracterize what we are saying. Our portrait of order and coherence in policy comes from a long-term perspective. We spent Chapters 8 and 9 looking at a good deal of seeming disorder in policymaking. The closer one gets to the process, the more difficult it is to see anything resembling coherence. A political decision tomorrow could take a multiplicity of forms. A minister might resign or be removed or a government might be unmade and remade over a question of religious tolerance, union activity, application of welfare rules, rearrangement of tax rates, corruption, and so on (Browne et al. 1988). Over the course of several years, however, one can be reasonably confident that what the sequence of elections, parliaments, governments, and ministers has produced will mostly be in line with what the parliament would want, and parliaments will have been occupied by parties of varying strength who represent fairly much what the people have said they want. All of this may sound like the good luck of political statistics, which in a search for a central tendency smoothes out ragged variations. It is, of course. But in a substantive sense the central tendency represents the long-term output of the system. It is more than an artefact, or simply good luck, that it coincides with the settled preferences of the various participants. Democracy, for all its institutional variations and for all its value-based tensions, holds dear a decisive principle. Its institutions must honour and its pursuit of goals must accommodate this idea. Democratically derived power is provisional power. The same voice that can order the unlocking of forces in the Pandora's box of democratic decision-making can at the next moment reconsider its decision and order those forces back into the box.

13

Unifying Theories of Democracy Through the Median Mandate

This book has gone from a general consideration of representative democracy (see Chapter 1), to a specific median mandate theory of how it works and on what basis it can be justified (see Chapter 2), and on to detailed analyses of how well contemporary democracies function in accordance with the theory (see Parts II–IV). In the process we have addressed many of the classical questions of democratic theory. Does a prospective majority emerge? Is it possible to infer a popular majority view either as one centred on a median or one revealed in a negative vote against the government? Can and does a popular majority, in any form, empower its policy views in government? How accurately, and how reliably can a popular majority preference translate into a similar position in government? What role do party systems play in the translation? What role do electoral systems play in the translation? Even if the policy views of an electoral majority and a government are brought into alignment, can such political views really influence a decision-making process characterized by incremental change and possibly dominated by the bureaucracy?

All these questions have been considered and received at least a partial answer at some point in this book. Our purpose here is to bring them together in an integrated account, based on a validated median mandate view of the democratic process. We begin with the general view of the party mandate and where it stands in light of our analysis.

13.1 THE PARTY MANDATE

We considered both the government and the median forms of party mandate theory in Chapter 2, setting out the essential assumptions of each in a series of propositions (see Tables 2.1 and 2.4). The government mandate is the classical version of the theory, giving a central role to political parties in channelling the preferences of the electorate through the policy programmes they offer. The party that receives majority endorsement in the election on this basis is then empowered to form a government that will put its programme into effect.

13.1.1 A Mandate From the Electorate

We could tell, even before getting much beyond the evidentiary starting point, that the idea of an electoral majority selecting a government under the government mandate version is seldom fulfilled. Either a mere plurality of votes is translated under SMD into a majority of seats, or a majority is constructed through party bargaining under PR. The electorate's role in selecting a governing majority is, at best, partial. Under SMD, electoral rules are partly responsible, and under PR party negotiations are partly responsible. In either case, there is no guarantee that a popular majority might not oppose government policy.

We turned then to consider what is required in order to be able to infer the existence of a majority. To infer that an electoral majority exists, one centred on a median voter, requires a common currency in the language of electoral politics. Parties have to use this language and the voters have to understand it. The evidence we reviewed strongly, virtually unequivocally, supports the proposition that such a common language exists in a form known to nearly everyone, everywhere, as the Left-Right dimension. Also, the direct evidence we have on party policy proposals at the time of elections tells us that parties are reliable carriers of identifiable Left-Right positions. Furthermore, party policy positions with respect to specific policy topics are usually arranged in properly aligned subsets of the general Left-Right dimension. Little about the parties' policy behaviour indicates that their presentations to electorates would be an obstacle to inferring the existence of an electoral majority based on the distribution of party votes along a Left-Right alignment.

It was possible that we need not go to the median-centred majority inference, for electors could be signalling their majority preference in the negative. While majorities seldom form in support of a new government, perhaps we could infer that they form in opposition to a failed government. The evidence for this could come from electors throwing the rascals out for bad economic times during a government's tenure and retaining credible governors following good economic times. We found modest evidence in line with this proposition, in the form of incumbents losing a percentage point and a half of their votes for particularly bad inflation. As it turns out, however, this positive evidence lends little support to the proposition that elections are used as accountability devices. Incumbents, on average, suffer larger vote percentage losses than 1.5 per cent through the ordinary ebb and flow of party vote fortunes. Moreover, at the time of the eleven elections when inflation rates were running more than 1 per cent worse than expected, and the incumbents did lose an extra point and a half, they were no more or less likely to leave office than if their fate had been decided by the flip of a coin. Upon considered reflection, the modesty of the evidence to support retrospective economic voting stands to theoretical reason. The thesis' basic assumption is that the voters' decision calculi are simple when the economy is running well or poorly. The decision is, in actual fact and logic, entirely problematic. The only firm expectation one can arrive at is that incumbents are unlikely to keep the extra votes they received in the election preceding their entry into government, where, of course, the extra votes were part of the reason they were in government.

A predominating fact about elections is that party support ebbs and flows around stable levels, in ways that make it possible to say there are 'forces restoring party competition'. A deviation from that normal situation at any given election is *expected* to disappear so that the starting point for a new election is the competitive balance that has been established over the long run. Viewed in the light of identifiable Left-Right party position taking, this pattern of vote dynamics carries with it the implication that there are stable, long-run, Left-Right positions of median voters in national electorates. There are such Left-Right electoral equilibria, and, what is more important, the equilibria *and* the fluctuations around them are the forces that mark the Left-Right positions of governments. Governments move left and right, on average through time, in synchronic rhythm with electoral Left-Right movements.

How can that be? Is there not substantial evidence of representational missteps, slippages, and, thereby, distortions due to electoral system mistranslations, party system voids in and around positions occupied by median voters, and narrowly self-interested parties negotiating which of them will enter governments? We find, indeed, that there are representational distortions everywhere we look, and we find that they are, just as expected, attributable to electoral systems, party systems, and party negotiations. Nevertheless, distortions do not cumulate across the steps in the representational process nor do they cumulate over time. Rather, across the steps and most especially over time, distortions cancel one another so that typically they do not amount to much in terms of representational bias. Biased representation is the exception, not the rule. In the intermediate and long run, the Left-Right positions of median voters translate rather faithfully into Left-Right positions of governments—more faithfully under PR compared to SMD, but with reasonable faithfulness almost everywhere.

The evidence with respect to the behaviour of both parties and electorates suggests that the median mandate could work without the need for an actual majority to emerge. What an election mandates is the position (or very close to it) that the majority *would* adopt if it *did* emerge. In those instances when a majority actually does endorse a position, however, it must include the median voter by definition. In this exceptional event government mandate reasoning, too, will work, but simply as a special case of the median mandate, a case where a spontaneous rather than just an inferred majority position exists.

13.1.2 The Median Mandate as Democratic Policy Process

Having established the plausibility of a median mandate at the electoral stage, the normative requirement for a representative system is to translate this into public policy. At the core of the mandate thesis is the idea that individual elections shape policy outcomes. The mechanism through which this occurs is the translation between median vote and median legislative party. The fact of the median legislative party being the prime policy mover rather than the median voter himself or herself is what makes the process representative. Median in this context is the Left-Right overall policy median, because the general debate that takes place between electors and parties during elections can only be conducted in broad terms (Downs 1957: 113–20; Pierce 1999). Within this framework the essential thing is that the median voter chooses the median legislative party which in turn shapes policy outputs, thus making the 'necessary connection' between popular preferences and public policy, the defining characteristic of democracy (Saward, 1998: 51).

13.1.3 Policy Effects of Individual Elections, Parliaments, and Governments

Our electoral evidence indicates that a transfer of the mandate between parties will result from a new election. However, the policy consequences of such new or renewed mandates are not revealed in the short run. The stated policy intentions of governments correlate only at modest levels with what the parliamentary centre parties said to their electorates they intended to do. Moreover, on the evidence from government policy declarations, we are left with an ambiguous understanding of whether a government's policy statements are more or less in line with the parliamentary centre, more or less in line with pre-election stated intentions of the parties in government, or more or less in line with an individual ministry's preferences.

Similar, perhaps even weaker, evidence exists when we turn to actual policies as our basis for asking whether parliament, government, or ministry holds responsibility for actual policies. On size of political economies in both the early 1980s and early 1990s, on two different indicators of welfare policy also for the early 1980s and early 1990s, and on international affairs policy as indicated by foreign aid and defence expenditures in the early 1980s and early 1990s, there is no strong and persistent effect on policies from either the Left-Right or the specific policy positions of parliaments, governments, or ministries. Each institutional actor appears more influential than the others every once in a while, but no one of them appears as a persistent and potent policy force.

One reaction at that juncture is to conclude that the representational process works well enough on its own political terms but does not mean much in policy terms. Preferences of voters translate into preferences of governors reasonably well, but there is some sort of disconnection between preferences and policy. Another possibility, however, is to step back from the process and look at the preference-to-policy linkage in its larger democratic context.

13.1.4 Long-term versus short-term change

Because of the slow nature of policy change within a country, the effects of individual elections can be properly estimated only in terms of changing the long-term equilibrium point which policy is moving towards. From a short-term perspective, change in policy between one government and the next is small, and may even be imperceptible. As a consequence, no clear preference-to-policy linkage emerges. In line with what we had already found, (*a*) a variety of actors—median voters themselves, median parties, governments, and ministries—seem to exert an effect somewhere, sometime, but (*b*) sometimes no political actor seems involved. One is left wondering about the regularity and orderliness of democratic decision-making (Kingdon 1984) and the power of elections to change things. By default, the major influence could be attributed to a bureaucracy, largely characterized by policy inertia that permits only limited, incremental change (Davis et al. 1966; King and Laver 1993).

Our overtime investigations of policies confirm this characterization, at least in regard to the pace of policy change. Policy is very slow moving. If a democratic will emerges to change, say, the size of a political economy by as much as 5 per cent, we can expect it to take more than four years to move halfway towards its intention. Given the electoral forces restoring party competition, which themselves move quite rapidly, it is reasonable to expect that by the time the new intentions found themselves not even quite halfway towards implementation, another new set of political intentions will be in place.

What is needed for a full understanding of the democratic policy process is a broader perspective, a time horizon that goes beyond the results of the last election and the preferences of the current parliament and government. The merit of our pooled over-country, over-time data is that they permit this broader perspective (McDonald et al., 1999). Taking that perspective we see that cross-national differences on policy matter enormously, and that they cumulate through successive individual elections as the elections become reflected, again successively, in parliamentary median preferences. Within countries, individual elections have an impact. And, while the impact is not, possibly, discernible as between two governments, it is important in substituting one long-term equilibrium point for another and in making some progress towards it. What emerges in the long run are national policy regimes proceeding along tracks set by the averaged Left-Right disposition of their parliaments, which themselves are mostly in line with the long-term preferences of their electorates.

The fact that the next election result often reverses the policy movement set in motion after the previous election does nothing to detract from the importance of the individual election. The intelligence of democracy is about having the freedom to reconsider and alter direction as the effects of the incremental changes are evaluated at the margin (Lindblom 1959). And individual election outcomes are central to this process, as they must be if the popular will is to be translated into public policy. If overtime fluctuations in popular feeling create a median preference equilibrium point, reflected in a settled national policy regime, then that is a fair outcome for democracy. It is one that derives from a series of varying election outcomes and appropriate policy responses to them.

These facts, inferences, and interpretations square with two sets of attitudinally grounded analyses of democracy. In one, Edward Muller and Mitchell Seligson use macro-level data to explore the causal structure leading to and maintaining democracy (Muller and Seligson 1994). Broadly construed, their intention was to sort out structural features—economic, political, and social—in contrast to civic culture attitudes of a nation's public which influence the maintenance and strengthening of democratic regimes. With one important exception, they found civic culture attitudes play no essential role. The exception is public attitudes towards the pace of policy change. High levels of public support for gradual change—relative to levels of support for revolutionary change or for vigorous defence of the status quo—promote democracy. Given that policy change in a democracy is gradual, it makes sense that attitudes supportive of a gradual pace would provide a foundation on which to build and rest a democracy.

Another attitude, which we will call political patience, has also been shown to play a key role in democracies. Democracy requires open competition; some have even defined it expressly in terms of the competitive struggle for power (e.g. Schumpeter 1942). From competition come winners and losers, and being one or the other has consequences for a person's willingness to support democracy (Anderson and Guillory 1997). Over the long haul, however, an especially important contribution to maintaining democracies comes from the consent of losers (Anderson et al. forthcoming). Gradual policy change is one way to keep the consent of those who recently lost. Were pension systems, tax codes, access to medical care, infrastructure investment, national security provisions, monetary policy, and the like to change abruptly with each switch in the direction of political winds, the ability to adjust one's personal situation to the new political reality would significantly raise the stakes for being a winner. And even then, laying secure plans for what one should do to improve one's lot in life while in a winning situation might prove impossible. Gradual change, for all that it fails to accomplish, leaves most people with knowledge of how to run their lives in their own interests.

13.1.5 Overall Policy Orientations Versus Specific Ones

Pluralism sees different actors as being decisive in different policy areas (Dahl 1960). General mandate theory has assumed that electors, parties, and governments operate within the same policy space, which makes a clear line of linkage between them easy to maintain.

Our own design entertains the possibility that the unified Left-Right space of election debate may break down into its component parts after the end of the campaign. Competences over different areas are given to ministers and ministries, with the legislative and cabinet agendas organized departmentally. The difficulty this potentially creates for a median mandate theory of representation is that median parties in the specific areas may create and run each specific policy, in contrast to having policy created and coordinated in line with the general Left-Right parliamentary median endorsed by the electorate.

There is, of course, a reasonably high chance that the party of the general Left-Right median parliamentarian will also be at the median in each separate policy area, but it is not guaranteed. Some slippage can and, as we have seen, does occur in actual representational practice. Not unnaturally, given the procedural segmentation of policy, the composition of governments and the ministry allocation to parties are influenced by the party at the median in each specific policy area (see Figure 12.3). Fortunately, from the viewpoint of the median mandate thesis, the overall median party continues to be the main influence over actual policy outputs, in the long run. Thus the slippage between electorally endorsed Left-Right positions and specific policy ones does not impede the 'necessary connection' between popular preferences and public policy. The coordination across policy areas is mediated through the overall median party. Will this always happen? We cannot say. But as it has occurred over a quarter of a century in twenty-one democracies there is a fair presumption that it will. The overall median party seems generally to be placed in a powerful decision-making position.

The specific policy areas that we have analysed are of course central areas of policy and thus major components of overall Left-Right differences themselves. Other areas of policy further removed from these (e.g. environment, culture, agriculture) may show more slippage as a result. Representation, like other democratic mechanisms, can be a clumsy device. What we see here is that it works reasonably in the central areas of policy. And that is a reassuring result.

13.2 UNIFYING THEORIES OF REPRESENTATIVE DEMOCRACY ROUND THE MEDIAN MANDATE

Few contemporary theorists, analysts, or commentators contest the normative aspirations of democracy. And no more than a few would object to the observation that the twenty-one democracies we analysed here have succeeded in responding to democratic aspirations over the course of their individual democratic histories—not uninterruptedly but generally. Large, well-reasoned, and long-considered doubts exist, however, about how and why this is so. One line of argument maintains that these democracies, and all successful democracies generally, are able to take account of citizen preferences by organizing themselves through pluralistic decision-making (Dahl 1960). An especially appealing and powerful variant of Dahl's democratic pluralism is Arend Lijphart's 'consensus democracy'. This maintains that majorities manufactured from electoral pluralities, and probably even those created by electoral majorities, do not work as effectively to bring citizen interests into the governing process as relying on institutional devices and cultural dispositions to thwart the creation of an actual majority and, in its stead, invite representative elites from all pillars of society to take part in setting the agenda and deciding its outcomes. A third line of argument, a liberal democratic thesis closely associated with William Riker, implicitly refuses to embrace pluralism, in general or in its consensus democracy form, because both are too divorced from what he calls the 'the keystone democratic institution', the ballot box. Because it can be shown that any multi-option collective decision is almost assuredly unstable and subject to devious manipulation, his liberal democracy thesis opts prescriptively for a majoritarian two-party system and descriptively for elections holding policymakers accountable for what they have chosen to do. Remembering, as Downs observed and as the clarity of responsibility thesis of elections has since sought to demonstrate, consensus democracy (multiparty, PR) systems are less susceptible to enforcing accountability, they are not well adapted to liberal democracy. A fourth line of argument, articulated by Powell and his collaborators, postulates 'two visions of democracy'. Each is to be evaluated on its own terms. In one vision, Lijphart's consensus democracy, elections are used to bring elites together for negotiations; in the other, Riker's liberal (aka, majoritarian) democracy, elections are used to hold leaders of the majority party accountable for what their party did (or did not do) while holding the reins of power.

The median mandate embraces many of the observations that have given rise to these four theses. It does so, however, while refusing to cede the central idea that elections create a necessary correspondence between citizen preferences and government policies. Pluralism exists under the median mandate, but its long-run effects are coordinated by elections. The appeal of consensus democratic arrangements, compared to majoritarian ones, is a consequence of their greater reliability in translating public preferences into policy. The theoretically ineradicable instability of collective decisions that gives rise to calls for liberal democracy is apparent in short-run decisions under the median mandate. But the thesis also calls attention to how elections produce long-run equilibria around which the short-run instability swirls. And, in the end, given a theory of democracy in which elections create a necessary correspondence between public preferences and public policy, there is no need to retreat to two incommensurable visions of democracy, each operating according to its own standards and neither of which, in any case, is really democratic.

13.2.1 Pluralism and the Median Mandate

An important theoretical advantage of the median mandate is that it explains why ideas such as pluralist democracy seem a good way to make sense of chaotic short-term political processes. At a certain point all the authorized democratic actors—median voters, median parties, governments, ministries—get a look in, though not in an orderly way nor necessarily in the areas where they are really authorized by an electorate. But it is because the process lacks electoral authorization that pluralism falls short of guaranteeing a 'necessary link' between popular preferences and policy. On this score, its democratic credentials have been harshly criticized. Interpreting those credentials through the median mandate, as a reaction to the froth and change of everyday politics and short-term decision-making but with due attention to long-term dynamics responsive to settled popular preferences, is therefore better for understanding the processes at work and their democratic credibility.

Pluralism under the median mandate is reminiscent of Lindblom's claim that the intelligence of democracy comes from *not* granting unconditional power to a central decision-maker. Instead, power is dispersed among a number of independent actors no one of whom can be said to be in control, unconditionally, but all of whom adapt their preferences and strategies to the preferences and strategies of others. For Lindblom the process is pluralism describable in other words, as *partisan mutual adjustment*. This is appropriate and accurate, so far as it goes. The median mandate goes farther and specifies how partisan mutual adjustments are coordinated by elections.

13.2.2 Consensus Democracy and the Median Mandate

Consensus democracy privileges extensive negotiation and compromise among all parties, whether in government or not. Decisions may take longer, therefore, but they are thoroughly worked out and more acceptable to everyone than under majoritarian systems. Party leaders can then sell agreements to their supporters as the best feasible policy. There is comparative evidence that such policies are indeed better in a number of ways than 'majoritarian' policies (Lijphart 1999).

In many ways 'consensus democracy' represents a return to older conceptions of representation, where elected parliamentarians could act on their own conceptions of what was good for their constituents rather than being mandated by them. Seen in this light it is not very democratic—there is clearly no necessary connection between popular preferences and public policy. Indeed, if the two conflict, the party leaders' job is to reconcile preferences to policy rather than the other way round. This contrasts with 'majoritarian democracy' where the current majority (or, generally, plurality with a manufactured legislative majority) can impose whatever policy it wants, subject to practical constraints.

Our analysis of policy regimes suggests that neither side may be quite as free as this implies to create or impose policy, given the constraints and the slow nature of change. More importantly, however, median mandate ideas suggest that consensus democracy may not be undemocratic at all under a universal criterion of democracy. Provided that the median legislative party, with the pivotal position in parliamentary negotiations, is the choice of the median voter—as in these PR systems it generally is—then consensus democracy *is* making the 'necessary connection' between majority preferences and public policy. The 'Power of the Median' should ensure that the agreed policy settles at or near the point favoured by it, which is the optimal social-political solution anyway.

Consensus democracy thus fares quite well under a median criterion. 'Majoritarian democracy' (in practice 'pluralitarian democracy') does less well. To the extent the median in parliament diverges from the voter median, democracy is actually being distorted, though of course if a true majority emerges it becomes a special case of the median mandate. From a democratic point of view, and applying the median criterion, most SMD systems need to be modified towards PR. If PR produces more of a multiparty system this will result in electoral preferences being more sensitively interpreted and a median-median translation made with more accuracy and much more reliability.

Finally, as regards the 'better' policies discovered by Lijphart in consensus democracies, the median mandate reveals how policies follow from preferences, not processes, which is how things should be if it is the process of democracy that is at work. Once we enter a control for the preferences of electors and more especially their agent, the median party in parliament, it is preferences that stand up as determining, while the process of negotiation becomes simply the way in which they are effected.

13.2.3 Liberal Democracy and the Median Mandate

One of the troubling theoretical problems for contemporary democracy is the revelation that collective decision-making leads to incoherence (Arrow 1963; Riker 1980, 1982). Elections may, therefore, not be very democratic after all inasmuch as the policies that emerge lack the necessary correspondence to majority preferences. Worse, policies decided collectively can end up anywhere in a policy space (McKelvey 1979; Schofield 1985). Worst, *where* they end up can depend on the art and manipulative skill of a single clever individual, determined to make his or her preference the policy by which all have to abide. This reasoning could lead to despair over the democratic credentials of any and every policy (Rae 1971) and the futility of science of politics as applied to democracy (Ordeshook 1986).

The median mandate's salve for such despair comes in part from the structure-induced equilibrium, described in general theoretical terms by Shepsle and Weingast (1981) and in specific electoral terms by Niemi (1969, 1984). Political parties do much to carry electorates towards equilibrium outcomes. That is not all, however, for it is not enough by itself. Any single outcome is arguably not at an equilibrium point. According to the median mandate, and on our evidence in support of it, no single political outcome is an equilibrium outcome. Nor can we report that many individual outcomes are especially close to their equilibrium points. The ultimate remedy for this in a democracy, helped as it may be from time to time by structure-induced equilibria, is one that Riker himself recognized early on (Riker 1964)—democratically derived power is provisional. Even though a policy today can end up anywhere in the policy space, there is a tomorrow for democrats. When it arrives, the median mandate implies that an inconsonant outcome is likely to be reconsidered and brought back into line with the long-run preferences of electors.

Democratic instability, therefore, is very much evident in the theoretical light cast by the idea of a median mandate. But it is short-run instability. All manner of governments can form, all sorts of parties sit in ministries; all sorts of disconnections and distortions in translating the preferences of one set of actors in the sequence into the preferences of the next set of actors in the sequence and then into policy are apparent. Equally apparent, however, is the long-run equilibrium around which the short-run instability revolves. The operation of a democratic system is not well analogized by looking at it as if it were a celestial system subject to mechanical causes and effects, describable by mathematically formulated physical laws. It is better compared to a biological system where the characteristics and behaviours of individual creatures are not entirely predictable but where we understand their adaptive equilibria in the aggregate and in the long run.

13.2.4 Two Visions of Democracy and the Median Mandate

The median mandate is grounded in a universal standard. This runs contrary to a relativist view that different visions of democracy set their own criteria against which to be judged. The most eloquent recent plea for 'two visions of democracy' to run independently comes from Powell (2000). In his view, majoritarian democracy (even the diluted version in which pluralities take the place of majorities) has its own criteria of clarity and decisiveness by which it ought to be judged, as should the SMD system on which it is based. On the other hand, 'consensus democracies', PR-based with many parties, have values of compromise and quality of outputs, which need to be accepted on their own terms. There are no universal standards of 'democracy' that Powell thinks need be applied. Both systems have regular elections of course, and that entitles them to be called 'democracies'. But elections do not need to function in the same way or promote the same values. The two systems are incommensurable under the two visions since each generates and applies its own standards, which stress goals and strategies quite different from each other.

Powell's postmodernist dualism stems from the critique of majoritarian systems associated with Lijphart's 'consensus democracy' and with pluralism and from the defence of majoritarian systems by liberal democratic theory as articulated by Riker. The median mandate thesis concurs with Powell's general conclusion—both systems can be defended. However, it leads us to that conclusion through very different theoretical and evidentiary terrain than that traversed by the 'two visions'. And when we do arrive at our conclusion that both can be defended, we are still able to say that PR-based systems have better democratic credentials. There is a unique meaning to democracy that enables us to judge between different forms of it.

We recognize that Powell is correct about the two principal sets of rules by which democracies operate. Still, and perhaps precisely because there are two general sets of rules, it is surely correct to maintain that we must apply the same criteria in order to evaluate them. Otherwise political theory as we know it would cease to exist. We could not even compare Dutch with American democracy, as each country would have its own unique traditions and criteria to apply. The end result would be the old country-by-country analyses, telling the story of each national democracy and undermining the theoretical generalizing ambitions of modern political science. Cutting through all of this is the fact that democracy *is* a universal concept in the sense of bringing popular preferences necessarily into decision-making. Democracy in any country can be judged by its success in doing so. In this context, the median mandate provides the best practical way of operationalizing the 'necessary link'—certainly under representative democracy.

13.3 THE MEDIAN MANDATE AND DIRECT DEMOCRACY

The driving force behind moves to direct democracy in the modern world comes from a perception that it makes this necessary link between popular preferences and public policy in a way that representative democracy cannot. There could hardly be a simpler way of ensuring the connection than having the whole population voting on separate policies as they come up, particularly if popular pressure can initiate the vote. Supporters of representative democracy in fact often argue in terms of insulating public policy from 'popular passions' and leaving it to the calm deliberation of elected representatives (for a review of such arguments, see Budge 1996).

Although proponents of both the representative and direct 'visions' argue in such traditional and contrasting terms surprisingly often, the presence of political parties competing over policy has long outdated them. Party activity has brought direct and representative voting closer together—in many ways both can be regarded as variants of party democracy. By their nature parties tend to take sides in debates, particularly where central areas of policy are involved. Indeed, by defining and discussing the alternatives in direct voting they help set choices just as we have seen them doing in representative democracy. On the other side, general elections are not really held to choose individual representatives but rather to decide what the balance of party strength will be in the legislature (or governing institutions, in the case of the USA) and thus, ultimately, what programmatic mix will prevail as public policy.

In a real sense, therefore, thanks to parties, all elections have become policy-based. This has subverted the two-stage interpretation of general elections as having only to do with electing representatives who will then make better policy for you than you can yourself, though consensus democracy can be seen as an update on this idea. The importance of the median mandate interpretation is that it sees elections as determining legislative deliberation through the empowerment of the median party by the median voter.

If modern direct and representative democracies are both based on party-guided policy votes, the differences between them boil down to the level of generality at which popular decisions are made. Under representative democracy, votes take place on general policy for a three-to five-year period. Under direct democracy, individual policies are decided one by one. This difference in levels of aggregation might produce different outcomes (see Table 1.2). But, of course, so do the different representative voting procedures.

To fully enforce the necessary democratic connection between preferences and policy in the modern world we probably need parties, legislatures, governments, *and* direct voting on specific policies. Elected governments are necessary to carry through politics and administration, and legislatures to support, criticize, and choose them. Parties are essential for organizing elections and interpreting their outcomes in legislative terms. They need to give some indication of what they will do in policy terms, otherwise a median mandate will not work. When it does, it ensures the necessary linkage between preferences and policymaking in central areas, that is, those linked to the Left-Right differences in terms of which general election debates are carried on.

There remain, however, many policy areas only loosely linked to this central debate or indeed quite divorced from it. Here the median parliamentary party is not democratically empowered because such issues are always crowded out by more pressing ones (and may not even align with Left-Right positions anyway). Here, then, direct voting must surely be the only way of making popular preferences prevail. Problems of aggregation with general programmes do not matter since policy is decided separately in these areas anyway.

It is significant that contemporary practice, in democracies with a strong element of direct voting, is to hold referendums and initiatives precisely in such policy areas—not economic or social policy but environment, morals, territorial powers, constitutional matters and so on (Butler and Ranney 1994). The median mandate interpretation of representative democracy as a method of policy aggregation and transmission of central policy preferences helps us understand better why this division of spheres might hold. Even direct and representative democracy can be seen in this light not as two rival and exclusive 'visions' of 'doing democracy' but as complementary ways of ensuring its necessary link between popular preferences and policy.

13.4 THE 'BIG QUESTIONS' ANSWERED THROUGH THE MEDIAN MANDATE

With this discussion we have traversed many of the central questions of democratic theory and practice. Like its main rival, the government mandate (which it encapsulates as a special case), the median mandate is a general theory of democracy—describing how it works and also how it ought to work. It confronts the central finding which discredits its rival—majorities rarely emerge spontaneously—by substituting the median for an actual majority vote. The median voter's position estimates what the majority will would be if it were concretely embodied. Under equality of votes it is also the socially optimal policy position, a satisfying symmetry with the expression of the majority position.

Any fears that we are simply endorsing a majority steamroller, with no safeguards for minority rights, should be allayed by the consideration that a median mandate would work equally well if intensity of feeling were taken into account, as under a Borda procedure (Budge 1996: 163–6). There is no difficulty in finding the median under weighted voting. It is simply likely to be a different median from that found under equality of votes.

In either case, the election rules can make sure that the median electoral position is reflected in the median party in parliament. The best election rules are those that ensure the translation is made accurately and reliably. This points to some kind of PR as opposed to an SMD plurality system. The choice between these systems could be taken on incommensurable criteria of representativeness and compromise versus decisiveness. We can cut this knot, with the consideration that as democrats we ought maximize democracy rather than secondary values that might be found in greater measure under other systems of government. PR is clearly the system that most accurately and reliably lines up median vote with median party (see Table 2.5). It should therefore be preferred.

In any case the contrast between the decisiveness and responsiveness of SMD majoritarian systems and multiparty coalition PR systems has often been overdrawn. On accuracy of responsiveness, our own analyses (see Tables 11.1 and 11.2) indicate there is little difference between the systems. Nor is there much evidence to suggest that one system facilitates control over policy more than the other. Both confront a slow, constrained process of policy change in which the changing parties in control can intervene. But they make a long-term mark only if their policy is actually a settled, long-term choice of voters confirmed in two or three successive elections. Where dominance changes hands after one election, policy is as like as not to veer back to where it was. The resulting long-term equilibrium value, or long-term policy regime as we have termed it, remains stable under these circumstances. But it is certainly capable of being affected by political parties, where their appeal can overcome for a sustained period the 'forces restoring democratic competition'.

These forces undermine any notions of government accountability, as all governments lose votes without a great deal of regard to their performance. These same forces however also act on the position of the median party, usually changing it and its policy disposition between one parliament and another. Governments may not be held accountable as such. Here again we see the median mandate solving a difficulty of the government mandate. Some parties in a coalition government will have to continue if its successor is to get a majority: which, therefore, should voters target to punish? In the case of median parties there is only one, and it will cease to be the median if enough voters shift.

In many areas, median mandate theory solves classic dilemmas of democratic politics more concisely and elegantly than either the government mandate or convergence theory (which indeed quite fails to tackle many of the classic governmental problems of democracy). Its theoretical potential to deal with these is enhanced by our empirical validation of it as the working explanation of democracy. This implies that the central conceptual doubts about democracy can be disposed of not only in principle but now also in practice. Contemporary democracy works largely as it is intended to. Its workings not only follow the prescriptions of the median mandate but can be justified as effecting it.

Bibliography

Achen, Christopher H. (1975). 'Mass Political Attitudes and the Survey Response', *American Political Science Review*, 69: 1218–31.

—— (1977). 'Measuring Representation: Perils of the Correlation Coefficient', *American Journal of Political Science*, 21: 805–15.

—— (1978). 'Measuring Representation', *American Journal of Political Science*, 22: 475–510.

Adams, James (2001). 'A Theory of Spatial Competition with Biased Voters', *British Journal of Political Science*, 31: 121–58.

—— and Ernest Adams (2000). 'The Geometry of Voting Cycles', *Journal of Theoretical Politics*, 12: 131–54.

Aldrich, John H. (1983). 'A Downsian Spatial Model with Party Activism', *American Political Science Review*, 77: 974–90.

—— (1995). *Why Parties: The Origins and Transformation of Political Parties in America* (Chicago: University of Chicago Press).

Anderson, Christopher J. (1995). *Blaming the Government: Citizens and the Economy in Five European Democracies* (Armonk, NY: M. E. Sharpe).

—— and Christine Guillory (1997). 'Political Institutions and Satisfaction with Democracy', *American Political Science Review*, 91: 66–81.

—— André Blais, Shaun Bowler, Todd Donovan, and Ola Listhaug (2005). *Losers' Consent: Elections and Democratic Legitimacy* (Oxford: Oxford University Press).

ASPA (American Political Science Association) (1950). *Towards a More Responsible Two-Party System* (New York: Rinehart).

Arrow, Kenneth J. (1963). *Social Choice and individual Values*, 2nd edn. (New Haven, CT: Yale University Press).

—— (1969). 'Values and Collective Decision Making', in Peter Laslett and W. G. Runciman (eds.), *Philosophy, Politics and Society*, Third Series (Oxford: Blackwell), pp. 215–32.

Auer, Andreas and M. Bützer (eds.) (2001). *Direct Democracy: The Eastern and Central European Experience* (Burlington, VT: Ashgate).

Austen-Smith, David and Jeffrey Banks (1988). 'Elections, Coalitions and Legislative Outcomes', *American Political Science Review*, 82: 405–22.

—— and Jeffrey Banks (1990). 'Stable Portfolio Allocations', *American Political Science Review*, 84: 891–906.

Axelrod, Robert (1970). *Conflict of Interest* (Chicago: Markham).

Balinski, M. L. and H. P. Young (1978). 'Stability, Coalitions and Schisms in Proportional Representation Systems', *American Political Science Review*, 78: 848–58.

Bara, Judith (1999). 'Tracking Estimates of Public Opinion and Party Policy in Britain and the US', Paper presented at ECPR Joint Sessions, Mannheim.
Barry, Brian M. (1970). *Sociologists, Economists and Democracy* (London: Collier-Macmillan).
Bartolini S. and Peter Mair (1990). *Identity, Competition and Electoral Availability: The Stabilisation of European Electorates, 1885–1985* (Cambridge: Cambridge University Press).
Black, Duncan (1958). *The Theory of Committees and Elections* (Cambridge, UK: Cambridge University Press).
Boix, Carles (2000). 'Partisan Governments, the International Economy, and Macroeconomic Policies in Advanced Nations, 1960–93', *World Politics*, 53: 38–73.
—— (2001). 'Democracy, Development and the Public Sector', *American Journal of Political Science*, 45: 1–17.
Bonner, R. J. (1967). *Aspects of Athenian Democracy* (New York: Russell & Russell).
Brams, Steven (1976). *Paradoxes in Politics: An Introduction to the Nonobvious in Political Science* (New York: Free Press).
Browne, Eric C. and Mark Franklin (1973). 'Aspects of Coalition Payoffs in European Parliamentary Democracies' *American Political Science Review* 67: 453–69.
——John P. Frendreis and Dennis W. Gleiber (1984). 'An "Events" Approach to the Problem of Cabinet Stability', *Comparative Political Studies* 17: 167–97.
Buchanan, James and Gordon Tullock (1962). *The Calculus of Consent* (Ann Arbor, MI: University of Michigan Press).
Budge, Ian (1994). 'A New Spatial Theory of Party Competition: Uncertainty, Ideology and Policy Equilibria', *British Journal of Political Science*, 14: 443–67.
—— (1996). *The New Challenge of Direct Democracy* (Cambridge: Polity Press).
—— (2001). 'Validating the Manifesto Research Group Approach: Theoretical Assumptions and Empirical Confirmations', in Michael Laver (ed.), *Estimating the Policy Positions of Political Actors* (London: Routledge), pp. 50–65.
—— and D. J. Farlie (1983). *Explaining and Predicting Elections* (London: Allen & Unwin).
—— and Richard I. Hofferbert (1990). 'Mandates and Policy Outputs: U.S. Party Platforms and Federal Expenditures', *American Political Science Review*, 84: 111–31.
—— and Hans Keman (1990). *Parties and Democracy: Coalition Formation and Government Functioning in Twenty States* (New York: Oxford University Press).
—— Ivor Crewe, David McKay, and Kenneth Newton (1998). *The New British Politics* (London: Pearson Longman).
—— H.-D. Klingemann, Andrea Volkens, Judith Bara, Eric Tannenbaum, et al. (2001). *Mapping Policy Preferences: Estimates for Parties, Voters and Governments 1945–1998* (Oxford: Oxford University Press).
—— David Robertson, and Derek John Hearl (eds.) (1987). *Ideology, Strategy and Party Change* (Cambridge: Cambridge University Press).
Butler, David E. and Austin Ranney (eds.) (1994). *Referendums around the World*, (London: Macmillan).
Cain, Bruce (1992). 'Voting Rights and Democratic Theory: Toward a Colour-Blind Society' in Bernard Grofman and Chandler Davidson (eds.), *Controversies in*

Minority Voting Rights: The Voting Rights Act in Perspective, (Washington DC: The Brookings Institution) pp. 261–77.

Cameron, David R. (1978). 'The Expansion of the Political Economy', *American Political Science Review*, 78: 1243–61.

Campbell, James E. (1985). 'Explaining Presidential Losses in Midterm Congressional Elections', *Journal of Politics*, 47, 1140–57.

—— (1986). 'Predicting Seat Gains from Presidential Coattails', *American Journal of Political Science*, 30: 165–83.

—— (1991). 'The Presidential Surge and Its Midterm Decline in Congressional Elections, 1868–88', *Journal of Politics*, 53: 477–87.

—— (1997). 'The Presidential Pulse and the 1994 Midterm Congressional Election', *Journal of Politics*, 59: 830–57.

Castles, F. (ed.) (1982). *The Impact of Parties* (London: Sage).

—— and Peter Mair (1984). 'Left-Right Political Scales: Some Expert Judgements', *European Journal of Political Research*, 12: 73–88.

Converse, Philip E. (1964). 'The Nature of Belief Systems in Mass Publics', in David Apter (ed.), *Ideology and Discontent* (New York: Free Press).

—— (1966). 'The Concept of a Normal Vote', in A. Campbell, Philip E Converse, Warren E. Miller, Donald E. Stokes (eds.), *Elections and the Political Order* (New York: Wiley), pp. 9–39.

—— (1969). 'Attitudes and Non-Attitudes: Continuation of a Dialogue', in Edward R. Tufte (ed.), *The Quantitative Analysis of Social Problems* (Reading, MA: Addison Wesley).

—— and Roy Pierce (1986). *Political Representation in France* (Cambridge, MA: Harvard University Press).

Coughlin, Peter J. (1992). *Probabilistic Voting Theory* (Cambridge: Cambridge University Press).

Cox, Gary (1997). *Making Votes Count Strategic Coordination in the World's Electoral Systems* (Cambridge and New York: Cambridge University Press).

Dahl, Robert A. (1956). *A Preface to Democratic Theory* (Chicago: University of Chicago Press).

—— (1960). *Who Governs?* (New Haven, CT: Yale University Press).

—— (1989). *Democracy and Its Critics* (New Haven, CT: Yale University Press).

—— (1998). *On Democracy* (New Haven, CT: Yale University Press).

—— and Charles Lindblom (1954). *Politics, Economics and Welfare* (New Haven CT: Yale University Press).

—— and Edward R. Tufte (1973). *Size and Democracy* (Stanford: Stanford University Press).

Davis, O. A., A. H. Dempster, and Aaron Wildavsky (1966). 'A Theory of the Budgetary Process', *American Political Science Review*, 60: 529–47.

De Jouvenal, Bertrand (1961). 'The Chairman's Problem', *American Political Science Review*, 55: 368–72.

DeSwaan, Abram D. (1973). *Coalition Theory and Cabinet Governments* (Amsterdam: Elsevier).

Downs, Anthony (1957). *An Economic Theory of Democracy* (New York: Harper).

Dorussen, Han and Harvey D. Palmer (2002). 'The Context of Economic Voting: An Introduction', in Han Dorussen and Michaell Taylor, (eds.), *Economic Voting* (London: Routledge).

Duverger, Maurice (1954). *Political Parties: Their Organization and Activities in a Modern State*, B. North and R. North (trans.) (New York: John Wiley).

Dye, Thomas R. (1966). *Politics, Economics and the Public* (Chicago, IL:Rand McNally).

Edgeworth, Frances Y. (1898). 'Miscellaneous Applications of the Calculus of Probabilities—Continued', *Journal of the Royal Statistical Society* 51: 534–44.

Eldersveld, Samuel J. (1950). 'Polling Results and Prediction Techniques in the British Election of 1950', in James C. Pollock, Lionel Laing, Samuel Eldersveld, Thomas J. Jenkin, and Richard Scammon (eds.), *British Election Studies, 1950* (Ann Arbor, MI: George Wahr).

Enelow, J. M. and Melvin J. Hinich (1984). *The Spatial Theory of Voting* (Cambridge: Cambridge University Press).

Engle, Robert F. and Clive W. J. Granger (1987). 'Cointegration and Error Correction: Representation, Estimation and Testing', *Econometrica*, 55: 251–76.

Epstein, Leon (1967). *Political Parties in Western Democracies* (New York: Praeger).

—— (1988). 'The Puzzle of Midterm Loss', *Journal of Politics*, 50:1011–29.

—— (1979). 'The SRC Panel Data and Mass Political Attitudes', *British Journal of Political Science*, 10: 52–73.

Erikson, Robert S., Michael B. MacKuen, and James A. Stimson (2001). *The Macro Polity* (New York: Cambridge University Press).

Esping-Andersen, Gøsta (1990). *The Three Worlds of Welfare Capitalism* (Princeton, NJ: University Press).

Ferejohn, John (1999). 'Cautionary Notes', in Robert Richie and Steven Hill (eds.), *Reflecting all of Us: The Case for Proportional Representation* (Boston: Beacon).

Fiorina, Morris (1981). *Retrospective Voting in American National Elections* (New Haven, CT: Yale University Press).

Gabel, Matthew J. and John D Huber (2000). 'Putting Parties in Their Place: Inferring Party Left-Right Ideological Positions from Party Manifestos Data', *American Journal of Political Science*, 44, 94–103.

Gallup, George, Jr. (1972, 1978, 1979–88). *The Gallup Poll* (New York: Random House: Scholarly Research Institute, Wilmington, DE).

—— (1976). *The GallupInternational Opinion Polls*, (New York: Random House; Westport, CT: Greenwood Press).

Gallup Political and Economic Index (1966–1995). (London: The Gallup Poll).

Grofman, Bernard (1996). 'Political Economy: Downsian Perspectives', in R. E. Goodin and H-D Klingemann (eds.), *A New Handbook of Political Science*, Chapter 30 (Oxford: OUP), pp. 691–701.

Guinier, Lani (1994). *The Tyranny of the Majority: Fundamental Fairness in Representative Democracy* (New York: Free Press).

Hausman, J. A. (1976). 'Specification Tests in Econometrics', *Econometrica*, 46: 1251–71.

Hearl, Derek John (2001). 'Checking the Party Policy Estimates', in Budge, et al. op.cit, pp. 11–125.

Hermans, F. A. (1938), [reprinted 1968]. 'The Dynamics of Proportional Representation', in Harry Eckstein and David E. Apter (eds.), *Comparative Politics: A Reader* (London: Free Press), pp. 254–80.
Hinich, Melvin J. (1977). 'Equilibrium in Spatial Voting: The Median Voter Result is an Artefact', *Journal of Economic Voting Theory*, 16: 208–19.
Hofferbert Richard I. and Hans-Dieter Klingemann (2002). 'Remembering the Bad Old Days', *European Journal of Political Research*, 46: 41–65.
——, Ian Budge and Michael D. McDonald (1993). 'On Party Platforms and Government Spending: Reply', *American Political Science Review* 87: 781–6.
Huber, John D. and Ronald Inglehart (1995). 'Expert Interpretations of Party Space and Party Locations in 42 Societies', *Party Politics*, 1: 73–111.
—— and G. Bingham Powell, Jr. (1994). 'Congruence Between Citizens and Policymakers in Two Visions of Liberal Democracy', *World Politics*, 46l: 291–326.
Inglehart, Ronald and Hans-Dieter Klingemann (1976). 'Party Identification, Ideological Preference, and the Left-Right Dimension among Western Mass Publics', in Ian Budge et al. (eds.), *Party Identification and Beyond* (London: John Wiley), pp. 243–73.
Iversen, Torben (1994). 'Political Leadership and Representation in West European Democracies: A Test of Three Models of Voting', *American Political Science Review*, 88: 45–74.
Jacobson, Gary C. (1997). *The Politics of Congressional Elections*, 4th edn. (New York: Longman).
Janda, Kenneth, Robert Harmel, and Edith Goff (1995). 'Changes in Party Identities: Evidence from Party Manifestos' *Party Politics*, 1: 73–111.
Kateb, George (1981). 'The Moral Distinctiveness of Representative Democracy', *Ethics*, 91: 357–74.
Katz, Richard S. (1980). *A Theory of Parties and Electoral Systems* (Baltimore: John Hopkins).
—— and Peter Mair (1995). 'Changing Models of Party Organization and Party Democracy: The Emergence of the Cartel Party', *Party Politics*, 1: 5–28.
Kavanagh, Dennis (1981). 'The Politics of Manifestos', *Parliamentary Affairs*, 34: 7–27.
Kendall, M.J. and K. Stuart (1950). 'The Law of the Cubic Proportion in Election Results', *British Journal of Sociology* 1: 183–96.
Kim, Hee Min and Richard Fording (1998). 'Voter Ideology in Western Democracies', *European Journal of Political Research*, 33: 73–97.
—— —— (2001). 'Extending Party Estimates to Voters and Governments', in Budge, Klingemann, et al., op. cit., Chapter 8.
King, Gary and Andrew Gelman (1991). 'Systemic Consequences of Incumbency Advantage in the U.S. House.' *American Journal of Political Science*, 35: 110–38.
—— and Michael Laver (1993). 'On Party Platforms and Government Spending', *American Political Science Review*, 87: 774–80.
—— and Michael Laver (1999). 'Many Publications but Little Evidence', *Electoral Studies* 18: 597–8.
Kingdon, John (1984). *Agendas, Alternatives and Public Policies* (Boston: Little Brown).

Klingemann, H. D. (1995). 'Party Positions and Voter Orientations', in Klingemann H. D. and Dieter Fuchs (eds.), *Citizens and the State* (Oxford: Oxford University Press), pp. 183–205.

—— R. I. Hofferbert, et al. (1994). *Parties, Policies and Democracy* (Boulder, CO: Westview).

Knutsen, Oddbjorn (1998). 'Expert Judgements of the Left-Right Location of Political Parties: A Comparative Longitudinal Study', *West European Politics*, 21: 63–94.

Laver, Michael (2001). 'The Policy Space of Party Manifestos', in Michael Laver (ed.), *Estimating the Policy Positions of Political Actors* (London: Routledge).

—— and Ian Budge (eds.) (1992). *Party Policy and Government Coalitions* (London: St Martin's).

—— and John Garry (2000). 'Estimating Policy Positions from Political Texts', *American Journal of Political Science*, 44: 619–34.

—— and W. Ben Hunt (1992). *Policy and Party Competition* (New York: Routledge).

—— and Norman Schofield (1990). *Multiparty Government: The Politics of Coalition in Europe* (New York: Oxford University Press).

—— and Kenneth Shepsle (1996). *Making and Breaking Governments* (Cambridge: Cambridge University Press).

Le Duc, L. Richard Niemi, Pippa Norris (1996). *Comparing Democracies* (Thousand Oaks, CA: Sage).

Lewis-Beck, Michael and Martin Paldam (2000). 'Introduction', *Electoral Studies*, 19: 113–23.

Lijphart, Arend (1968). *The Politics of Accommodation* (New Haven, CT: Yale).

—— (1977). *Democracy in Plural Societies: A Comparative Exploration* (New Haven, CT: Yale University Press).

—— (1984). *Democracies: Patterns of Majoritarian and Consensus Government* (New Haven, CT: Yale University Press).

—— (1994). *Electoral Systems and Party Systems: A Study of Twenty-Seven Democracies, 1945–1990* (Oxford: Oxford University Press).

—— (1999). *Patterns of Democracy: Government Forms and Performance in Thirty-Six Countries* (New Haven, CT: Yale University Press).

Lindblom, Charles E. (1959). 'The Science of Muddling Through', *Public Admin Review*, 19: 79–88.

—— (1965). *The Intelligence of Democracy: Decision Making Through Mutual Adjustment* (New York: Free Press).

Lipset, Seymour Martin and Stein Rokkan (eds.) (1967). *Party Systems and Voter Alignments* (New York: Free Press).

Lupia, Arthur (1994). 'Shortcuts Versus Encyclopaedias: Information and Voting Behaviour in California Insurance Reform Elections', *American Political Science Review*, 88: 43–76.

—— and Matthew D. McCubbins (1998). *The Democratic Dilemma: Can Citizens Learn What They Need to Know?* (New York: Cambridge University Press).

Mackie, Thomas. and Richard Rose (1991). *International Almanac of Electoral History*, 3rd edn. (Washington, D.C.: Congressional Quarterly).

Madison, James, with Alexander Hamilton and John Jay (1788/1911). *The Federalist Papers* (London: Dent).

Mair, Peter and Cas Mudde (1998). 'The Party Family and Its Study', *Annual Review of Political Science*, 1, 211–29.

March, James G. (1957–58). 'Party Legislative Representation as a Function of Election Results', *Public Opinion Quarterly*, 21: 521–42.

Marcus G. E. and R. L. Hanson (eds.). (1993). *Reconsidering the Democratic Public* (University Park, PA: University of Pennsylvania Press).

May, J. D. (1978). 'Defining Democracy: A Bid for Coherence and Consensus', *Political Studies*, 26:1–14.

McDonald, Michael D and Silvia M. Mendes (2001). 'The Policy Space of Party Manifestos', in Michael Laver (ed.), *Estimating the Policy Position of Political Actors* (London: Routledge), pp. 90–114.

—— Ian Budge, and Richard I. Hofferbert (1999). 'Party Mandate Theory and Time Series Analysis', *Electoral Studies*, 18: 587–96.

—— Ian Budge, and Paul Pennings (2004). 'Choice Versus Sensitivity', *European Journal of Political Research*, 43: 845–68.

—— Silvia M. Mendes, and Ian Budge (2004). 'What Are Elections For?' *British Journal of Political Science*, 34: 1–26.

McKelvey, R. D. (1979). 'General Conditions for Global Intransitives in Formal Voting Models', *Econometrica*, 47: 1085–111.

McLean, Iain S. (1989). *Democracy and New Technology* (Cambridge: Polity Press).

Meffert, Michael, F., Helmut Norpoth, and Anirudh V. S. Ruhil (2001). 'Realignment and Macropartisanship', *American Political Science Review*, 95: 953–62.

Mendelson, Matthew and Andrew Parkin (eds.) (2001). *Referendum Democracy* (London: Palgrave).

Michels, Roberto (1949). *Political Parties* (Glencoe, IL: Free Press).

Mill, J. S. (1861/1910). *Utilitarianism, Liberty, Representative Government* (London: Dent).

Miller, Warren, Roy Pierce, Jacques Thomassen, Richard Herrera, Sören Holmberg, Peter Essaiasson, and Bernhard Wessels (1999), *Policy Representation in Western Democracies* (Oxford: Oxford University Press).

Muller, Edward and M. Seligson (1994). 'Civic Culture and Democracy: The Question of Causal Relationships', *American Political Science Review* 88: 635–52.

Müller, Wolfgang C. and Kaare Strom (2000). *Coalition Government in Western Europe* (Oxford: Oxford University Press).

Nannestad, Peter and Martin Paldam (1994). 'The VP-function: A Survey of the Literature on Vote and Popularity Functions after 25 Years', *Public Choice*, 79: 213–45.

—— —— (2002). 'The Cost of Ruling', in Dorussen and Taylor (eds.), op.cit., pp. 17–44.

Niemi, Richard (1969). 'Majority Decision Making with Partial Unidimensionality', *American Political Science Review*, 63 (June), 489–97.

—— and Herbert F. Weisberg (1984). 'Do Voters Think Ideologically?', in R. G. Niemi and H. F. Weisberg (eds.), *Controversies in Voting Behaviour* (Washington, D.C.: Congressional Quarterly), pp. 131–280.

OECD (various dates). *Cross-National Political and Social Indicators* (Paris, France).
Oppenheimer, Bruce I., James A. Stimson, and Richard W. Waterman (1986). 'Interpreting U.S. Congressional Elections: The Exposure Thesis', *Legislative Studies Quarterly*, 11: 227–47.
Ordeshook, Peter (1986). *Mathematical Political Theory* (Cambridge: Cambridge University Press).
Owen G. and Bernard Grofman (1995). 'A Two-Stage Model of Two-Party Competition.' Paper delivered at Public Choice Society Meeting, Long Beach, California.
Page, B. I. and R. Y. Shapiro (1983). 'Effects of Public Opinion on Policy', *American Political Science Review*, 81: 23–43.
Paldam, Martin (1991). 'How Robust is the Vote Function? A Study of 17 Countries over Four Decades', in Helmut Norpoth, Michael S. Lewis-Beck, Jean-Dominique Lafay (eds.), *Economics and Politics: The Calculus of Support* (Ann Arbor, MI: University of Michigan Press).
Palmer, Harvey D. and Guy Whitten (1999). 'The Electoral Impact of Unexpected Inflation and Economic Growth', *British Journal of Political Science*, 29: 623–39.
—— —— (2002). 'Economics, Politics and the Cost of Ruling in Advanced Industrial Democracies: How Much Does Context Matter?', in Han Dorussen and Michaell Taylor, (eds.), *Economic Voting* (London, UK: Routledge).
Panebianco, Angelo (1988). *Political Parties: Organizations and Power* (Cambridge: Cambridge University Press).
Pierce, Roy (1999). 'Left-Right Space' in Warren Miller et al., *Policy Representation in Western Democracies* (Oxford: Oxford University Press) pp. 25–63.
Pitkin, Hanna Fenichel (1967). *The Concept of Representation* (Berkeley, CA: University of California Press).
Polsby, Nelson W. and Aaron B. Wildavsky (1971). *Presidential Elections: Strategies of American Electoral Politics*, 3rd edn. (New York: Scribner).
Powell, G. Bingham (2000). *Elections as Instruments of Democracy: Majoritarian and Proportional Visions* (New Haven, CT: Yale University Press).
—— and Georg Vanberg (2000). 'Election Laws, Disproportionality and Median Correspondence: Implications for Two Visions of Democracy,' *British Journal of Political Science*, 30, 383–411.
—— and Guy Whitten (1993). 'A Cross-National Analysis of Economic Voting Taking Account of the Political Context', *American Journal of Political Science*, 37: 341–414.
Price, Simon and David Sanders (1993). 'Modelling Government Popularity in Postwar Britain: A Methodological Example', *American Journal of Political Science*, 37: 317–34.
Rabinowitz, George and Stuart Elaine Macdonald (1989). 'A Directional Theory of Issue Voting', *American Political Science Review*, 83, 93–121.
—— —— and Ola Listhaug (1991). 'New Players in an Old Game: Party Strategy in Multiparty Systems', *Comparative Political Studies*, 24:147–85.
Rae, Douglas W. (1971). *The Political Consequences of Electoral Laws* (New Haven, CT: Yale University Press).
Rallings, Colin (1987). 'The Influence of Election Programmes: Britain and Canada 1945–1979', in Budge, Robertson, Hearl (eds.), op.cit., pp. 1–14.

Ranney, Austin (1975). *Curing the Mischief of Faction: Party Reform in America* (Berkeley and Los Angeles: University of California Press).

Riker, William H. (1964). *Democracy in the United States*, 2nd edn. (New York: Macmillan).

—— (1966). *The Theory of Political Coalitions* (New Haven, CT: Yale University Press).

—— (1980). 'Implications from the Disequilibrium of Majority Rule for the Study of Institutions', *American Political Science Review*, 74: 432–46.

—— (1982). *Liberalism Against Populism: A Confrontation Between the Theory of Democracy and the Theory of Social Choice* (San Francisco: W. H. Freeman).

Robertson, David (1976). *A Theory of Party Competition* (London and New York: Wiley).

Rose, Richard (1980). *Do Parties Make a Difference?* (London: Macmillan).

Royed, T. (1996). 'Testing the Mandate Model in Britain and the US: Reagan and Thatcher', *British Journal of Political Science*, 26: 44–80.

Sani, Giacomo and Giovanni Sartori (1983). 'Polarization, Fragmentation and Competition in Western Democracies,' in Hans Daalder and Peter Mair, (eds.), *Western European Party Systems* (London: Sage), pp. 307–40.

Saward, Michael (1998). *The Terms of Democracy* (Cambridge: Polity Press).

Schattschneider, E. E. (1960). *The Semi-Sovereign People: A Realist's View of Democracy in America* (New York: Holt Rinehart & Winston).

Schlesinger, Joseph (1975). 'The Primary Goals of Political Parties: A Clarification of Positive Theory,' *American Political Science Review*, 69, 840–9.

Schofield, Norman (1985). *Social Choice and Democracy* (Berlin: Springer).

Schumpeter, Joseph A. (1942). *Capitalism, Socialism and Democracy* (New York: Harper & Row).

Shepsle, Kenneth and B. Weingast (1981). 'Structure-Induced Equilibrium and Legislative Choice', *Public Choice*, 37: 503–19.

Snedecor, George W. and William G. Cochran (1967). *Statistical Methods* (Ames, IA: Iowa State University Press).

Spafford, Duff (1971). 'A Note on the "Equilibrium" Division of the Vote', *American Political Science Review*, 65: 180–83.

Stimson, James A. (2001). 'Party Proximity to the Median Voter in US Presidential Elections', Department of Political Science, University of North Carolina: Chapel Hill.

—— Michael B. McKuen, and Robert S. Erikson (1995). 'Dynamic Representation', *American Political Science Review*, 89: 543–65.

Stokes, Donald E. and Gudmund R. Iversen (1962). 'On the Existence of Forces Restoring Party Competition', *Public Opinion Quarterly*, 26: 159–71.

Strom, Kaare (1990). *Minority Government and Majority Rule* (Cambridge: Cambridge University Press).

—— and Wolfgang C. Muller (1999). 'Political Parties and Hard Choices', in Wolfgang C. Muller and Kaare Strom (eds.), *Policy Office or Votes? How Political Parties in Western Europe Make Hard Decisions* (Cambridge: Cambridge University Press).

Sullivan John L. and Robert E. O'Connor (1972). 'Electoral Choice and Popular Control of Public Policy', *American Political Science Review*, 66: 125–39.
Taagepera, Rein and Matthew Shugart (1989). *Seats and Votes: The Effects and Determinants of Electoral Systems* (New Haven, CT: Yale University Press).
Tufte, Edward R. (1973). 'The Relationship between Seats and Votes in Two-Party Systems', *The American Political Science Review*, 67: 540–54.
—— (1974). *Data Analysis for Politics and Policy* (Englewood Cliffs, NJ: Prentice-Hall).
—— (1975). 'Determinants of the Outcomes of Midterm Congressional Elections,' *American Political Science Review*, 69: 812–26.
—— (1978). *Political Control of the Economy* (Princeton, NJ: Princeton University Press).
United Nations (various dates). *United Nations Demographic Yearbook* (New York).
Van der Brug, Wouter (2001). 'Analyzing Party Dynamics by Taking Partially Overlapping Snapshots', in Michael Laver (ed.), *Estimating the Policy Positions of Political Actors* (London: Routledge), pp. 115–132.
Van Roozendall, Peter (1990). 'Centre Parties and Coalition Formation: A Game Theoretic Approach', *European Journal of Political Research*, 18: 325–48.
—— (1992). 'The Effect of Dominant and Central Parties on Cabinet Composition and Duration', *Legislative Studies Quarterly*, 17: 5–36.
Volkens, Andrea (1994). *Dataset CMP94: Programmatic Profiles of Political Parties in 27 Countries, 1945–1992* (Berlin: WZB).
Volkens, Andrea, Kai-Uwe Schnapp, and Jurgen Lass (1992). *Data Handbook on Election Results and Seats in the National Parliaments of 26 Contemporary Democracies, 1945–1990* (Berlin: Wissenschaftszentrum).
Waterman, Richard W., Bruce I. Oppenheimer, and James A. Stimson (1991). 'Sequence and Equilibrium in Congressional Elections: An Integrated Approach', *Journal of Politics*, 53: 373–93.
Weale, Albert (1999). *Democracy* (Cambridge: Politiy Press).
Weissberg, Robert (1978). 'Collective Versus Dyadic Representation in Congress', *American Political Science Review*, 72, 537–47.
Wessels, Bernhard (1999). 'System Characteristics Matter: Empirical Evidence from Ten Representation Studies', in Warren Miller, Roy Pierce, Jacques Thomassen, Richard Herrera, Soren Holmberg, Peter Esaiasson and Bernhard Wessels (eds.), *Policy Representation in Western Democracies*, (Oxford: Oxford University Press).
Whitten, Guy and Harvey D. Palmer (1999). 'Cross-National Analysis of Economic Voting', *Electoral Studies*, 18: 49–67.
Woldendorp, Jaap, Hans Keman, and Ian Budge (1993). 'Political Data 1945–1990: Party Government in 20 Democracies' *European Journal of Political Science*, 24: 1–120.
—— —— —— (1998). 'Party Government in 20 Democracies: An Update (1990–95)', *European Journal of Political Science*, 33: 125–64.
—— —— —— (2000). *Party Government in 48 Democracies (1945–1998)* (Amsterdam: Kluwer Academic).
Wright, William (1971). 'Comparative Party Models: Rational Efficient and Party Democracy', in William Wright (ed.), *A Comparative Study of Party Organization* (Columbus, OH: Charles Merrill), pp. 17–54.

Index

The letter n indicates a textual note, f a figure and t a table.

age distribution: and welfare
    policies 221, 223, 223 n11
Arrow conditions: elections 46 n1
Australia: and distortions 131; elections
    in 66t, 75t, 76, 79t, 81, 82t, 85t,
    104, 105t, 133t; and electoral
    responsiveness 190t, 196t, 198t;
    and foreign aid 163f; and
    government spending 156f, 179t;
    political parties in 114, 115; and
    public economy 175t; voters
    in 115, 121t, 126t, 128t; and
    welfare state 160f
Austria: coalitions in 119; elections
    in 66t, 75t, 80t, 81, 83t, 84t, 94 n2,
    104, 105t, 133t; and electoral
    responsiveness 186, 190t, 195, 196t,
    198t; and foreign aid 163f; and
    government spending 156f, 179t;
    and public economy 175t; voters
    in 121t, 126t, 128t; and welfare
    state 160f

Belgium: elections in 67t, 70 n4, 71, 75t,
    76, 77, 79t, 81, 82t, 85t, 105t, 133t;
    and electoral responsiveness
    190t, 196t, 198t; and foreign
    aid 163f; and government
    spending 156f, 179t; and public
    economy 174f, 175t; voters in
    121t, 126t, 128t; and welfare
    state 160f
bias: representation 122–4, 130–5,
    187–8, 229
Britain *see* United Kingdom
budgets: government spending 51

Calculus of Consent 15
Canada: elections in 66t, 71, 72, 74t, 76,
    80t, 81, 83t, 84t, 104, 105t, 133t;
    electoral responsiveness in 185–6,
    190t, 196t, 198t; and foreign
    aid 163f; and government
    spending 156f, 179t; and public
    economy 174f, 175t; voters in 121t,
    126t, 128t; and welfare state 160f
'central' parties 12 *see also* median
    parties
centre ground 30
choices: and parties 61–90; and
    voters 33–4, 61
Christian parties 112, 196
cleavages: political divisions 31–2
coalitions 6, 10, 39, 95, 183–4, 196
communications 30–31, 47
comparative investigations 49–57
Comparative Manifesto
    Project 199–201
consensus democracies 29, 119,
    164, 224t, 225, 232–3, 234–5,
    236, 238
Conservative Party (UK) 7t, 8
control: and government
    policies 151–2, 164
convergence: party policies 53, 62–73,
    89–90

declarations: governments 50, 141,
    145–53, 165, 194
defence spending governments 161–4,
    168, 175t, 177, 179t, 223
Denmark: and defence 162; elections
    in 69t, 71, 74t, 75, 76, 79t,

Denmark: and defence (*contd.*)
81, 82t, 84t, 105t, 131, 131–2, 133t; and electoral responsiveness 190t, 195, 196t, 198t; and foreign aid 163f; and government spending 156f, 179t; and public economy 175t; voters in 121t, 126t, 128t, 200t; and welfare state 160f
differentiation: political parties 73–7
dimensionality 54
direct democracy 239–40
distortion: representation 122–30, 132–5, 142, 229
Downs' spatial model: elections 25 n3

economic policies: governments 209, 210, 211–12
Economic Theory of Democracy (Downs) 89, 90
economic voting *see* retrospective economic voting
economies *see* market economies: and government policies; public economies: government policies on
election programmes 51
elections: and democracy 8–11, 61, 193, 239; and governance 3–8; and political parties 39–40; and policymaking process 184; *see also* voting
electoral majorities 4–5, 6–7, 14, 22–3, 42, 228
electoral processes 11–15
electoral responsiveness 184–93
electorates: and mandates 228–9
electors 4–5, 10, 11, 32–3, 46, 47, 89 *see also* elections; voters
elites 118–19, 122
equilibria: policy 173–9; polictical 181–3
Eurobarometer Surveys: voters' ideologies 199–201

Finland: elections in 69t, 72, 75t, 80t, 81, 83t, 85t, 104, 105t, 107 n8, 133t; and electoral responsiveness 190t, 196t, 198t; and foreign aid 163f; and government spending 156f, 179t; and public economy 175t; voters in 121t, 126t, 128t; and welfare state 160f
Fording, R *see* Comparative Manifesto Project
foreign affairs *see* defence spending
France: elections in 67t, 71, 74t, 80t, 81, 83t, 84t, 132, 133t; and electoral responsiveness 190t, 196t, 198t; and foreign aid 163f; and government spending 156f, 179t; and public economy 175t; and representation 136; voters in 121t, 126t, 128t, 200t; and welfare state 160f

general elections: United Kingdom 7–8 *see also* elections
Germany: elections in 62–3, 64t, 65, 67t, 71, 75t, 80t, 81, 82t, 85t, 104, 105t, 133t; and electoral responsiveness 190t, 196t, 198t; and foreign aid 163f; and government spending 156f, 179t; and public economy 174f, 175t; voters in 121t, 126, 128t; and welfare state 160f
government declarations 50, 141, 148, 165, 194
government mandates 5, 20–25, 116, 227 *see also* median mandates; single-party governments
government minorities 22–3
government spending *see* public economies: government policies on
governments: and policies 142–53, 214–25
gradation and polarization 77
Greece 8, 201t

Holland *see* Netherlands

Iceland: elections in 70t, 72, 74t, 79t, 81, 83t, 85t, 133t; and electoral responsiveness 190t, 196t, 198t; and

government spending 156f; and public economy 175t; and representation 136; voters in 121t, 126t, 128t
ideologies: parliaments 194 *see also* Eurobarometer Surveys: voters' ideologies
incrementalism: policies 171–80
indicators: goverment declarations 115–6; goverment left–right 113–4; normal vote 112–3; party policy positions 90; policy outputs 142, 166–8
inflation: effects on voting 97–9, 109
international relations 150, 151, 161–4, 210, 211t, 213, 223–5 *see also* defence
Ireland: elections in 66t, 71, 72, 80t, 81, 82t, 85t, 104, 105t, 133t; and electoral responsiveness 190t, 195, 196t, 196t, 198t; and foreign aid 163f; and government spending 155, 156f, 179t; and public economy 175t; voters in 121t, 126t, 128t
issues: and parties 77–89
Italy: elections in 67t, 71, 73–4, 75t, 76, 80t, 81, 83t, 85t, 104, 105t, 132, 133t; and electoral responsiveness, 190t, 196t, 198t; and foreign aid 163f; and government spending 156f, 179t; and public economy 175t; voters in 121t, 126t, 128t, 200t; and welfare state 160f

Kim, H-M *see* Comparative Manifesto Project

Labour Party (United Kingdom) 7t, 8
leapfrogging: parties 65–70
Left-Right dimensions 32–3, 35–8, 39–40, 53, 54–5, 73–88, 102–5, 114–15, 131, 144, 145–8, 189–90, 194, 197, 200–201, 205–8, 209, 215,218,219,221–23, 228

see also choices: and parties; convergence: party policies
liberal democracies 237
liberalism *see* neo-liberalism
Luxembourg: elections in 67t, 71, 74t, 77, 79t, 81, 83t, 85t, 131–2, 133t; and electoral responsiveness 190t, 196t, 198t; and foreign aid 163f; and government spending 155, 156f, 179t; voters in 121t, 126t, 128t, 200t

majoritarian democracies 236, 238
majorities, electoral *see* electoral majorities
mandates 3–4, 13, 14, 15–17, 18–29, 49–57, 89–90, 91–115, 143, 227, 240–42
manifestoes 37, 38, 145 *see also* Comparative Manifesto Project
market economies: and government policies 148, 149, 150t
media *see* communication
median mandates 25–9, 31, 101–8, 227, 240–42; and policies 203; and political preferences 203–4; and representational process 135–7
median parties 6–7, 10, 13, 40–42, 56 *see also* 'central' parties
median voters 4–5, 10, 11, 46, 47, 102–8, 182, 199; and Left-Right positions 145–8, 151, 200–201t, 208, 210; and policies 142–3, 178–80, 187, 188f, 230; and representation 116–37
militarism *see* international relations: governments
minimalist mandates 92–3
ministries: and policies 142
minority government 22–3

Netherlands: elections in 63, 68t, 70 n5, 71, 73, 74t, 77, 79t, 81, 82t, 84t, 105t, 133t; and electoral responsiveness 190t, 195, 196, 198t; and foreign aid 163f; and

Netherlands (*contd.*)
    government spending 156f, 179t; and public economy 174f, 175t; voters in 121t, 126t, 128t, 200t; and welfare state 160f
'New Labour' party (UK) 8
New Zealand: and distortions 131; elections in 66t, 75t, 76, 80t, 81, 83t, 85t, 105t, 133t; and electoral responsiveness 190t, 196t, 198t; and foreign aid 163f; and government spending 156f, 179t; and public economy 175t; voters in 121t; 126t; and welfare state 160f
Norway: elections in 69t, 71, 74t, 76, 77, 79t, 81, 82t, 84t, 104, 105, 133t; and electoral responsiveness 190t, 196t, 198t; and foreign aid 163f; and government spending 156f, 179t; political parties in 114; and public economy 175t; voters in 114–5, 121t, 126t, 128t; and welfare state 160f

PR *see* proportional representation (PR)
parliaments: and choices 61–90; and ideologies 194; and policies 183, 209–14
parties: and coalitions 95; and convergence 53, 62–73, 89–90; and differentiation 73–7; and election programmes 51; and electors 38; and issues 77–89 and Left-Right dimension 37; and mandates 21, 29, 227–33; and policies 8, 13, 25–6, 55–6, 183–4, 191–2; and preferences 50 *see also* Christian parties; Conservative Party (UK); New Labour party (UK)
party issues 77–89
party systems 9, 13
peace *see* international orientation: governments
planned economies *see* market economies: and government policies
pluralism 234, 235
pluralities: governments 22–3, 52
plurality parties 8
policies: governments 142–153, 154–68, 209–14; incrementalism in 171–80; and political parties 9, 13, 25–6, 34–5, 52, 53, 55–6
policy changes: governments 231–3
policy preferences: voters 30–48, 50, 53, 54, 178, 205
policy regimes 173–78, 203–26
policy spaces 38–40, 43–7
political dynamics 181–4
political preferences 203–8
Portugal: elections in 67t, 70 n3, 72, 79t, 81, 83t, 85, 133t; and electoral responsiveness 190t, 196t, 198t; and foreign aid 163f; and government spending 156f, 179t, 217 n7; and public economy 175t; voters in 121t, 126t, 128t
proportional representation (PR) 9–10, 12, 13, 23–4, 27–8, 29, 52, 76, 77, 89, 90, 97, 118, 119–20, 125–30, 131, 132–7, 185–6, 189, 193, 194–5, 196–7, 198, 214, 228, 236, 238, 241
public economies: government policies on 154–8, 173–8, 216–20

referendums 13, 240
regimes *see* policy regimes
representation: voters 116–37
representative democracy 234–5
retrospective economic voting 92, 108–9

Scandinavia *see also under individual countries*; cleavages in 31–2
Single Member District (SMD) systems 9, 12–13, 76–7, 99, 118, 119–20, 125–30, 131, 133–5, 136, 213, 228, 236, 241; election results in 22–3, 27–8, 52–3, 106; and electoral responsiveness 185, 189, 193, 194–5, 196, 198
single-party governments 56

social spending 223
Spain: elections in 66–7t, 71, 74t, 79t, 81, 83t, 84t, 132, 133t; and electoral responsiveness 190t, 196t, 198t; and foreign aid 163f; and government spending 156f, 179t, 217 n7; and public economy 175t; voters in 121t, 126t, 128t, 200t
surveys *see* Eurobarometer Surveys
Sweden: elections in 69t, 71, 74t, 80t, 81, 83t, 84t, 104, 105t, 133t; and electoral responsiveness 185–6, 190t, 196t, 198t; and foreign aid 163f; and government spending 156f, 179t; and proportional representation 118; and public economy 175t; voters in 121t, 126t, 128; and welfare state 160f
Switzerland: 69t, 71, 74t, 80t, 81, 82t, 84t, 104, 105t, 133t; and electoral responsiveness 190t, 195, 196t, 198t; and foreign aid 163f; and government spending 156f, 179t; voters in 121t, 126t, 128t; and public economy 174f, 175t; and welfare state 160f

time frames: and policies 143–4

unemployment: effect on voting 97, 109
United Kingdom: cleavages in 32; distortions in 127, 129; elections in 66t, 71, 75t, 76, 80t, 81, 83t, 85t, 104, 105t, 132, 133t; and electoral responsiveness 190t, 196t, 198t; and foreign aid 163f; and government spending 156f, 179t; median parties in 7–8t; and policy profiles 47; and proportional representation 129; and public economy 174f, 175t, 219 n8; and representation 136; Single Member District (SMD) systems in 118; voters in 121t, 126t, 128t, 200t; and welfare state 160f
United States: elections in 63–6, 71, 73, 74t, 76, 79t, 82t, 84t, 104, 105t; and defence 162; and electoral responsiveness 190t, 196t, 198t; and foreign aid 163f; and government spending 156f, 179t; and public economy 175t; voters in 115; and welfare state 160f *see also* retrospective economic voting

vote losses: governments 101
voters 8, 21, 30–48, 50, 53, 54, 61, 206–8 *see also* elections; electors; mandate theory; Eurobarometer Surveys: voters' ideologies; median mandates; median voters
voting 12, 50, 51–2, 97–9, 108–9, 192 *see also* elections; electors; mandates

welfare policies: governments 149–50, 158–61, 174–5, 179t, 210, 211t, 212–13, 220–23